Oxford Smart

Key Stage 3 Science

Activate

2

Curriculum Editor:

Dr Andrew Chandler-Grevatt

Philippa Gardom Hulme • Jo Locke • Helen Reynolds

OXFORD
UNIVERSITY PRESS

Contents

Physics 2 Unit Opener 162

Introduction

Learning objectives

Each spread has a set of learning objectives. These tell you what you will be able to do by the end of the lesson.

Reactivate your knowledge

Here you will find some short questions that will help to remind you what you already know about a topic.

Maths skills

Scientists use maths to help them solve problems and carry out their investigations. These boxes contain activities to help you practise the maths you need for science. They also contain useful hints and tips.

Link

Links show you where you can learn more about something mentioned in the topic.

Summary Questions

1 Each spread has a set of Summary Questions. Questions with one dot symbol ask you to recall information.

2 Questions with two dot symbols are a bit more challenging.

3 Questions with three dots are more challenging. You will need to think carefully and apply your knowledge.

Welcome to your *Activate* Student Book

This introduction shows you all the different features *Activate* has to support you on your journey through Key Stage 3 Science.

Being a scientist is great fun. As you work through this Student Book, you'll learn how to work as a scientist, and get answers to questions that science can answer.

This book is packed full of activities to help build your confidence and skills in science.

Q These boxes contain short questions. They will help you check that you have understood the text.

Working scientifically

Scientists work in a particular way to carry out fair and scientific investigations. These boxes contain activities and hints to help you build these skills and understand the process so that you can work scientifically.

Key words

The key words in each spread are highlighted in bold and summarised in the key-word box. They can also be found in the Glossary.

Literacy skills

As a scientist, you need to be able to communicate and share your ideas. These boxes contain tasks and tips to help build your reading, writing, listening, and speaking skills.

Opener

Each unit begins with an opener spread. This introduces you to the awe and wonder of science and helps you to understand your place in the scientific world.

It asks some important questions that you will find the answers to in the unit, and shows you the key topics you will study.

Chapter map

This shows all the chapters in this unit and what each one contains.

Each chapter has an opener spread to reactivate what you already know, and to show you what's coming up in the chapter. It also shows you the Working Scientifically and Maths skills that you will learn. The chapter map shows how far through the unit you have progressed.

Summary

This summarises the key ideas you have learnt so far and shows you your progress through the unit.

Metacognition and self-reflection

You can use these techniques to reflect on your own strengths and challenges when working through the chapter.

End-of-chapter questions

You can use these exam-style questions to test how well you know the topics in the chapter.

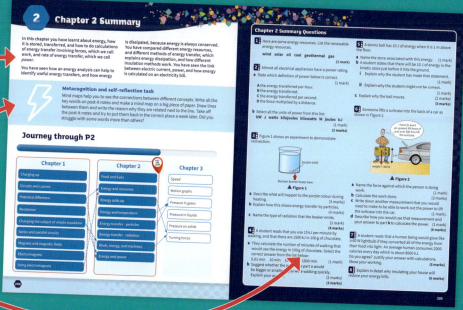

Strategies for effective learning

Throughout your time in school, your teachers will have taught you several different strategies to help you to be an effective learner. Sometimes these strategies will be useful for specific subject skills, and sometimes they are useful when learning independently. To be an effective learner it is important that you have a good understanding of <u>what</u> strategies you have available, <u>how</u> you need to use them, and <u>why</u> they are useful.

The EVERY method for calculations

What: The EVERY method is an approach you can use to complete calculations in science. Each of the letters in EVERY represent a different step in the process, and should be used every time.

Equations
Values
Enter values
Rearrange
Your answer and units

How: You can use the EVERY method anytime you are asked to complete a calculation in science. Here is an example of how to use the EVERY method:

A bike is travelling at 5 m/s for 100 s, calculate the <u>distance</u> the bike has travelled.

E	$s = d \div t$
V	$s = 5\,m/s \quad d = ? \quad t = 100\,s$
E	$5 = d \div 100$
R	$(\times 100)\, 5 = d \div 100\, (\times 100)$
	$(\times 100)\, 5 = d \div \cancel{100}\,\cancel{(\times 100)}$
	$d = 5 \times 100$
Y	$d = 500\,m$

Why: Students often find calculations challenging in science. This strategy is something that you can use to make it easier. As you progress into GCSE study, following this method will also be helpful in your exams because it is common to receive marks for your working out when completing calculations.

Graphic organisers

What: A graphic organiser is a great way to transform key ideas into simplified visual summaries. They are particularly useful for showing the stages in a process or the links between key ideas. In **Table 1**, there are various examples of graphic organisers and when you could use them.

Task	Suggested graphic organisers	
grouping, classifying, or summarising your ideas	 spider diagram	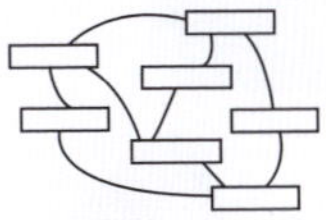 concept map
sequencing events or ordering ideas	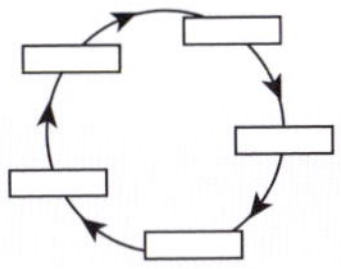 cycle circle	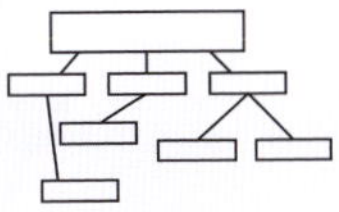 flow chart
making links between ideas	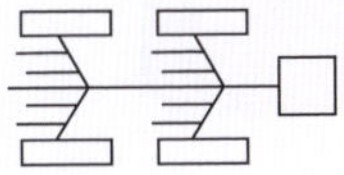 fishbone	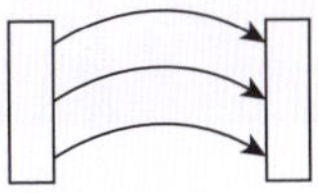 bridge
making comparisons	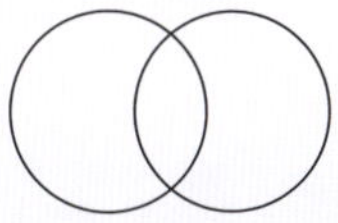 Venn diagram	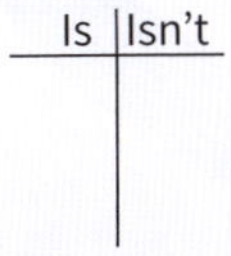 T chart

▲ **Table 1** Graphic organisers and when to use them.

How: You first need to decide which graphic organiser you need. Once you have done this, you need to pick out the key words, equations, and ideas from your chosen topic. It is important to remember that this needs to be a simple and clear summary, so you will not be writing lots of information on it. Finally, start to populate your graphic organiser.

Why: Although a fully completed graphic organiser can be used when you revise for a test, the process of filling one in is beneficial too. By thinking carefully about how the information can fit into a simple graphic organiser, you are reviewing the content, making links between everything you have learnt, evaluating what information is necessary, and summarising it. All of these are very important skills that an effective learner has.

Discuss

Think and discuss with your partner what type of graphic organiser you would use to compare:

- the organelles within a plant and an animal cell
- the relative sizes of the parts of our Universe.

3

Using strategies effectively

The Plan, Monitor, and Evaluate cycle is a structure you can follow to help you approach a new task like an expert learner. Below are examples of how an expert learner would use this structure to successfully select and use the strategies their teacher has taught them.

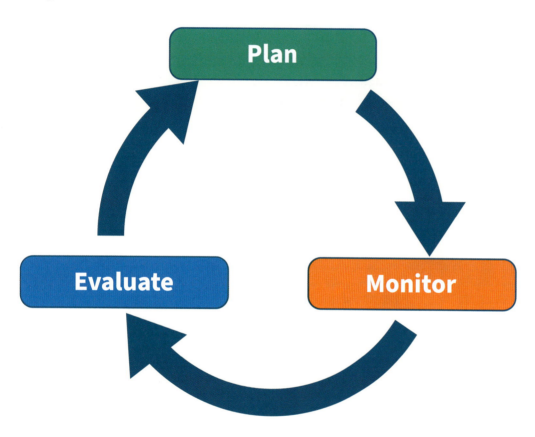

Discuss

Think and discuss with a partner your answers to these questions:

- How should you plan your approach to a question?
- What are some examples of monitoring your progress?
- Why is the evaluation phase important?

Plan

Before you start a new task, whether it be revision at home or a science question in class, you need to plan your approach. This includes deciding what scientific content needs to be included, selecting an appropriate strategy to use, and then checking back on previous work to see what success looks like.

What does this look like in practice?

When completing revision, it may be appropriate to summarise a process using a graphic organiser. Before you start, you would plan your approach by reflecting on the different types of graphic organiser and seeing which one suits the process you need to summarise. Next, you would check back to the last time you created a graphic organiser and see what success looks like. Finally, you would carefully review your notes to select what information you need to include.

Evaluate

When you have completed the task, you need to evaluate how you have done. During this phase you would look at what you have done, and decide what was successful and what needs to be improved upon next time. You would also start to put a brief plan in place for what you would do if you were to complete the task again.

What does this look like in practice?

When you have completed an extended answer, and your teacher has marked your work, you would evaluate your performance. To do this, you should look at what you have done correctly and what areas need to be improved upon. After this, you would make a small note about what you would do differently next time. This is very useful because it will help you to plan your approach the next time you complete a similar task.

Monitor

Monitoring your progress is where you pause and double check that your chosen strategy is correct, and that you are including everything that is needed. It may even be appropriate to stop and change your approach.

What does this look like in practice?

When using the **EVERY** method to complete a calculation, you would pause and re-read the question to double check the values given, and to make sure you have put them in the right place in the equation. You may even check to see whether you have converted the units correctly before carrying on and finishing the question.

Welcome

In this book you will look further at the planning of investigations, focusing on ensuring data is precise and reproducible, and produce risk assessments to make sure you and others around you are kept safe.

You will analyse data in more detail, exploring the different types of relationship that exist between variables and use secondary data to improve the confidence in your conclusions. You will also begin to analyse sources to check for their reliability.

Thinking about the whole of science, you will study how our understanding of science develops over time, the importance of peer review in verifying research work, and how scientists communicate information with different audiences.

Working Scientifically

Where can science take you?

Scientists work in every field imaginable, and can therefore be found working for a huge range of employers including universities, hospitals, and the government. Regardless of the career a scientist chooses to follow their goal is to add knowledge and insight to the wider scientific community, to pave the way for further discoveries in the future, and to help ignite interest and enthusiasm in the next generation of scientists - you.

Being able to work scientifically equips you with many skills, and prepares you for a wide range of jobs, careers, and interests you may wish to follow in the future.

Engineer

Meteorologist

Astronaut

Nutritionist

Microbiologist

Geologist

Working Scientifically and the world

We all have a responsibility to protect and enhance the living world, and the physical environment in which we live. The ability to think like a scientist is important to ensure that all of us listen to the scientific evidence, for example about climate change, take account of what it is saying to us, and then act in a way which is the most beneficial to the planet. The collective actions of many people make an enormous difference, and are critical in ensuring a stable, sustainable future not only for human beings, but for all species on Earth.

BIG QUESTIONS

How do scientists keep safe?
Before carrying out any scientific investigation a risk assessment is carried out. This identifies any hazards and the control measures that must be followed to make sure no one is injured.

How can you trust a scientific claim?
One of the key skills of a scientist is to think critically: what is the basis for the claim, who wrote it, and why? Only when we know the answers to these questions can we make a reasoned decision on whether to believe a piece of information, or not.

Why do scientists change their minds about how things happen?
The development of new technology, carrying out different experiments and new ways of thinking can all provide new evidence. This can result in scientists having to amend a previous idea or change their thinking entirely.

Working Scientifically through Book 2

YOU ARE HERE

Planning investigations 2

There are a few things that you should consider before you begin a scientific investigation.

Presenting data 2

Presenting data is a vital part of an investigation. How can we do this?

Analysing and evaluating 2

Once we have our results, we can use them to understand science better.

Communicating scientific information

Science is amazing but can be complicated. How do we help others learn about science?

Using evidence and sources

How can we assess the results and evidence of other scientists?

Development of scientific understanding

How do scientists work together over time to understand the world?

Learning objectives

After this topic, you will be able to:

- write a hypothesis for a scientific investigation
- describe the difference between precise and accurate data
- write a risk assessment for a scientific investigation.

Reactivate your knowledge

1 What is a prediction?
2 What information helps you to keep safe during an investigation?
3 What is accurate data?

▲ **Figure 1** Scientists collect data about bungee cords. This information is then used each time a person jumps.

Link ↗

You learnt about predictions and variables in Working scientifically 1.1 *Asking scientific questions*.

Link ↗

You learnt about accurate data in Working scientifically 1.3 *Planning investigations*.

Key words 🔑

prediction, hypothesis, independent variable, dependent variable, accurate, precise, spread, repeatable, reproducible, hazard, risk, control measure

Bungee jumping gives you a huge adrenaline rush as you freefall through the air, but is it safe? A detailed risk assessment is performed before every jump to ensure all risks are minimised (Figure 1).

What is a hypothesis?

You should be used to making **predictions** about your investigations. Scientists back up their predictions with reasons why they think something will happen, using scientific knowledge. This is known as a **hypothesis**.

Katie and Tom decide to investigate the link between the thickness of a piece of elastic and how much it stretches (Figure 2). Their hypothesis is:

'The thicker the piece of elastic, the lower the extension will be when a force is applied. This is because a thicker piece of elastic contains more bonds, which all need to be stretched to make the elastic get longer.'

▲ **Figure 2** Katie and Tom discuss the hypothesis.

Reactivate your knowledge answers
1 What you think will happen in an investigation 2 Risk assessment 3 Data that is close to the true value

They make a list of variables. In their plan they:

- identify the **independent variable** – the thickness of the elastic
- identify the **dependent variable** – the extension of the elastic
- identify all the variables they need to control, and say how they will control them.

> **A** Write down one variable Katie and Tom need to control.

How do you collect accurate and precise data?

It is important to collect data that is both **accurate** and **precise** (Figure 3). Accurate data is close to the true value of what you are trying to measure. This means you have taken steps to minimise the effect of random and systematic errors. Precise data means getting similar results if you repeat a measurement. This means that precise data has a very small **spread**.

If Katie and Tom repeat their investigation several times, their data should be similar. The data is then said to be **repeatable**. Therefore, repeatable data is also referred to as being precise.

Sometimes the same experiment is repeated by other students, or by using a different method or equipment. If these experiments produce similar data then the data is said to be **reproducible**.

How do you write a risk assessment?

You may need to complete a risk assessment for an investigation before you carry it out. A risk assessment usually consists of three sections: **hazard**, **risk**, and **control measure**. Figure 4 shows an example of a risk assessment.

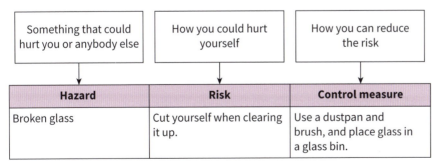

Something that could hurt you or anybody else	How you could hurt yourself	How you can reduce the risk
Hazard	**Risk**	**Control measure**
Broken glass	Cut yourself when clearing it up.	Use a dustpan and brush, and place glass in a glass bin.

▲ **Figure 4** A risk assessment table.

> **B** State a risk associated with using a lit Bunsen burner.

not accurate · accurate
not precise · not precise

not accurate · accurate
precise · precise

▲ **Figure 3** Be aware that sometimes readings can be precise but not accurate. These are often the most misleading.

Summary Questions

1 Match the key term to its definition.

accurate data	the chance someone could be hurt
precise data	close to the true value
hazard	repeat measurements with a small spread
risk	something that could hurt you or anybody else

(3 marks)

2 Describe the difference between repeatable data and reproducible data. (2 marks)

3 A group of students are asked to heat a beaker of water up to boiling point. Complete a risk assessment for this investigation, identifying **two** hazards. (6 marks)

Learning objectives

After this topic, you will be able to:

- select the appropriate graph to display data
- present data as a pie chart or a histogram
- calculate the mean, mode, and median of a set of data.

Reactivate your knowledge

1 What is continuous data?
2 What is discrete data?
3 What are some different ways data can be presented?

▲ **Figure 1** Data can be presented in a number of different ways.

Link ↗

You learnt about categorical, discrete, and continuous data in Working scientifically 1.5 *Presenting data*.

Averages

A group of 5 students scored the following marks on their biology test:

17   11   14   17   16

Calculate the mean, mode, and median scores.

Key words

discrete, categorical, bar chart, pie chart, continuous, line graph, histogram, mean, mode, median

Graphs and charts are used by scientists to share information. How do you know which type of chart to use (**Figure 1**)?

Which chart should you choose?

The chart you decide to use depends on the type of data you have collected. If you have **discrete** or **categorical** data you should choose a **bar chart** or a **pie chart**. If you have **continuous** data you should plot a **line graph** or a **histogram**.

> **A** State the type of chart you would use to display the method of transport students use to get to school.

How do you plot a pie chart?

Pie charts are used to show percentages, or proportions of a total. The whole pie chart represents 100%. It is then divided into sections to represent the data values. To work out the size of each section:

1 Calculate the total of the values to be plotted.

2 Calculate the angle of each section of the pie chart using the formula:

$$\frac{\text{data value}}{\text{total value}} \times 360$$

Katie and Tom collected data on the ages of 90 people who completed a bungee jump. They plotted a pie chart to display their results, shown in Figure 2.

> **B** State which age range contained the fewest bungee jumpers.

Reactivate your knowledge answers
1 Data that can have any value within a range 2 Data that can have only whole-number values 3 Bar chart, line graph, pie chart

How do you plot a histogram?

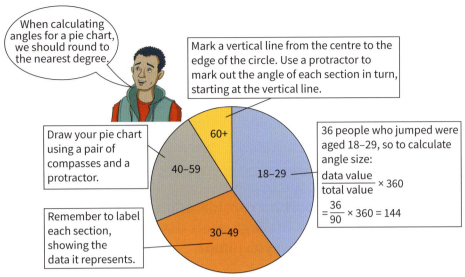

▲ **Figure 2** The students' results are plotted on a pie chart.

A histogram is a chart that is used to visualise the shape of a set of data. It presents continuous data in groups, which makes it easier to see certain information; for example, which is the most common value.

To ensure the bungee jumps are safe, measurements are taken of the jumpers' mass. Tom and Katie plot the mass of the jumpers in the past month as a histogram (Figure 3).

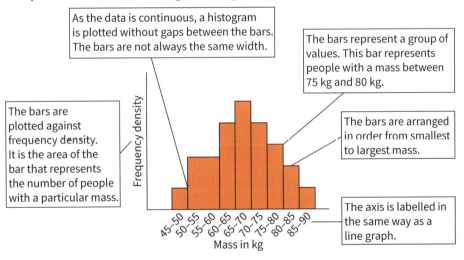

▲ **Figure 3** The features of a histogram.

What are the different types of average?

When looking at a data set, scientists often calculate averages. There are three different types of average:

- **Mean** – calculated by adding up all of the values, and dividing by the number of results.
- **Mode** – the most common value or group (modal group).
- **Median** – the middle value, when the data are placed in numerical order.

Summary Questions

1 Match the type of average measure to the method of calculation.

mean — place numbers from smallest to biggest, and find the middle one

mode — add up values, and divide by number of values

median — identify the value that occurs most

(2 marks)

2 A student collected the following data on the eye colour of members of their class:

Eye colour	Number of students
blue	4
brown	6
green	7
hazel	3

The student chose to display the data as a pie chart. Calculate the angle needed for each pie chart section. (4 marks)

3 A student collected the following data about students' heights within their class:

Student	Height in cm
1	121
2	122
3	162
4	156
5	149
6	164
7	160
8	122
9	158
10	154

a Calculate the mean, mode, and median height. (3 marks)

b Explain which average would give the best measure of the average height of students within the class. (3 marks)

Learning objectives

After this topic, you will be able to:

- identify linear and directly proportional relationships
- take readings from a graph using a line of best fit
- describe how to improve confidence in a conclusion.

Reactivate your knowledge

1 What does a line of best fit show?
2 What shape should a line of best fit be?
3 Which type of average identifies the middle value in a data set?

▲ **Figure 1** Scientific measurements are used to adjust the bungee cord before every jump.

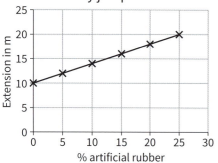

▲ **Figure 2** A graph showing how the bungee cord material affects its extension.

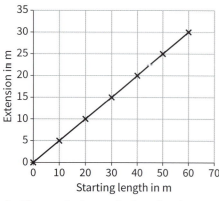

▲ **Figure 3** A graph showing how the starting length of the bungee cord affects its extension.

Safety is the most important consideration when you want to do a bungee jump. How do the organisers use data to ensure you don't hit the ground when you jump?

How do you identify a linear relationship?

Bungee jump organisers need to take both the type and length of a bungee rope into account when deciding how to adjust the cord for a jumper (Figure 1). A group of scientists completed two investigations to collect this data for a group of jump organisers. Their results are shown in Figure 2 and 3.

This graph shows a **linear relationship**. It is a straight-line graph. In this type of relationship, increasing the independent variable causes an increase in the dependent variable. So, in this example, the more artificial rubber the bungee rope contains, the more the rope extends.

> **A** Using Figure 2, state the extension for a bungee rope made of 25% artificial rubber.

The graph in Figure 3 shows a special type of linear relationship, known as a **directly proportional relationship**. It is a straight-line graph that passes through the origin (0,0).

In this type of relationship, doubling the independent variable causes a doubling of the dependent variable. So, in this example, doubling the starting length doubles the extension.

> **B** State how you can tell if a straight-line graph shows a directly proportional relationship.

Reactivate your knowledge answers
1 The pattern/trend in data 2 Curved or straight (going through/close to as many points as possible) 3 Median

Analysing data using a graph

Bungee jump organisers do not have to take measurements on how to adjust a bungee cord for every different jumper's mass. They can determine this information from a graph, by reading from the **line of best fit** based on earlier experiments.

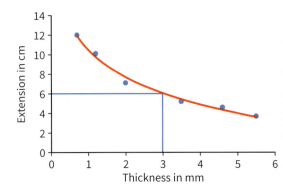

To determine the extension for a 3-mm-thick piece of elastic, draw a vertical line from 3-mm thickness to the line of best fit. Then draw a horizontal line to the y-axis, and read off the scale. In this example, the extension is 6 cm.

▲ **Figure 4** Katie and Tom decided to draw a curved line of best fit. A straight line would not fit their data.

The graph in Figure 4 shows the data Tom and Katie collected about how the thickness of a piece of elastic affected how far it stretched.

> **C** Use the graph to determine how long the extension of a piece of elastic will be if it has a thickness of 5 mm.

Conclusions and limitations

Katie and Tom correctly predicted that a thicker piece of elastic would stretch less when a force is applied. However, Katie and Tom can only draw a limited conclusion, as they can only be certain that the pattern holds true for the thicknesses of elastic they investigated.

The greater the range of the independent variable, the more certain you can be that a pattern holds true for all values. The range and interval for the variables that you use can depend on the equipment available, the measuring instruments, or the time available.

How can you improve confidence in your conclusion?

Katie wondered what real bungee cords were like. She looked up some data on the internet and found a graph showing how the thickness of bungee cords affected how much they stretch. Graphs or data that someone else has collected is known as **secondary data**. The data Katie found show the same pattern as their graph. This allowed Katie and Tom to have more confidence in their conclusion. Repeating an experiment several times also helps to improve your confidence in a conclusion.

Key words

linear relationship, directly proportional, line of best fit, secondary data

Summary Questions

1 Copy and complete the following sentences.

Patterns in data can be shown by adding a line of _____ _____ to your graph.

Data that forms a straight-line graph shows a _____ relationship.

Data that forms a straight-line graph that passes through the origin shows a _____ _____ relationship.

Data collected from other sources, such as the internet, is called _____ data. (4 marks)

2 Describe **three** ways you can increase your confidence in a conclusion. (3 marks)

3 Using data from Figure 3, explain why the relationship between the length of a bungee cord and its extension is described as directly proportional. (4 marks)

Learning objectives

After this topic, you will be able to:

- describe the key features of effective communication
- describe how to adapt communication for different audiences.

Reactivate your knowledge

1 How can you display data visually?
2 What should you include in observational drawings?
3 Name three sections which should be included in a scientific investigation.

▲ **Figure 1** Scientists publish their research in journals, which are read by other scientists. Articles about science are also published in newspapers and magazines.

Check it out

You might find it difficult to work out when your own writing is not clear. Next time you write something, ask someone else to read it and underline sections that they don't understand.

When scientists carry out research they often need to share their discoveries with a wide range of audiences. During a global pandemic, for example, scientists will appear regularly on the TV, on social media, and in the newspapers to explain their most recent findings to the public (Figure 1).

How do you plan your communication?

When you need to **communicate** ideas you need to think about how you are going to do it. Here are some questions that you should think about each time before starting:

- Who is the **audience**?
- What is the **purpose**?
- What is the best structure?
- How can I make it clear, **concise**, correct, and **coherent**?

Concise writing means that you describe or explain as much as possible using the minimum number of words.

Coherent writing is logical, well-organised, and easy to understand.

> **A** Write down two different audiences you may need to communicate with.

How do you write effectively for an audience?

Good communication should be used for all styles of writing, for example, when writing an article or preparing a presentation. To ensure your communication is effective you should:

- use clear language and well-formed sentences
- read any source material carefully, and rewrite anything that is not clear
- check there are no mistakes in spelling, punctuation, or grammar

Reactivate your knowledge answers
1 Using line graphs, pie charts, bar charts, and histograms 2 Clear labels (and where relevant, magnification/scale)
3 For example, hypothesis, method, results table, graph, conclusion

- put paragraphs in a sensible order to 'tell your story'
- use linking words to help the reader connect sentences and paragraphs
- use diagrams, charts, and graphs to communicate data.

All of these ideas help to make sure the audience understands what you are saying, and why you are saying it.

How should you write for a scientific audience?

When you write up an investigation, you are probably writing for your teacher or other students. A scientific investigation report should include:

- a hypothesis or prediction
- a method, written in the third person, with a labelled diagram of your equipment
- a risk assessment
- your results table and analysis of the data
- your conclusions and evaluation.

You should take care to use the correct scientific vocabulary; words often have a different meaning in science than in everyday life.

How do you write for different audiences?

There are many other types of audience. You will communicate effectively if you adapt your writing to suit the audience. Table 1 shows some examples.

What you are writing	How to adapt your writing
an information leaflet for primary pupils	• use simpler words • use shorter sentences
a newspaper article for the general public	• illustrate ideas with real-life examples • use vivid words, describing real things • if you are making a claim, make sure that you clearly state the evidence that you are using • make a list of the points and cover one in each paragraph
a scientific article	• use diagrams to make the meaning clear • use scientific vocabulary, units, and chemical notation accurately

▲ **Table 1** Different types of science writing and ways to adapt to your audience.

> **B** Write down one thing that you should include in a newspaper article but not in a scientific article.

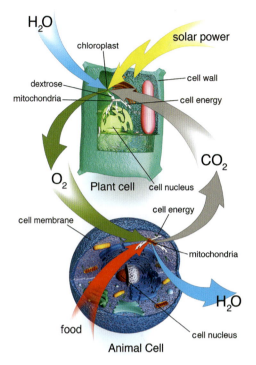

▲ **Figure 2** Diagrams are very important if you want to communicate clearly. It would take many paragraphs to describe what this diagram shows.

Key words

communication, audience, purpose, concise, coherent

Summary Questions

1 List four strategies that you should use when you are writing about a science investigation. (4 marks)

2 Compare writing for a science journal with writing for the general public. (4 marks)

3 Write a leaflet aimed at primary school students based on Katie and Tom's investigation into elastic bands and explain how your writing is suitable for the audience. (6 marks)

Learning objectives

After this topic, you will be able to:

- describe what peer review is
- describe how to assess sources of evidence
- identify possible sources of bias.

▲ **Figure 1** Scientists collect a range of evidence through observations, chemical tests, and measurements.

Link

You learnt about effective communication in *Working scientifically 2.4 Communicating scientific information*.

▲ **Figure 2** Journalists for science magazines often use the peer-reviewed articles that scientists publish in journals for their articles.

Historians use evidence to make conclusions about the past. Police need evidence to convict people of crimes. Scientists collect evidence through data (Figure 1). However, scientific evidence has to be checked before it is accepted as true.

How good is the evidence?

Not all **evidence** carries equal weight. For example, you may hear someone say:

'I know what they say about smoking, but my grandfather smoked every day for 50 years and he didn't get cancer.'

This is not scientific evidence. It is called **anecdotal** evidence. You cannot reason from this one example that smoking doesn't cause cancer. Scientific evidence is checked by other scientists.

What is a peer review?

Scientists make hypotheses, devise ways to test their hypotheses, collect evidence, and write up their investigation. This is not the end of their work. They then submit their work to a scientific **journal**. The editor of the journal sends it to other scientists working in the field who judge whether the work is correct. This is called **peer review**.

This is a checking system to make sure that the work is accurate, and that you can believe the conclusions that have been made. Work that has not gone through this process is not scientific evidence.

A State where scientists publish their results.

How do you interrogate sources?

How do you know if an information source can be trusted? To judge the reliability of evidence you need to consider the answers to a range of questions as shown in Table 1. The more reliable the source, the more valuable the information.

What to look for	Questions to ask
Who are the authors?	• Are they qualified scientists? • Is this their field of study?
Where is the **research** published?	• Has it been published in a peer-reviewed journal?
When was the research published?	• Are the data still up to date?
What were the findings of the research?	• Does it agree with current scientific thinking? • Did the author give a scientific explanation of the findings?
Does the scientist have a vested interest in the results?	• Who is the funder of the research? • Does the scientist work for a company that would like the conclusion to be a certain way?
Were there enough data to justify the conclusion?	• How many data points were collected? • What was the range and interval of measurements? • Was the sample big enough? • Were all the categories (of age/gender etc.) involved that should be?
What does other research into this area say?	• Are the findings backed up by other research? Who did that research?

▲ **Table 1** Questions to determine the reliability of evidence.

> **B** Write down three things you need to comment on when you judge the reliability of a source.

Who funds scientific research?

- Governments. Scientists write grant proposals to get money to do research. For example, for universities to develop vaccines. The government gets its money from taxpayers.
- Companies. For example, a car company might fund research into how to reduce vehicle emissions.
- Non-profit organisations, such as charities. For example, the British Heart Foundation might research the effect of a particular diet on the risk of heart disease.

What is bias?

If someone has a **bias** it means that they have a preference for something, which can be unfair. Biased information may be:

- a personal opinion – for example, a scientist developing a health product may claim it tastes sweeter even though it has less sugar
- a statement that has no factual basis – for example, a vitamin supplement may claim to 'help manage stress levels' but not be backed up by scientific evidence
- prejudiced towards or against another person, product, situation, or idea. For example, a scientist researching the impact of a new drug may focus on the health benefits, rather than highlight any side effects, if they work for the drug company.

Key words

evidence, anecdotal, journal, peer review, research, bias

Summary Questions

1 Copy and complete the following sentences.

biased   funding
peer reviewed   reliable

When a scientist checks another scientist's work, we say it has been _____ _____.

This makes the evidence in the work more _____.

Evidence may be _____ if the person doing the research could benefit from it, or if the person _____ the research could make money from the results. (4 marks)

2 In 1972, John Sawyer, a meteorologist, published evidence in the scientific journal 'Nature'. It said there is a link between man-made CO_2 and a rise in global temperatures.
a Explain why this evidence is probably reliable. (2 marks)
b Explain why a journalist may be biased in their reporting of this claim. (5 marks)

3 A food company produces a new low-fat dessert, which it claims is 'the after-dinner treat that keeps your heart healthy'. The claim is based on research completed by the company's own team of scientists.

Suggest some possible reasons for the research being biased, and how this may affect the reliability of the company's health claims. (4 marks)

Learning objectives

After this topic, you will be able to:

- describe what is meant by the scientific method
- describe the difference between a theory, a law, and a model
- describe how our understanding of science changes over time.

Reactivate your knowledge

1 Give some examples of scientific evidence.
2 What is a hypothesis?
3 Where do scientists publish the results of their research?

Key words

scientific method, observation, model, law, theory

From the Middle Ages until Victorian times, most people thought that disease was caused by a poisonous vapour (miasma) that came from decaying matter. How did scientists change our thinking?

The scientific method

Throughout your work in science, you are using the **scientific method**. This is an evidence-based approach to developing our understanding of the world around us (Figure 1).

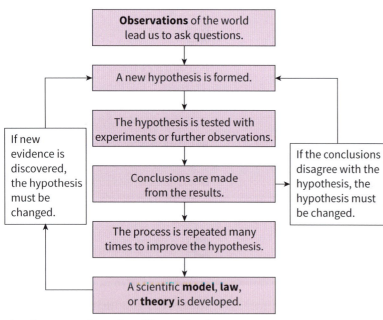

▲ **Figure 1** The scientific method involves a cyclical process of forming and testing hypotheses.

A model is a way of representing something that is too difficult to display because it is too big, too small, or too complicated. The mental image it gives you enables you to explain or predict the results of experiments.

A law is a scientific rule that is supported by evidence, such as 'energy cannot be created or destroyed'. Scientific laws do not explain why something happens.

Scientific theories are explanations of the world around us, based on evidence produced using the scientific method. This evidence must also be peer reviewed. Examples include the theory of evolution and the Big Bang theory.

A State the difference between a theory and a law.

Reactivate your knowledge answers

1 Measurements, observations 2 A description of what you think will happen, backed up with scientific reasoning
3 Scientific journals

Why do scientific ideas develop over time?

Although scientific models, laws, and theories are supported by experimental evidence, sometimes a new piece of information is discovered; for example, as a result of new technology or from another scientist having a different way of thinking. This might mean that the scientific idea is:

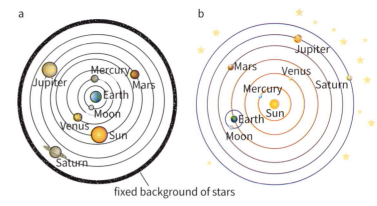

fixed background of stars

▲ **Figure 2** Ptolemy's Earth-centred model of the Solar System (a) and Copernicus's Sun-centred model (b).

- improved, because the new evidence tells us new information
- completely changed, because the new evidence proves that the existing idea cannot be true.

How did our understanding of the Solar System develop?

Since ancient times, humans have studied the night sky. A model of the Solar System was developed by Ptolemy in around 150 CE. It is known as the geocentric model. Ptolemy believed the Earth was at the centre of the Solar System (Figure 2a).

Ptolemy's model was based on careful observations of the movement of planets through the night sky. However, it did not always accurately predict the planets' positions.

> **B** Which parts of the Solar System did Ptolemy get correct in his geocentric model?

Almost 1500 years later, Nicolaus Copernicus developed a new model of the Solar System – the heliocentric (Sun-centred) model. From observational evidence, he discovered that the Earth rotates on its axis. In the Copernican model, the planets orbit the Sun in perfectly circular orbits (Figure 2b).

In 1609, Johannes Kepler refined the Solar System model after studying data on the planets' positions. Kepler realised that the orbits were not perfectly circular. This improved Copernicus's model, and led more astronomers to support the heliocentric model.

At around the same time, Galileo Galilei developed the first telescope. This allowed him to view some of the moons orbiting Jupiter. He realised these were like the planets orbiting the Sun. This development provided further evidence for the heliocentric model.

Summary Questions

1 Copy and complete the following sentences.

method   model   evidence   explanation   law

A scientific theory is a well-thought-out _____ of a scientific event. It is backed up by _____ that has been collected using the scientific _____ . A scientific _____ describes how a system will behave, but does not explain why. A _____ visually represents a complicated concept. (5 marks)

2 Describe two reasons why a scientist may change a hypothesis. (2 marks)

3 Suggest three reasons why most astronomers in the 1600s rejected the heliocentric model, even after the work of Kepler and Galileo was published. (3 marks)

Welcome

Biology is the study of living things. You will compare the effects of healthy and unhealthy lifestyles on your body. You will look at why organisms need energy to function well and how plants produce their own food using energy from the Sun.

You will explore the relationships between organisms–how they interact with each other and their environment, and why this is important for survival. You will also study how organisms have changed over time in response to changes in their surroundings.

2 Biology

Where can biology take you?

A good knowledge of biology is important for many different parts of your life. Every experience you have as a human being will build on this knowledge. As you learn more about the world around you, you will keep on discovering how living organisms are affected by, and have an effect on, their environment.

Studying biology equips you with many skills, and prepares you for a wide range of jobs, careers, and interests you may wish to follow in the future.

Vet

Physiotherapist

Sports coach

Marine biologist

Midwife

Commercial flower grower

Medical researcher

Environmentalist

Biology and the world

Biologists have a responsibility to look after the living environment, and increase our understanding of the natural world. We are experiencing climate change and environmental damage caused by human activity in all parts of the world. There has never been a more important time for us to understand how we can act together to protect all living species, and maintain or bring back the natural habitats of plants, animals, and microorganisms.

BIG QUESTIONS

Why do organisms need to eat to survive?
Observing what happens when people eat the wrong types of foods, provides clues of the role different food groups play within the body.

How do plants make food?
Providing plants with different raw materials has enabled scientists to discover what plants need to survive, and how we can help plants to grow more rapidly.

Why don't we all look the same?
Amazingly, plant experiments revealed the ways in which organisms reproduce, which explains how we inherit information from our biological parents.

Journey through B2

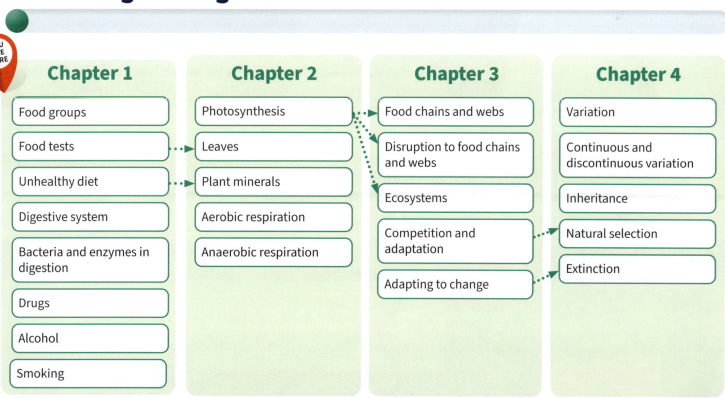

YOU ARE HERE

Chapter 1
- Food groups
- Food tests
- Unhealthy diet
- Digestive system
- Bacteria and enzymes in digestion
- Drugs
- Alcohol
- Smoking

Chapter 2
- Photosynthesis
- Leaves
- Plant minerals
- Aerobic respiration
- Anaerobic respiration

Chapter 3
- Food chains and webs
- Disruption to food chains and webs
- Ecosystems
- Competition and adaptation
- Adapting to change

Chapter 4
- Variation
- Continuous and discontinuous variation
- Inheritance
- Natural selection
- Extinction

In this chapter you will learn about the components of a balanced diet and how much of each component you should eat to remain healthy. You will also test a range of foods to identify which nutrients they contain.

You will study the main organs in the digestive system and the role enzymes and some bacteria play in digestion.

Finally, you will look at the effects of drugs on the body, focusing on smoking and alcohol.

Reactivate your knowledge

1 Draw a plate containing a healthy meal. Label the food groups contained in each type of food.

2 Name some organs in the digestive system. Add a note describing what they do.

3 Make a list of some medical and non-medical drugs.

You already know

A healthy diet contains lots of fruit and vegetables and only a small amount of fat and sugar.

An organ system is a group of different organs that work together to perform a certain function.

Glucose and oxygen diffuse into cells from the blood.

People can take medicines when they are unwell to make them feel better.

 How to calculate percentages.

 How to work scientifically to: make a prediction.

Journey through B2

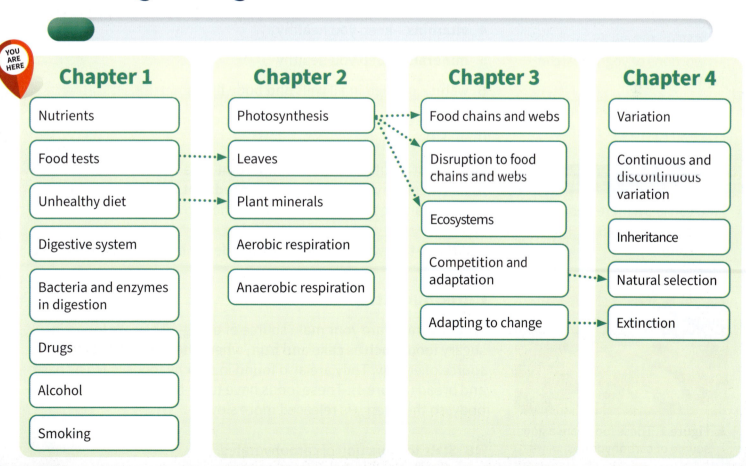

Chapter 1

- Nutrients
- Food tests
- Unhealthy diet
- Digestive system
- Bacteria and enzymes in digestion
- Drugs
- Alcohol
- Smoking

Chapter 2

- Photosynthesis
- Leaves
- Plant minerals
- Aerobic respiration
- Anaerobic respiration

Chapter 3

- Food chains and webs
- Disruption to food chains and webs
- Ecosystems
- Competition and adaptation
- Adapting to change

Chapter 4

- Variation
- Continuous and discontinuous variation
- Inheritance
- Natural selection
- Extinction

1.1 Nutrients

Learning objectives

After this topic, you will be able to:

- describe what is meant by a balanced diet
- name the seven components of a balanced diet, giving examples
- describe the role of each component of a balanced diet.

Reactivate your knowledge

1 Name the organ in the body where food is broken down.
2 What is meant by an organ system?
3 Name the organ system in the body where food is broken down.

Key words

nutrient, carbohydrate, lipid, protein, vitamin, mineral, fibre, balanced diet

How much yoghurt?

A family-size 500 g yoghurt pot contains 55 g of sugar. A recommended portion is 100 g.

1 Calculate how many portions of yoghurt are in the 500 g pot.

2 Calculate how much sugar each portion contains.

Link

You can learn more about balanced diets in B2 1.3 *Unhealthy diet*.

▲ **Figure 1** These foods are a good source of carbohydrates.

We all know that sweets should only be eaten as a treat, and you have probably heard many times that you should eat a balanced diet. But what does this mean, and why is it important?

Nutrients are important substances that your body needs to survive and stay healthy. There are different types of nutrients. We get most of them from food. The types of nutrient are:

1 **carbohydrates** – provide energy

2 **lipids** (fats and oils) – provide energy

3 **proteins** – used for growth and repair

4 **vitamins** – keep you healthy

5 **minerals** – keep you healthy

6 water – needed in all cells and body fluids

We also need **fibre** to provide bulk to food and keep it moving though the gut.

Fibre is not a nutrient but it is important for a healthy diet. To remain healthy you must eat a **balanced diet**. This means eating food containing the right nutrients in the correct amounts.

A Name the two nutrients that provide the body with energy.

Carbohydrates

Carbohydrates are your main source of energy. They are found in sugary foods such as cake and fruit, where they provide a quick source of energy. They are also found in starchy foods, such as pasta and bread (Figure 1). These foods have to be broken down by the body, so the energy is released more slowly.

B State the function of carbohydrates.

Reactivate your knowledge answers
1 Stomach 2 Group of organs working together to perform a function 3 Digestive system

Lipids

Lipids include fats and oils (Figure 2). They have three important jobs. They:

- provide you with a store of energy
- keep you warm, by providing a layer of insulation under your skin
- protect organs like your kidneys and heart from damage.

Proteins

Proteins (Figure 3) are needed to repair body tissues and to make new cells for growth. Your muscles, organs, and immune system are mostly made of proteins.

> **C** Give two example of foods that have a high protein content.

Vitamins and minerals

Vitamins and minerals are essential substances for keeping you healthy, but you only need tiny amounts. Vitamins are needed for you to grow, develop, and function normally. For example, vitamin A is needed for good eyesight. Vitamin D is needed with the mineral calcium to maintain healthy teeth and bones. Fruits and vegetables are a good source of vitamins and minerals.

Water

Your cells are made up of about 70% water. To keep them healthy you need to constantly replace the water your body loses in sweat, tears, urine, faeces, and exhaling. You should drink over a litre of water every day. This can come from drinking water, but tea, fruit juice, and squash all count.

> **D** Explain why you need to drink more water on a hot day.

Fibre

Fibre is a type of carbohydrate but it is not classed as a nutrient. However, it is an important part of your diet as it adds bulk to your food (Figure 4). This means it keeps food moving through the gut, and waste is pushed out of the body more easily, helping to prevent constipation.

▲ **Figure 2** These foods have a high fat content.

▲ **Figure 3** These foods are a good source of protein.

Summary Questions

1 Match each nutrient to its role in the body.

carbohydrates	growth and repair
lipids	remain healthy
protein	provide energy
vitamins and minerals	provide bulk to food
water	energy store and insulation
fibre	needed in cells and bodily fluids

(5 marks)

2 Describe the role of lipids in the body. (2 marks)

3 a Explain how carbohydrates allow the body to function. (2 marks)

b Explain how eating a fibre-rich diet helps prevent constipation. (2 marks)

▲ **Figure 4** Fibre-rich foods.

Learning objectives

After this topic, you will be able to:

- name the chemicals used to test foods for starch, lipids, sugar, and protein
- state the positive result for each food test
- describe how to test foods for starch, lipids, sugar, and protein.

Reactivate your knowledge

1   Name the nutrient that is used for growth and repair.
2   What is the main function of carbohydrates?
3   What is meant by a balanced diet?

Key words

food test, starch, iodine, lipid, sugar, Benedict's solution, protein, biuret solution

You may be able to guess by looking at some foods which nutrients they contain. For example, you may know that oily foods contain lipids. Scientists use food tests to find out which nutrients are in a food product.

How can you test foods?

A different chemical test exists for each type of nutrient. For most **food tests**, you will need a solution of the food. To prepare a food solution:

1   crush the food using a pestle and mortar
2   add a few drops of water and mix well.

You should use a special type of water called distilled water – this is pure water that contains no other chemical substances.

How do you test for starch?

To test for **starch**, you use **iodine** solution. Iodine solution is an orange-yellow liquid.

1   Add a few drops of iodine solution to the food solution.
2   If the solution turns a dark blue-black colour, the food contains starch (Figure 1).

A   Potatoes contain starch. State the colour a potato would appear after iodine has been added.

How do you test for lipids?

To test for **lipids** in a solid piece of food, you use a piece of filter paper.

1   Rub some of the food onto a piece of filter paper.
2   Hold the paper up to the light.
3   If the paper has gone translucent, the food contains lipids.

▲ **Figure 1** Iodine changes from orange-yellow to blue-black if starch is present.

To test for lipids in a food solution, you use ethanol. Ethanol is a colourless liquid.

1   Add a few drops of ethanol to the food solution.

2   Shake the test tube and leave for one minute.

3   Pour the ethanol into a test tube of water.

4   If the solution turns cloudy, the food contains lipids (Figure 2).

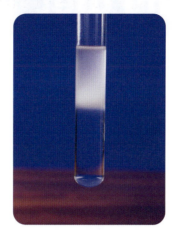

▲ **Figure 2** Ethanol forms a cloudy solution if lipids are present.

B   Describe how you would test a chip to see if it contains fat.

How do you test for sugar?

To test for simple **sugars** such as glucose you use **Benedict's solution**. Benedict's solution is a blue liquid.

1   Add a few drops of Benedict's solution to the food solution.

2   Heat the test tube in a water bath.

3   If the solution turns orange-red, the food contains sugar (Figure 3).

▲ **Figure 3** Benedict's solution turns orange-red if a food contains sugar.

C   Identify which of the following foods would turn orange-red if Benedict's solution were added: vegetable oil, boiled sweets, flour.

How do you test for protein?

To test for **protein**, you use **biuret solution**. This is a pale-blue liquid.

1   Add a few drops of biuret solution to your food solution.

2   If the solution turns purple, the food contains protein (Figure 4).

▲ **Figure 4** Biuret solution turns purple if a food contains protein.

D   Describe how you can tell that a solution made from fish contains protein.

Risky food tests

Before carrying out a food test, a risk assessment must be performed.
Biuret solution is an irritant. Suggest some actions you should take to minimise the risks of working with this chemical.

Summary Questions

1 Complete the table using the words below.

turns blue-black
turns orange-red
makes paper translucent
turns purple

Nutrient	Colour change if nutrient present
starch	
lipids	
sugar	
protein	

(4 marks)

2 A student wants to test their cereal for sugar.

a Describe how to prepare a food solution of a breakfast cereal. (2 marks)

b Name the chemical that would be used to test the cereal for the presence of sugar. (1 mark)

3 Explain which chemicals would produce a positive food test result for a birthday cake. (4 marks)

Learning objectives

After this topic, you will be able to:

- describe some health issues caused by an unhealthy diet
- state what is meant by a vitamin or mineral deficiency
- compare the energy requirements of different people.

Reactivate your knowledge

1 Give one problem that may be caused by eating an unhealthy diet.
2 Name the two types of nutrient that provide the body with energy.
3 Name a good source of vitamins and minerals.

Key words

malnourishment, starvation, obese, deficiency

▲ **Figure 1** This food pyramid shows a healthy balanced diet.

Energy requirements

If a person changes job, their energy requirements may change. To calculate percentage change, use the following formula:

$$\frac{\text{new value} - \text{original value}}{\text{original value}} \times 100$$

Using the graph in Figure 3, calculate the percentage change for a female office worker who becomes pregnant.

You may have seen pictures of people who are either extremely overweight or underweight. Both of these conditions can be caused by malnourishment. This means the people may have eaten the wrong amount or the wrong types of food.

Where does your energy come from?

You need energy for everything you do, even to sleep. This energy comes from your food. You can see how different types of food make up a balanced diet in Figure 1. The largest part of your diet should be carbohydrate-based. Lipids, oils, and sweets should only be eaten in very small quantities.

The energy in food is measured in joules (J) or kilojoules (kJ). 1 kilojoule is the same as 1000 joules. If you look on a food label it will tell you how much energy is stored in that food.

A Write down the number of joules in 2 kJ.

Why is it unhealthy to be underweight?

Some people do not eat enough food. In extreme cases this is known as **starvation**. If the energy in the food you eat is less than the energy you use, you will lose body mass. This leads to you being underweight. Underweight people:

- often suffer from health problems, such as a poor immune system
- lack energy to do things, and are often tired
- are likely to suffer from a lack of vitamins or minerals.

B State three problems caused by being underweight.

Reactivate your knowledge answers
1 Become overweight or underweight/lack energy/any other sensible suggestion 2 Lipids and carbohydrates 3 Fruits/vegetables

Why is it unhealthy to be overweight?

Some people eat too much, or eat too many fatty foods. If the energy content in the food you eat is more than the energy you use, you gain body mass. This is stored as fat under the skin. If a person becomes extremely overweight, they are said to be **obese**. Overweight people have an increased risk of:

- heart disease
- stroke
- diabetes
- some cancers

> **C** State three diseases that obese people are more likely to suffer from.

What are vitamin and mineral deficiencies?

If a person does not have enough of a certain vitamin or mineral, they are said to have a **deficiency**. This can damage a person's health. For example, a vitamin A deficiency can lead to 'night blindness'. This makes it difficult for you to see clearly in dim light. A vitamin D deficiency can lead to a condition called rickets, where your bones become weak (Figure 2).

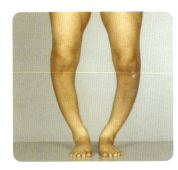

▲ **Figure 2** This person is suffering from rickets.

How much energy do you need?

Your body needs energy to function properly. The amount of energy you need depends on your age (as this affects your growth rate), your body size, and how active you are. The more exercise you do, the more energy your body requires (Figure 3).

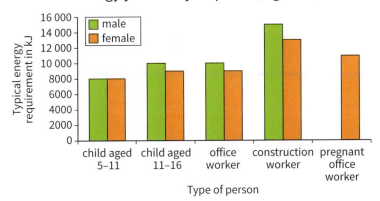

▲ **Figure 3** Daily energy requirements for different types of people.

> **D** Identify which of the following people needs more energy to do their job – a farmer, a computer programmer, a librarian.

Link ↗

You can learn more about energy in food in P2 2.1 *Food and fuels*.

Summary Questions

1 Copy and complete the following sentences.

You gain the _____ you need to survive from food. Energy is measured in _____.

If you take in more energy than you need, you can become _____. This increases the risk of diseases such as _____. An underweight person is often _____. (5 marks)

2 Use the graph in Figure 3 to answer the following questions.

a Calculate the amount of extra energy a female office worker would need each day if she became pregnant. (2 marks)
b A male office worker starts a new job as a construction worker. Calculate the percentage increase in his daily energy needs. (4 marks)

3 Use the information in the graph in Figure 3 to estimate the daily energy requirements of a female science teacher. Justify your answer. (3 marks)

Learning objectives

After this topic, you will be able to:

- describe the process of digestion
- describe the function of the main structures in the digestive system.

Reactivate your knowledge

1 What is the function of the digestive system?
2 Name some organs in the digestive system.
3 Name the food component that adds bulk to food.

Key words

digestive system, digestion, stomach, small intestine, rectum, anus, large intestine, gut, villi

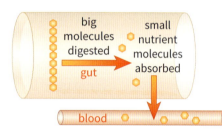

▲ **Figure 1** The small nutrient molecules produced in digestion pass into the bloodstream.

You may sometimes notice your stomach rumbling. This is a hint that you need to eat. You know that food contains nutrients. But how does your body get nutrients out of food?

What is the digestive system?

The **digestive system** is a group of organs that work together to break down food. The nutrients in most of the food you eat are large molecules, like lipids and proteins. During **digestion** these large molecules are broken down into small nutrient molecules. These nutrients can then pass into the blood where they are used by the body (Figure 1).

> **A** Compare the size of food molecules before and after digestion.

Structures in the digestive system

Your digestive system digests the food that you eat. Figure 2 shows the digestive system and its different parts.

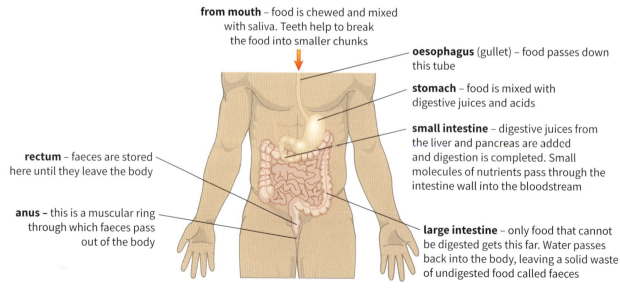

from mouth – food is chewed and mixed with saliva. Teeth help to break the food into smaller chunks

oesophagus (gullet) – food passes down this tube

stomach – food is mixed with digestive juices and acids

small intestine – digestive juices from the liver and pancreas are added and digestion is completed. Small molecules of nutrients pass through the intestine wall into the bloodstream

rectum – faeces are stored here until they leave the body

anus – this is a muscular ring through which faeces pass out of the body

large intestine – only food that cannot be digested gets this far. Water passes back into the body, leaving a solid waste of undigested food called faeces

▲ **Figure 2** Structures in the digestive system – often referred to as your **gut**.

Reactivate your knowledge answers
1 Break down food 2 Stomach/intestine/mouth 3 Fibre

B List the organs in the order that food passes through them in the digestive system.

Moving through the digestive system

Fibre in your food isn't digested but adds bulk to the food. Muscles push against this, forcing food along the gut (Figure 3). Eating lots of fibre-rich foods such as vegetables and wholemeal bread helps prevent constipation.

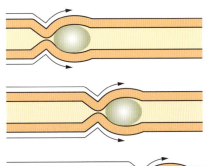

C Describe how food moves along the gut.

▲ **Figure 3** Muscles in the wall of the gut squeeze food along – a bit like squeezing a tube of toothpaste.

Passing into the blood

The small molecules of nutrients produced during digestion pass into the bloodstream through the wall of the small intestine. They are then transported around the body.

The small intestine needs to absorb the nutrients quickly, before the undigested food passes out of the body. The small intestine is specially adapted to this function. The wall of the small intestine is thin. It is also covered with tiny structures called **villi** (Figure 4). These stick out of the wall and give it a big surface area. They also contain blood capillaries to carry away the absorbed food molecules.

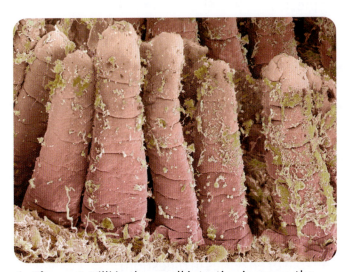

▲ **Figure 4** Villi in the small intestine increase the surface area so more nutrients can be absorbed.

Link ↗

You learnt about molecules in C1 2.3 *Compounds*.

Wordbank 🎯

Make a wordbank by listing all the scientific terms about digestion. You can refer to your wordbank as you progress through this topic.

Summary Questions

1 Match each organ below to its role in digestion.

stomach	food is chewed and mixed with saliva
small intestine	water is absorbed back into the body
large intestine	food is mixed with acid and digestive juices
rectum	faeces are stored here until they pass out of the body
mouth	small molecules of nutrients are absorbed into the bloodstream

(4 marks)

2 Describe the process of digestion using a named nutrient. (3 marks)

3 Explain the structural adaptations of the small intestine. (4 marks)

Learning objectives

After this topic, you will be able to:

- describe the role of bacteria in digestion
- define what is meant by an enzyme
- describe the role of enzymes in carbohydrate, protein, and lipid digestion.

Reactivate your knowledge

1 What is meant by a unicellular organism?
2 What happens during digestion?
3 What food group does starch belong to?

▲ **Figure 1** Some foods, called probiotic foods, contain bacteria that help digestion in the body. Live yoghurts are a good source of these bacteria.

Have you seen the TV adverts that say that yoghurts and yoghurt drinks are good for your digestive system? They contain bacteria, which are important for digestion (Figure 1).

How do bacteria aid digestion?

Your large intestine contains bacteria. They live on the fibre in your diet. They make important vitamins such as vitamin K. (Vitamin K is a group of vitamins that the body needs for blood clotting, helping wounds to heal.) These vitamins are then absorbed into your body and help to keep you healthy.

A State why bacteria are important in your digestive system.

What's in digestive juices?

Your teeth begin digestion by breaking down food into smaller pieces. The digestive juices in your gut contain

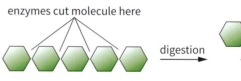
enzymes cut molecule here   digestion

▲ **Figure 2** Enzymes chop large molecules into smaller molecules.

enzymes. These are special proteins that can break large molecules of nutrients into small molecules.

Large molecules in your food like starch, a type of carbohydrate, are made of lots of smaller molecules joined together. Enzymes chop these large molecules into the smaller molecules they are made from (Figure 2).

Enzymes are known as biological **catalysts** – they speed up digestion without being used up.

B State the role of enzymes in digestion.

Key words

enzyme, catalyst, carbohydrase, protease, lipase, bile

What happens to the bread you eat?

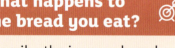

Describe the journey bread takes through your body and how it is digested. Present its journey as a flow diagram. Hint – bread contains a lot of starch.

Reactivate your knowledge answers
1 Organism made of only one cell 2 Breakdown of large food molecules into small molecules 3 Carbohydrates

Different types of enzyme

Different types of enzyme break down different nutrients. The three main types of digestive enzymes are – **carbohydrase**, **protease**, and **lipase**.

Carbohydrase

Carbohydrase is an enzyme that breaks down carbohydrates into sugar molecules (Figure 3). Carbohydrates are digested in the mouth, stomach, and small intestine. Carbohydrase present in your saliva breaks down the starch in bread into sugar.

Protease

Protease is an enzyme that breaks down proteins into amino acids (Figure 4).

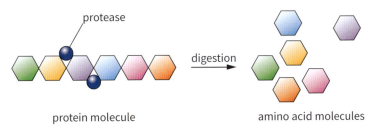

protease

digestion

protein molecule

amino acid molecules

▲ **Figure 4** Protein is broken down into amino acids.

Proteins are digested in the stomach and small intestine. Acid in the stomach helps digestion and kills harmful microorganisms in food.

Lipase

Lipase is an enzyme that breaks down lipids into fatty acids and glycerol (Figure 5). Digestion of lipids takes place in the small intestine. It is helped by **bile**, a substance made in the liver. Bile breaks the lipids into small droplets that are easier for the lipase enzymes to work on.

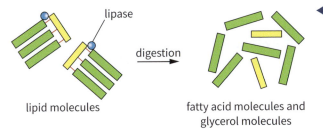

lipase

digestion

lipid molecules

fatty acid molecules and glycerol molecules

◀ **Figure 5** Lipids are broken down into fatty acids and glycerol.

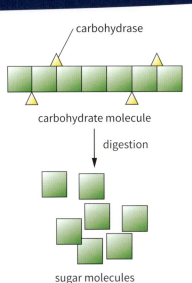

carbohydrase

carbohydrate molecule

digestion

sugar molecules

▲ **Figure 3** Starch is broken down into sugar molecules.

Summary Questions

1 Copy and complete the following sentences.

Carbohydrates/proteins are broken down into sugars by the enzyme **lipase/carbohydrase**.
Proteins are broken down into **amino acids/lipase** by the enzyme **carbohydrase/protease**.
Lipids are broken down into **lipase/fatty acids and glycerol** by the enzyme **lipase/carbohydrase.**   (6 marks)

2 a State where bacteria are found in the digestive system.   (1 mark)

b Name the source of nutrition for bacteria in the human digestive system.   (1 mark)

c Describe **one** benefit of having bacteria in the digestive system.   (1 mark)

3 Explain the role of enzymes in digestion.   (4 marks)

1.6 Drugs

Learning objectives

After this topic, you will be able to:
- define what is meant by a drug
- describe the difference between recreational and medicinal drugs
- describe what happens during drug addiction.

Reactivate your knowledge

1 Name two things you should do to stay healthy.
2 Name some medicines people take when they feel unwell.
3 Name the organ system that controls body reactions.

Key words

drug, medicinal drug, recreational drug, addiction, withdrawal symptoms

Some drugs can seriously damage your health, or even be deadly. Some can save your life, and are used widely in medicine. So what's the difference?

What are drugs?

Drugs are chemical substances that affect the way your body works. They alter the chemical reactions that take place inside your body. Sometimes these changes are helpful but in many cases they are harmful.

There are two types of drugs – **medicinal drugs** and **recreational drugs**.

> **A** State what is meant by a drug.

What are medicinal drugs?

Medicinal drugs are used in medicine. They benefit your health in some way. They may be used to treat the symptoms of a condition; for example, paracetamol is taken to relieve pain. Other drugs can cure an illness. For example, antibiotics are often used to treat chest infections (Figure 1).

However, even medicinal drugs can cause harm if you do not take them in the right way. Some medicinal drugs also have unwanted side effects. When prescribing drugs, doctors have to weigh up the benefits of a person taking a drug against any possible risks.

> **B** Explain why a person may take a medicinal drug.

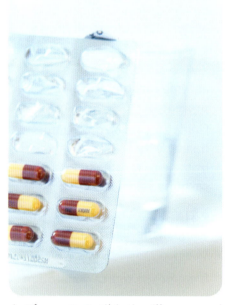

▲ **Figure 1** Antibiotic pills are used to treat bacterial infections.

Reactivate your knowledge answers
1 Eat a balanced diet/exercise regularly/sleep well 2 E.g., cough medicine, aspirin, paracetamol 3 Nervous system

What are recreational drugs?

Recreational drugs are drugs that people take for enjoyment, to help them relax, or to help them to stay awake. Recreational drugs normally have no health benefits and in many cases are harmful.

C Give two reasons why a person might take a recreational drug.

Recreational drugs are not prescribed by a doctor. Many are illegal (Figure 2) – this means that you are breaking the law if you take them. Even very small amounts of these drugs can damage your body. Examples of these drugs include heroin, cocaine, cannabis, and ecstasy.

D Name three illegal drugs.

Some recreational drugs, like those in Figure 3, are legal to use. They can still be harmful. These include:

- alcohol – drinking alcohol affects your nervous system and damages your liver.
- tobacco – smoking significantly increases your risk of cancer, as well as lung and heart disease.
- caffeine (Figure 3) – affects the nervous system, making you feel less tired.

▲ **Figure 2** Many recreational drugs are illegal.

▲ **Figure 3** Caffeine is a recreational drug that speeds up your nervous system.

Drug addiction

If your body gets used to the changes caused by a drug, it may become dependent on the drug. This means that you need to keep taking the drug to feel normal. If this happens you have an **addiction**. If a person with an addiction tries to stop taking the drug, they may suffer **withdrawal symptoms**. These can be very unpleasant and make it even harder to give up the drug. Withdrawal symptoms include headaches, anxiety, and sweating.

Summary Questions

1 Copy and complete the following sentences.

Drugs are _____ that affect the way your body works.

_____ drugs are taken for enjoyment. _____ drugs benefit health.

If you take drugs too often you may develop an _____. When addicted people stop taking drugs, they suffer _____, which can make it harder to give up.
(5 marks)

2 Describe **three** differences between medicinal drugs and recreational drugs. (3 marks)

3 Suggest and explain **two** impacts on society of drug addiction. (4 marks)

Learning objectives

After this topic, you will be able to:

- describe some effects of alcohol on the body
- describe some health problems caused by alcohol
- describe some effects of alcohol on conception and pregnancy.

Reactivate your knowledge

1 What is a drug?
2 What is a recreational drug?
3 What are withdrawal symptoms?

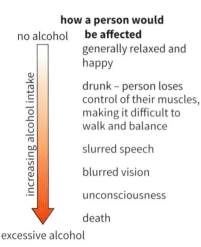

increasing alcohol intake

	how a person would be affected
no alcohol	generally relaxed and happy
	drunk – person loses control of their muscles, making it difficult to walk and balance
	slurred speech
	blurred vision
	unconsciousness
	death
excessive alcohol	

▲ **Figure 1** This diagram shows what happens to a person as they increase their alcohol intake.

Key words

ethanol, depressant, addiction, alcoholic, unit of alcohol

pint of lager	alcopop	glass of wine	shot of vodka
3	1.5	2	1

units of alcohol

▲ **Figure 2** How many units of alcohol are in each drink?

Many adults drink alcohol but it can be harmful. Drinking even small amounts of alcohol can change your behaviour. It can make some people feel relaxed and happy but others can feel aggressive or unhappy.

What is alcohol?

Alcohol contains the drug **ethanol**. When you drink alcohol, ethanol is absorbed into your bloodstream. It then travels to your brain, where it affects your nervous system (Figure 1). This chemical is called a **depressant** because it slows down your body's reactions.

> **A** Name the drug found in wine and beer.

If people drink a lot of alcohol regularly, they may need to drink greater and greater volumes to cause the same effect on their body. They may become addicted. People who have an **addiction** to alcohol are called **alcoholics**.

> **B** State what is meant by the word alcoholic.

How much alcohol can you drink safely?

Different alcoholic drinks contain different concentrations of alcohol. For example, spirits such as vodka and whisky contain more alcohol than beer.

To lower the risk of damage to your body from drinking alcohol, the government recommends that men and women do not drink more than 14 **units of alcohol** a week on a regular basis, and that that this number of units is spread over several days, if people do regularly drink 14 units. One unit of alcohol is 10 ml of pure alcohol (Figure 2).

Reactivate your knowledge answers

36

1 Chemical substance that alters the way the body works 2 Drug taken for pleasure 3 Unpleasant symptoms an addict experiences when they stop taking a drug

However, these are only guidelines because a person's height, weight, and sex affect the way they react to alcohol.

Dangers of alcohol

Drinking large volumes of alcohol over a long time can cause stomach ulcers, heart disease, and brain and liver damage.

Your liver breaks down harmful chemicals (including ethanol) into harmless waste products, which are then excreted from your body.

As a result of having to break down large amounts of ethanol, the livers of heavy drinkers become scarred (Figure 3). This means their liver works less efficiently, taking longer to break down alcohol and other chemicals. This condition is called cirrhosis of the liver, and can result in death.

◀ **Figure 3** Look at the difference in appearance of a diseased liver (left) and a healthy liver (right).

C Name three conditions whose risk is increased by drinking large amounts of alcohol over a long period.

Should pregnant women drink alcohol?

The Department of Health recommends that pregnant women do not drink any alcohol. Drinking alcohol increases the risk of miscarriage, stillbirth, premature birth, and low-birth-weight babies.

When a pregnant woman drinks alcohol, it diffuses into the baby's bloodstream through the placenta. It can then damage the developing organs and nervous system. Foetal Alcohol Syndrome (FAS) affects the way a baby's brain develops. It can result in children with learning difficulties, facial differences, and problems with the liver, kidneys, and other organs.

D Name three negative effects of alcohol on pregnancy.

Alcohol can also reduce fertility in both men and women. This means they are less likely to conceive (get pregnant). For example, alcohol reduces the number of sperm that a man produces. It also affects ovulation.

Units of alcohol

On drinks labels, the alcohol content is given as a percentage of the whole drink. Wine that says '10%' on its label is 10% pure alcohol.

Calculate the number of units of alcohol in a 200 ml glass of this wine. One unit = 10 ml of pure alcohol.

Summary Questions

1 Copy and complete the following sentences.

Alcoholic drinks contain the drug _____. This is a _____, because it affects the _____ system, slowing down your body's reactions. Drinking alcohol can lead to brain and _____ damage. (4 marks)

2 Drinking Alcohol can be harmful.

a Describe how alcohol causes an effect on the body. (3 marks)

b Describe the effect of alcohol on the liver. (2 marks)

3 Explain why it is important that pregnant women avoid alcohol. (4 marks)

1.8 Smoking

Learning objectives

After this topic, you will be able to:

- describe the effects of the components of tobacco smoke on the body
- describe some health problems caused by smoking
- describe some effects of smoking on pregnancy.

Reactivate your knowledge

1 What do the lungs do?
2 What is the role of red blood cells in the body?
3 Name two problems linked to drinking alcohol whilst pregnant.

▲ **Figure 1** The chemicals in tobacco smoke can be deadly.

Key words

passive smoking, tobacco, tar, nicotine, stimulant, carbon monoxide

Deadly smoke

Use the graph in Figure 2 to answer the following questions:

1 Which smoking-related diseases cause the greatest number of deaths?

2 How many more deaths occurred due to lung disease than heart disease?

3 How many times more likely is a smoker to die from lung and throat cancer, compared to a stroke?

Most people know that smoking harms your health, yet many people still smoke. Even breathing in the smoke of someone else's cigarette, like the person in Figure 1, can affect your health.

Why is smoking dangerous?

Smoking increases your chances of developing conditions such as breathing problems, cancer, heart attacks, and strokes. Smokers are much more likely to die prematurely than non-smokers. For example, male smokers are over 20% more likely to die from lung cancer than male non-smokers. Figure 2 shows the number of deaths by smoking-related diseases.

▲ **Figure 2** Graph to show the number of deaths from smoking-related diseases.

A Name three conditions a smoker is more likely to suffer from.

As well as affecting their own health, smokers can endanger the health of others. By breathing in other people's smoke, your risk of developing circulatory and respiratory conditions increases. This is known as **passive smoking**.

Smoking in pregnancy greatly increases the risk of miscarriage. It can also increase the risk of low-birth-weight babies and affects the foetus' development. Once a baby is born, passive smoking can also increase the risk of sudden-infant-death syndrome ('cot death') and respiratory illness, such as bronchitis and pneumonia.

B Explain why smoking is banned in public buildings.

Reactivate your knowledge answers
1 Take in oxygen and remove carbon dioxide 2 Transport oxygen 3 Miscarriage/stillbirth/premature births/low-birth-weight/FAS

What's in tobacco smoke?

Cigarettes contain **tobacco**. Tobacco smoke contains over 4000 chemicals, many of which are harmful. These include:

- **tar** – a sticky, black material that collects in the lungs (Figure 3). It irritates and narrows the airways. Some of the chemicals it contains cause cancer
- **nicotine** – an addictive drug that speeds up the nervous system. It is a **stimulant**, which makes the heart beat faster and narrows blood vessels
- **carbon monoxide** – a poisonous gas that stops the blood from carrying as much oxygen as it should. It binds to the red blood cells in the place of oxygen.

C Name the addictive component of tobacco smoke.

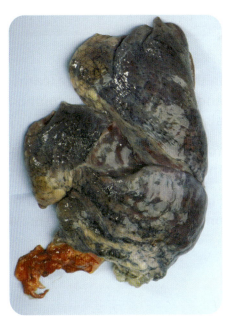

▲ **Figure 3** This diseased lung is full of tar. Healthy lungs should be pink.

How does smoking cause disease?

Some examples of the ways smoking causes disease are listed below:

- Respiratory infections – the cells lining your windpipe (trachea) produce mucus, which traps dirt and microorganisms. They also have cilia that sweep the mucus into your mouth for you to swallow into your stomach. This keeps your airways clean. Chemicals in tobacco smoke stop the cilia from moving (Figure 4). This allows mucus to flow into your lungs, making it harder to breathe and often causing infection. Smokers cough this mucus up, which can damage the lungs further.
- Heart disease – smoking causes a person's arteries to become blocked. This prevents blood flowing properly, and can cause a heart attack or stroke.
- Emphysema (a lung disease) – chemicals in tobacco smoke affect the alveoli in your lungs. Their walls become weakened so they do not inflate properly when you inhale. They may also burst during coughing. This reduces the amount of oxygen that can pass into the blood, making the person breathless.

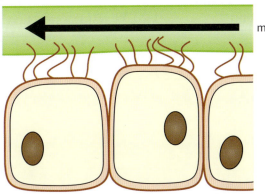

mucus

◀ **Figure 4** Smoking makes it harder for ciliated cells to sweep mucus from your airways.

Summary Questions

1 Match the chemicals in tobacco smoke to their harmful effect.

tar	addictive and makes the heart beat faster
nicotine	reduces the amount of oxygen the blood can carry
carbon monoxide	contains chemicals that cause cancer

(2 marks)

2 Describe **two** ways tobacco smoke can cause problems during pregnancy. (2 marks)

3 a Explain why smokers often cough a lot when they first wake in the morning. (2 marks)

b Explain why smokers are at greater risk of respiratory infections. (2 marks)

In this chapter you have learnt about the components of a balanced diet and how much of each component you should eat to remain healthy. You also tested a range of foods to identify which nutrients they contained.

You studied the main organs in the digestive system, and learnt about the role enzymes and some bacteria play in digestion.

Finally, you looked at both the positive and negative effects drugs have on the body, focusing on smoking and alcohol.

Metacognition and self-reflection task

Writing questions is a useful way of checking that you understand a concept. Write an exam-style question for each spread in the chapter as well as the mark scheme to go with it. Then test your questions out on fellow students. Which are the questions that they find trickiest to answer? Do they make the same mistakes?

Journey through B2

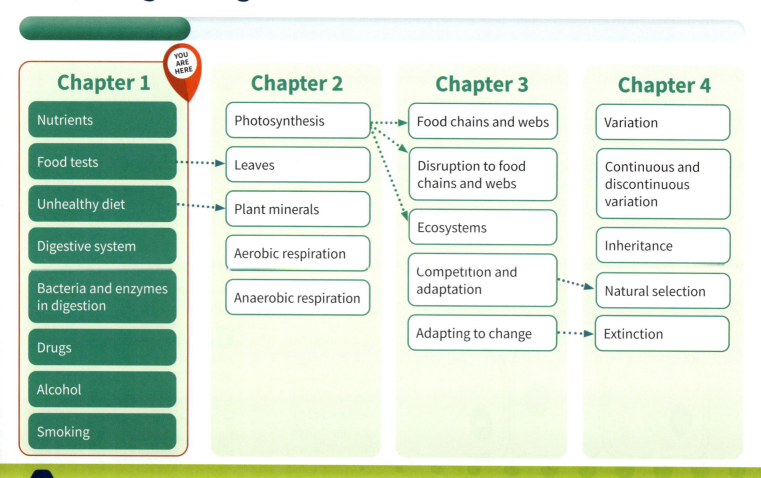

Chapter 1
- Nutrients
- Food tests
- Unhealthy diet
- Digestive system
- Bacteria and enzymes in digestion
- Drugs
- Alcohol
- Smoking

YOU ARE HERE

Chapter 2
- Photosynthesis
- Leaves
- Plant minerals
- Aerobic respiration
- Anaerobic respiration

Chapter 3
- Food chains and webs
- Disruption to food chains and webs
- Ecosystems
- Competition and adaptation
- Adapting to change

Chapter 4
- Variation
- Continuous and discontinuous variation
- Inheritance
- Natural selection
- Extinction

Chapter 1 Summary Questions

1 To remain healthy you must eat a balanced diet. Match the nutrient to its function in the body.

Nutrient	Function
carbohydrates	used for growth and repair
lipids	needed in small amounts to keep you healthy
proteins	provide energy
minerals	provide a store of energy and are used to insulate the body

(4 marks)

2 Figure 1 shows your digestive system.

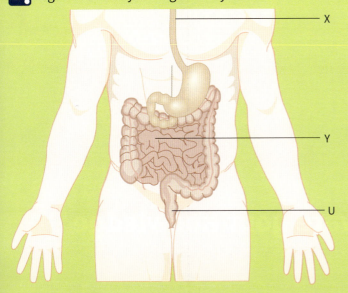

▲ **Figure 1**

a Name structure X. (1 mark)
b State what happens in structure Y. (1 mark)
c Identify which letter represents the structure that stores faeces until it leaves the body. (1 mark)
d State what happens in digestion. (2 marks)
(5 marks)

3 Describe the role of **two** components of a balanced diet. **(4 marks)**

4 A student wants to do a food test to find out which nutrients are in crisps. She starts by making a solution of the crisps.

a Name the piece of equipment she should use to break the crisps into small pieces. (1 mark)
b Suggest **two** safety precautions the student should take before performing a food test. (2 marks)
c Describe how the student should test the food solution for protein. (3 marks)
(6 marks)

5 People take drugs for a number of reasons.

a Describe the difference between medicinal drugs and recreational drugs. (2 marks)
b State how a drug causes an effect on the body. (1 mark)
c State the difference between a stimulant and a depressant. Give an example of each type of drug. (4 marks)
(7 marks)

6 Enzymes are special proteins that play a crucial role in digestion.
a Describe the role of enzymes in digestion. (1 mark)
b Explain why enzymes are called catalysts. (2 marks)
c Compare how carbohydrates and proteins are digested. (4 marks)
(7 marks)

7 Explain why a couple should avoid alcohol when trying to conceive, and why a pregnant woman should not drink any alcohol during pregnancy.
(6 marks)

8 Explain some health issues caused by an unhealthy diet. **(6 marks)**

2 Biological processes

In this chapter you will learn how plants make food through the process of photosynthesis and its importance for all life on Earth. You will also look at how leaves are adapted to maximise this process and the effects of minerals on plant growth.

You will study how energy is transferred from the food you eat to your cells, through the process of respiration. You will compare aerobic respiration to anaerobic respiration in animals, and fermentation in plants.

Reactivate your knowledge

1 Draw and label a diagram of a leaf cell or a root hair cell.

2 Draw an animal cell. Label the components and describe their function.

3 Use a table to compare the composition of inhaled and exhaled air.

You already know

The shape and structure of a specialised cell means it can perform a particular function.

Photosynthesis takes place inside chloroplasts.

Respiration takes place inside mitochondria.

Oxygen is used in respiration to transfer energy for the organism.

 How to take readings from a bar chart.

 How to work scientifically to: draw and label a diagram.

Journey through B2

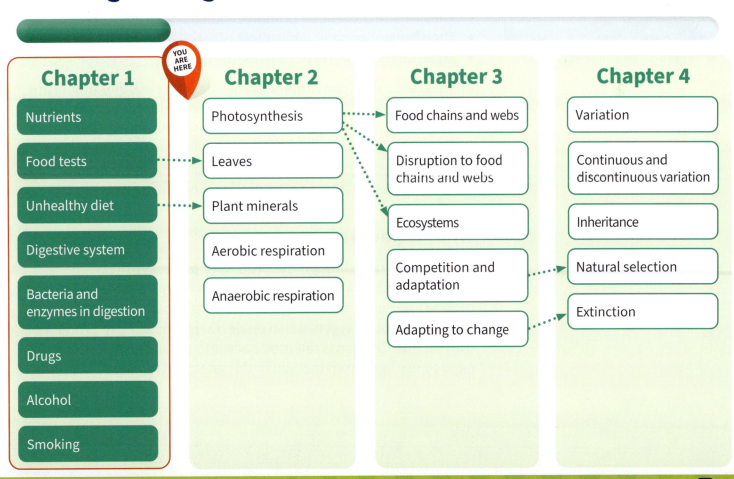

Chapter 1

- Nutrients
- Food tests
- Unhealthy diet
- Digestive system
- Bacteria and enzymes in digestion
- Drugs
- Alcohol
- Smoking

Chapter 2

YOU ARE HERE

- Photosynthesis
- Leaves
- Plant minerals
- Aerobic respiration
- Anaerobic respiration

Chapter 3

- Food chains and webs
- Disruption to food chains and webs
- Ecosystems
- Competition and adaptation
- Adapting to change

Chapter 4

- Variation
- Continuous and discontinuous variation
- Inheritance
- Natural selection
- Extinction

Learning objectives

After this topic, you will be able to:

- describe the process of photosynthesis
- state the word equation for photosynthesis
- describe how to test a leaf for the presence of starch.

Reactivate your knowledge

1 What substances does a plant need to grow?
2 Why are plants green?
3 Name three cell components only found in plant cells.

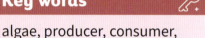

Key words

algae, producer, consumer, photosynthesis, chlorophyll

Unlike animals, plants do not have to eat other organisms to survive. Instead they make their own food using sunlight. How do they do this?

What is a producer?

Plants and **algae** are called **producers** because they make their own food. They convert materials found in their environment into glucose, a carbohydrate, using sunlight.

Algae, like those in Figure 1, are like plants because they are green organisms that make their own food. However, they differ from plants in the following ways:

- They can be unicellular or multicellular organisms.
- They live underwater while most plants live on land.
- Algae do not have leaves, stems, or roots.

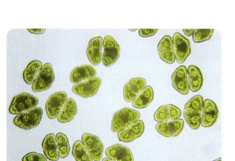

▲ **Figure 1** Algae live in water.

Animals are called **consumers** as they have to eat other organisms to survive. These can be plants or other animals. They break down the organism during digestion. This releases nutrients, which are then used by the body.

> **A** State whether a human is a producer or consumer.

What is photosynthesis?

Plants make food through the process of **photosynthesis**. Photosynthesis is a chemical reaction in which plants take in carbon dioxide and water and change them into glucose. This provides the plant with food. Oxygen is also made. Oxygen is a waste product of the reaction. Oxygen is released back into the atmosphere. Plants need to use light from the Sun in this chemical reaction.

The word equation below shows the process of photosynthesis.

$$\text{carbon dioxide} + \text{water} \xrightarrow{\text{light}} \text{glucose} + \text{oxygen}$$

(reactants)   (products)

> **B** Name the useful product of photosynthesis for plant growth.

Where does photosynthesis occur?

Photosynthesis mainly takes place in chloroplasts (Figure 2) in the leaf cells, though a small amount happens in the stem. Leaves and stems are green because they contain the green pigment **chlorophyll**. Chlorophyll uses light from the Sun. The energy transferred from the Sun is needed for the plant to change carbon dioxide and water into glucose and oxygen.

> **C** Name the part of the cell where chlorophyll is found.

Testing a leaf for starch

During photosynthesis, a plant produces glucose. It stores the glucose as starch in the leaf.

You can check that a plant has carried out photosynthesis by testing it with iodine.

Step 1 – Boil the leaf in water to remove the waxy layer.

Step 2 – Put the leaf into a test tube of ethanol and place into the boiling water. The ethanol dissolves the chlorophyll, removing it from the leaf.

Step 3 – Wash the leaf in water to remove the ethanol and soften the leaf (as the ethanol makes the leaf brittle).

Step 4 – Spread the leaf on a white tile and add a few drops of iodine. If the leaf turns black, starch is present.

▲ **Figure 2** Photosynthesis takes place inside chloroplasts in palisade cells in leaves.

Hypothesis

A hypothesis is an idea about why something happens. Look at the word equation for photosynthesis. Write a hypothesis for what would happen to the plant if you put it in a dark cupboard for a week.

Summary Questions

1 Copy and complete the following sentences.

Plants and ＿＿＿＿ are ＿＿＿＿. They use ＿＿＿＿ to make their own food. They use ＿＿＿＿ and water to make ＿＿＿＿ and oxygen using ＿＿＿＿ energy.
(6 marks)

2 State and explain whether photosynthesis would occur in the following situations:

a a bright sunny day (1 mark)
b at night (1 mark)
c in the root hair cells. (2 marks)

3 Explain why photosynthesis is important for all life on Earth.
(4 marks)

2.2 Leaves

Learning objectives

After this topic, you will be able to:

- describe the main adaptations of a leaf
- describe the role of stomata
- describe how water is transported through a plant.

Reactivate your knowledge

1 What are the main organs of a plant?
2 Why are plants called producers?
3 What do plants need to photosynthesise?

Leaves come in all shapes and sizes. Most are green (Figure 1) but have you ever looked closely at a leaf? Some, like stinging nettles, are covered in tiny hairs.

Structure of a leaf

Leaves are specially adapted for **photosynthesis**. Each component of a leaf has a special function that helps it to carry out photosynthesis. Most leaves:

- are green – they contain **chlorophyll**, which absorbs sunlight
- are thin – this allows gases to diffuse in and out of the leaf easily
- have a large surface area – to absorb as much light as possible
- have veins – which contain vessels (with tubes to transport water, and other tubes to transport sugars).

▲ **Figure 1** Most leaves are green because they contain chlorophyll.

> **A** Describe two adaptations of leaves for absorbing light.

The underside of a green leaf is lighter than the top. This is because the cells in the bottom of the leaf contain fewer **chloroplasts**, which means there is less chlorophyll. Most sunlight hits the top of the leaf, so this is where the chloroplasts need to be to absorb as much sunlight as possible.

> **B** State which part of the leaf contains the most chloroplasts.

The top of the leaf feels waxy, whereas the bottom is normally much drier. This waxy layer reduces the amount of water evaporating out of the leaf. The Sun heats up the top of the leaf, so without the waxy layer, a lot of water would escape from the leaf's top surface. You have to boil leaves before you can test them for starch to destroy the waxy layer so that the iodine can reach the cells.

> **C** State why the top surface of the leaf is covered in a waxy layer.

Key words

photosynthesis, chlorophyll, chloroplasts, stomata, guard cells

Surface area

A scientist calculated that one type of plant leaf had 9200 stomata per cm^2 on its lower surface. The leaf had a surface area of $10\,cm^2$. Estimate the number of stomata on the lower surface of the leaf.

Reactivate your knowledge answers
1 Root, leaf, flower, stem 2 They make their own food (photosynthesis) 3 Carbon dioxide, water, sunlight

How do gases get into and out of the leaf?

On the underside of the leaf, there are tiny holes called **stomata** (singular: stoma). They allow gases to diffuse into and out of the leaf:

- Carbon dioxide diffuses in. Carbon dioxide is a reactant in photosynthesis.
- Oxygen diffuses out. Oxygen is a product of photosynthesis.

Stomata are opened and closed by **guard cells** (Figure 2). These cells open the stomata during the day, and close them at night.

> **D** Describe the movement of gases through stomata during the day.

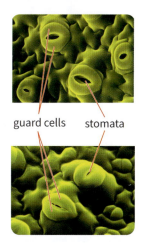

guard cells   stomata

▲ **Figure 2** Top - open stomata. Bottom - closed stomata.

How does water get into a plant?

Water diffuses into the root hair cells. It is then transported around the plant in water vessels (Figure 3).

Figure 4 summarises how the products and reactants of photosynthesis enter and leave a plant.

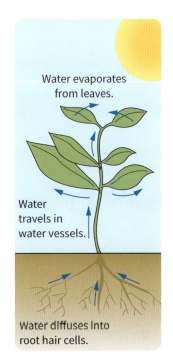

Water evaporates from leaves.

Water travels in water vessels.

Water diffuses into root hair cells.

▶ **Figure 3** As the water evaporates from the leaves, more water is drawn up through the plant. It is a bit like sucking on a straw! Water vapour is lost from the leaf through the stomata.

Link ↗

You learnt about evaporation in C1 1.5 *More changes of state.*

Summary Questions

1 Match each part of a leaf to its function.

stomata	reduces amount of water evaporating
waxy layer	allow gases to diffuse into and out of leaf
guard cells	transport water to cells in leaf
veins	open and close stomata

(3 marks)

2 Describe how water is transported through a plant.

(3 marks)

3 Explain why leaves are thin and have a large surface area.

(3 marks)

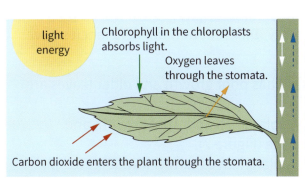

light energy

Chlorophyll in the chloroplasts absorbs light.

Oxygen leaves through the stomata.

Carbon dioxide enters the plant through the stomata.

Glucose (white arrows) is transported to all the parts of the plant. Water (blue dashed arrows) is transported from the roots to the stem and leaves.

▲ **Figure 4** The movement of products and reactants in photosynthesis.

Learning objectives

After this topic, you will be able to:

- describe how a plant uses minerals for healthy growth
- describe the symptoms of plant mineral deficiencies
- explain why farmers use fertilisers.

Reactivate your knowledge

1 How does water get into a plant?
2 Why do leaves have stomata?
3 Give three adaptations of a leaf.

▲ **Figure 1** A nitrate deficiency results in poor growth.

▲ **Figure 2** Purple leaves are a symptom of a phosphorus deficiency.

▲ **Figure 3** Magnesium deficiency results in yellow leaves.

Farmers and gardeners regularly check their plants for signs of poor health. If your plants start to wilt, they need watering. What does it mean if the leaves turn yellow?

What minerals do plants need?

For healthy growth, plants need a range of minerals. These include:

- **nitrates** (contain nitrogen) – for healthy growth
- **phosphates** (contain phosphorus) – for healthy roots
- **magnesium** – for making **chlorophyll**.

  A Name three minerals that plants need for healthy growth.

Where do plants get minerals from?

Plants get the minerals they need from the soil. The minerals are dissolved in soil water. They are absorbed into the root hair cells, and are then transported around the plant with the water in the water vessels.

  B Describe how minerals enter plants.

Mineral deficiency

If a plant does not get enough minerals, its growth will be poor. This is called a mineral **deficiency**. Different mineral deficiencies have different symptoms:

- Nitrate deficiency – plant has poor growth and older leaves are yellowed (Figure 1).
- Phosphorus deficiency – plant has poor root growth, and younger leaves look purple (Figure 2).
- Magnesium deficiency – plant leaves turn yellow (Figure 3).

Reactivate your knowledge answers

1 Through the roots (by diffusing into the root hairs) 2 To allow gases to diffuse into and out of the plant 3 Green/thin/large surface area/have stomata/have veins/waxy layer

C Identify the mineral missing from a plant with poor roots.

The chlorophyll molecule, which makes plants green, contains magnesium. If a plant does not get enough magnesium it can't make as much chlorophyll as it needs. This results in yellow leaves.

Nitrates are involved in making amino acids. The amino acids join together to form proteins. These proteins are needed for cell growth, to grow leaves and shoots.

Why do farmers use fertilisers?

When plants grow they remove minerals from the soil. These would normally be replaced when the plant dies, or when leaves are shed. However when crops are harvested this can't happen. To prevent future crops suffering from a mineral deficiency, farmers add chemicals to the soil to replace missing minerals – these chemicals are called **fertilisers** (Figure 4).

▲ **Figure 4** Farmers use fertilisers to add minerals to their crops.

Around the world, many farmers do not use chemical (artificial) fertilisers. Instead, they add minerals to the soil by spreading manure on their fields. Manure is dung from domestic animals or from people.

D List two ways farmers add minerals to the soil.

Link

You can learn more about the importance of minerals in B2 1.1 *Nutrients*.

Mineral deficiency

Produce a leaflet for farmers that could help them to decide which mineral their plant is missing. You should include an image of an unhealthy plant that farmers can compare to their own.

Key words

nitrate, phosphate, magnesium, chlorophyll, deficiency, fertiliser

Summary Questions

1 Copy and complete the following sentences.

To remain healthy, plants need to absorb _____ from the soil. These include phosphates, _____, and magnesium. They are absorbed through the _____ and then travel around the plant in the water _____.

(4 marks)

2 Explain why farmers use fertilisers. (2 marks)

3 Explain the role of nitrates in healthy plant growth.

(3 marks)

Learning objectives

After this topic, you will be able to:

- describe the process of aerobic respiration
- state the word equation for aerobic respiration
- describe how the reactants and products of respiration are transported to and from cells.

Reactivate your knowledge

1 Where in the cell does respiration occur?
2 Name the structure in the lungs where gas exchange occurs.
3 What is the function of red blood cells?

▲ **Figure 1** Physically active people like athletes need to eat lots of high-energy foods, as their bodies require energy to be transferred quickly.

You now know how organisms consume or produce glucose, but what happens next? Glucose is the key chemical that your body needs.

How do cells transfer energy?

Your body needs energy for everything it does. You need energy to move, to grow, and to keep warm (Figure 1). Energy is required constantly (even when you are asleep!) to keep your body functioning.

You get your energy from organic molecules in the food you eat.

To transfer the energy stored in food, glucose reacts with oxygen in a chemical reaction called **aerobic respiration**. This reaction transfers energy to your cells. The waste products carbon dioxide and water are also formed.

A Name the two substances required for aerobic respiration.

$$\text{glucose} + \text{oxygen} \longrightarrow \text{carbon dioxide} + \text{water (+ energy)}$$
$$\text{(reactants)} \qquad\qquad\qquad \text{(products)}$$

B Name the gas produced by aerobic respiration.

Defining respiration 🎯

Read through the information about respiration on these pages for three minutes. Close the book, and produce a definition and description of aerobic respiration. Swap your ideas with a partner. Together can you improve your definition?

Link ↗

You learnt about mitochondria in B1 2.2 *Plant and animal cells.*

Where does respiration happen?

Respiration happens inside tiny structures inside your cells called **mitochondria** (Figure 2). All cells contain mitochondria but different cells contain different amounts. Muscle cells carry out lots of respiration, so they contain large amounts of mitochondria.

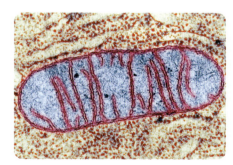

▲ **Figure 2** A mitochondrion.

Reactivate your knowledge answers
1 Mitochondria 2 Alveoli 3 Transport oxygen

How do glucose and oxygen get into cells?

Glucose and oxygen are transported by the blood. Figure 3 shows how.

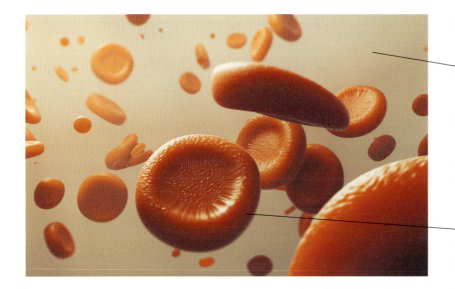

During digestion, carbohydrates are broken down releasing glucose molecules. These molecules are absorbed into the bloodstream through the wall of the small intestine.

Glucose dissolves in the liquid part of your blood called **plasma**. It then diffuses into the cells that need it for respiration.

When you breathe in, oxygen fills the alveoli in your lungs. The oxygen then diffuses into your bloodstream.

Oxygen joins to **haemoglobin** (a red pigment) in your red blood cells. When it reaches a cell requiring oxygen, the oxygen diffuses into the cell.

▲ **Figure 3** Glucose and oxygen are transported to the cells in the blood.

C State the process by which oxygen and glucose enter body cells.

How does carbon dioxide leave the body?

If carbon dioxide remained in your body, it would build up to a harmful level. You get rid of carbon dioxide when you exhale.

Carbon dioxide produced during respiration diffuses out of your cells and into the blood plasma. The blood transports it to the lungs, where it diffuses into the alveoli, and is then exhaled.

D Name two substances that are carried through the body in blood plasma.

Key words

aerobic respiration, mitochondria, plasma, haemoglobin

Summary Questions

1 Copy and complete the following sentences.

Energy is released in _____ inside your cells by the process of _____. _____ and oxygen react together to release _____. Carbon dioxide and _____ are produced as waste products. (5 marks)

2 Describe where and how respiration takes place. (4 marks)

3 Explain how oxygen and glucose are transported to cells for respiration. (4 marks)

Learning objectives

After this topic, you will be able to:

- compare the processes of aerobic and anaerobic respiration
- state the word equation for the process of anaerobic respiration
- state the word equation for fermentation.

1 What is the word equation for aerobic respiration?
2 Which part of the blood transports glucose?
3 Why do muscles need energy?

Key words

anaerobic respiration, oxygen debt, microorganism, fermentation

▲ **Figure 1** After heavy exercise, you breathe heavily to break down lactic acid in your muscles.

Useful microorganisms

Using the information on this double page, write a paragraph explaining how anaerobic respiration is used to make a useful product.

During a sprint race, athletes have very little time to breathe meaning their intake of oxygen is not very high. Respiration must constantly supply your body with energy, even when you are unable to breathe enough.

How do you respire without oxygen?

Anaerobic respiration is a type of respiration that does not use oxygen. Your body uses this type of respiration to transfer energy from glucose when there is not enough oxygen for aerobic respiration to take place.

Anaerobic respiration often happens during strenuous exercise, as the body requires extra energy to be transferred quickly (Figure 1). The body can transfer this extra energy for short periods of time without oxygen. The word equation for anaerobic respiration is:

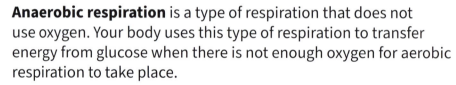

$$\text{glucose} \longrightarrow \text{lactic acid } (+ \text{ energy})$$
$$\text{(reactant)} \qquad\qquad \text{(products)}$$

A Describe the conditions in which anaerobic respiration occurs.

There are two reasons why the body normally respires aerobically:

1 Aerobic respiration transfers more energy per glucose molecule than anaerobic respiration.

2 The lactic acid produced from anaerobic respiration can cause painful cramps in your muscles.

When you have finished exercising you keep on breathing heavily.

The extra oxygen you inhale breaks down the lactic acid. The oxygen needed for this process is called the **oxygen debt**.

B Name the type of respiration that transfers the most energy.

Reactivate your knowledge answers
1 Glucose + oxygen → carbon dioxide + water (+ energy) 2 Plasma 3 To contract (to cause movement)

Do other organisms perform anaerobic respiration?

Other animals also use anaerobic respiration when they require a lot of energy quickly. For example, when a fox chases a rabbit, the cells in both organisms are likely to respire anaerobically.

Anaerobic respiration also takes place in plants and some **microorganisms** when there is no oxygen available. For example, the roots of plants in waterlogged soils respire anaerobically.

▲ **Figure 2** Yeast is a type of fungus.

Fermentation

Anaerobic respiration in some microorganisms produces ethanol and carbon dioxide instead of lactic acid. This process is called **fermentation**. Fermentation is a type of anaerobic respiration, as the microorganism respires without oxygen.

The word equation for fermentation is:

$$\text{glucose} \longrightarrow \text{ethanol} + \text{carbon dioxide} \ (+ \ \text{energy})$$
(reactant)   (products)

> **C** Describe the difference between anaerobic respiration in animals, and fermentation.

▲ **Figure 3** Yeast ferments the sugar in barley to make beer.

Yeast is an important microorganism in food production (Figure 2). It is needed to make bread, beer, and wine. These products are made using fermentation.

How do you make bread?

1 Flour, water, and yeast are mixed to make dough.

2 The yeast ferments carbohydrates in the flour into ethanol and carbon dioxide.

3 Carbon dioxide gas is trapped inside the dough and makes it rise.

4 The ethanol evaporates as the dough is baked.

5 Once baked, bread is produced.

How do you make beer and wine?

Beer (Figure 3) is made by fermenting barley grains; wine is made by fermenting grapes. In both cases, yeast ferments sugar into alcohol.

> **D** Name three products made using fermentation.

Summary Questions

1 Copy and complete the following sentences.

_____ respiration is a type of respiration that does not use _____. Anaerobic respiration in humans causes _____ to be transferred from glucose. _____ is produced as a waste product, which can build up in muscles and cause _____.

(5 marks)

2 Describe the main differences between aerobic and anaerobic respiration.

(3 marks)

3 Explain why cells in the body normally respire aerobically.   (4 marks)

In this chapter you have learnt how plants make food through the process of photosynthesis and its importance for all life on Earth. You also looked at how leaves are adapted to maximise this process and the effects minerals have on plant growth.

You studied how energy is transferred from the food you eat to your cells through the process of aerobic respiration. You then compared aerobic respiration with anaerobic respiration in animals, and fermentation in plants.

Metacognition and self-reflection task

Venn diagrams are a useful way to compare two similar processes. Produce a Venn diagram to compare the processes of aerobic and anaerobic respiration, and one to compare the processes of anaerobic respiration and fermentation. What do you notice about the two diagrams? Did you find one easier to complete than the other?

Journey through B2

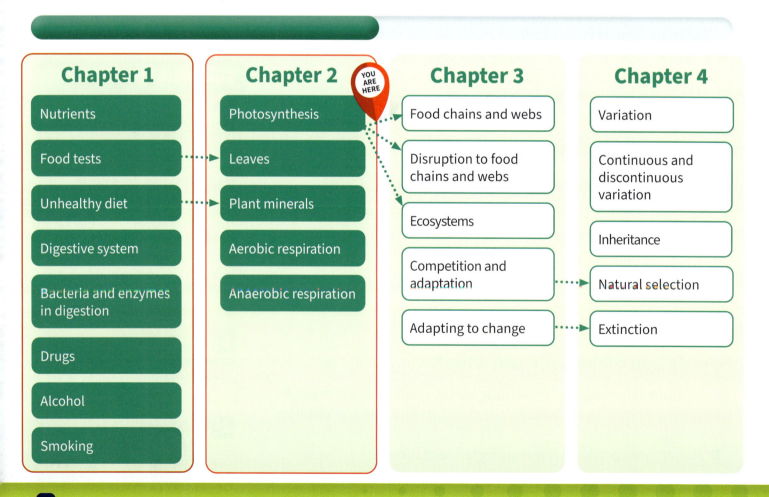

Chapter 1	Chapter 2	Chapter 3	Chapter 4
Nutrients	Photosynthesis	Food chains and webs	Variation
Food tests	Leaves	Disruption to food chains and webs	Continuous and discontinuous variation
Unhealthy diet	Plant minerals	Ecosystems	Inheritance
Digestive system	Aerobic respiration	Competition and adaptation	Natural selection
Bacteria and enzymes in digestion	Anaerobic respiration	Adapting to change	Extinction
Drugs			
Alcohol			
Smoking			

YOU ARE HERE

Chapter 2 Summary Questions

1

a Name the reaction that your body uses to transfer energy from glucose to cells. (1 mark)
b State where in a cell this reaction happens. (1 mark)
c Choose the correct term to complete the word equation below to represent this process:

glucose + **oxygen / carbon dioxide** →
water + **oxygen / carbon dioxide** (+ energy) (2 marks)
(4 marks)

2 Plants make food by the process of photosynthesis.

a Select the term that describes these organisms.
consumers herbivores producers (1 mark)
b State where in a cell photosynthesis occurs. (1 mark)
c Name the gas produced by photosynthesis. (1 mark)
d Plants store glucose as starch. Describe a positive test for starch. (2 marks)
(5 marks)

3 Plants need to take in minerals, such as magnesium, to remain healthy.

a State **one** other mineral needed by plants. (1 mark)
b Give **one** way farmers add minerals to the soil. (1 mark)
c Describe the role of magnesium in a plant. (3 marks)
(5 marks)

4 To check if a leaf has been photosynthesising you can check if it contains starch.

a Rearrange the statements below to show how to test a leaf for starch. The diagrams below show each step of the process. (3 marks)

  A Wash the leaf in water.
  B Boil the leaf in water.
  C Spread the leaf on a white tile and add a few drops of iodine.
  D Put the leaf into a test tube of ethanol and place in the boiling water.

A   **B**   **C**   **D**

b State the colour change you would see if starch is present. (2 marks)
c Glucose is converted to starch for storage by the plant. State one other use of glucose by the plant. (1 mark)
(6 marks)

5 Figure 1 shows equipment that can be used to study photosynthesis.

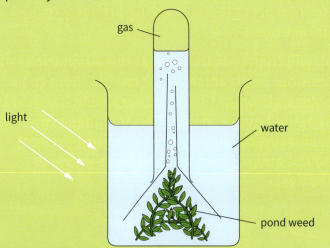

▲ **Figure 1**

a Name the gas given off by the plant. (1 mark)
b State the **two** reactants needed for photosynthesis. (2 marks)
c Describe the role of stomata in photosynthesis. (2 marks)
d Suggest and explain what would happen to the number of bubbles if the plant was placed in the dark. (3 marks)
(8 marks)

6 Explain how fermentation is used in food production. **(6 marks)**

7 Explain how leaves are adapted for photosynthesis. **(6 marks)**

Ecosystems and adaptation

In this chapter you will begin by looking at feeding relationships within food chains and how this can lead to a build up of toxic materials within organisms. You will then study the interdependence of organisms within a food web by looking at population changes. You will also interpret graphs showing predator–prey interactions.

You will then look in detail at the adaptations of a number of organisms that enable them to be successful competitors and survive in harsh and changing environments. This includes sampling ecosystems to identify the organisms present and the environmental conditions in which they live.

Reactivate your knowledge

1 Write an example of a food chain with at least three links.

2 Write down a list of 10 animals and sort them into predators and prey. Identify any features they have in common.

3 Choose an animal or plant and list three ways it is adapted to its habitat.

You already know

A food chain is a diagram that shows what living things eat.

Plants make food by the process of photosynthesis.

Plants are called producers because they make their own food using energy from the Sun.

Animals and plants are adapted to their environment to help them to survive.

 How to make sensible estimates in relation to everyday situations.

 How to work scientifically to: take measurements and make observations in one area.

Journey through B2

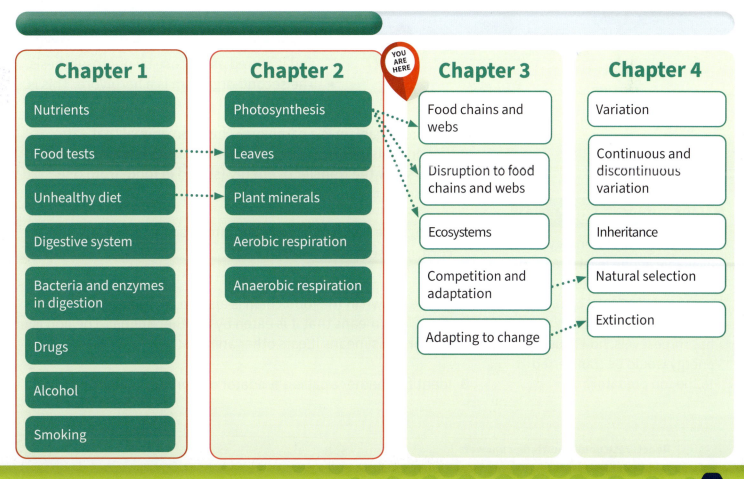

Chapter 1
- Nutrients
- Food tests
- Unhealthy diet
- Digestive system
- Bacteria and enzymes in digestion
- Drugs
- Alcohol
- Smoking

Chapter 2
- Photosynthesis
- Leaves
- Plant minerals
- Aerobic respiration
- Anaerobic respiration

YOU ARE HERE

Chapter 3
- Food chains and webs
- Disruption to food chains and webs
- Ecosystems
- Competition and adaptation
- Adapting to change

Chapter 4
- Variation
- Continuous and discontinuous variation
- Inheritance
- Natural selection
- Extinction

3.1 Food chains and webs

Learning objectives

After this topic, you will be able to:

- use relevant information to construct a food chain
- describe the feeding relationships between organisms in a food chain
- describe the feeding relationships between organisms within a food web.

Reactivate your knowledge

1 What is a producer?
2 What is a consumer?
3 What is the word equation for photosynthesis?

Key words

food chain, producer, prey, predator, food web, decomposers

To survive, you need to transfer energy from food to your cells. You need to eat plants or other animals. The animals you eat have to eat other animals or plants to survive. We can represent this information in diagrams called food chains and food webs.

What is a food chain?

A **food chain** is a diagram that shows what an organism eats (Figure 1). It shows the transfer of energy between organisms.

acacia tree (producer)   giraffe (herbivore)   lion (carnivore)

▲ **Figure 1** This food chain is from Africa.

Food chains have the following features:

- The first organism is a **producer**. Energy is transferred from the Sun to the organism and is stored as glucose by photosynthesis.
- The second organism is a herbivore. This is an animal that only eats plants.
- The third organism is a carnivore. This is an animal that eats other animals.
- Arrows show the transfer of energy (stored in food) from one organism to the next.

> **A** Arrange the following organisms into a food chain: owl, corn, mouse.

The giraffe shown in the food chain is also an example of a **prey** organism. This means that it is eaten by another animal. The lion is a **predator**. This means it eats other animals.

> **B** Identify whether a cat is a predator or a prey organism.

How much energy?

Around 10% of the energy available at one level of a food chain is transferred to the next level. If 1000 kJ of energy enters a food chain that has three levels, how much energy would be transferred to the top predator?

Reactivate your knowledge answers

1 Organism that makes its own food by photosynthesis   2 Organism that eats plants or animals to gain energy

3 Carbon dioxide + water $\xrightarrow{\text{light}}$ glucose + oxygen

58

How many levels are found in a food chain?

Most food chains have only four or five levels (Figure 2). If there were more, too little energy would be transferred to organisms at the top of the chain. As energy is transferred along the food chain, some is transferred to the surroundings by heat and in waste products. This means that at each level of the food chain, less energy is transferred to the organism in the level above.

acacia tree → impala → cheetah → lion

The lion is called the top predator – this means it is not eaten by any other animals. The top predator is always the last link in the food chain.

▲ **Figure 2** This food chain has four levels.

C Identify the herbivore in the food chain.

What is a food web?

Most animals eat more than one type of organism. For example, lions eat giraffes, cheetahs, leopards, and zebras. Scientists show this in **food webs** (Figure 3). A food web is a set of linked food chains. Food webs show the feeding relationships of organisms more realistically than food chains.

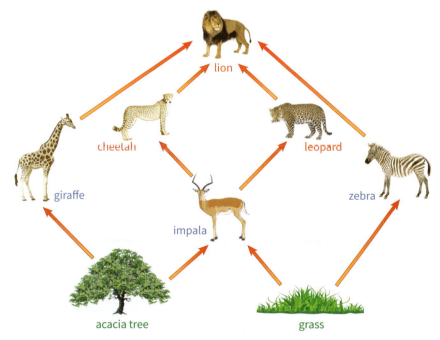

▲ **Figure 3** A food web showing feeding relationships in African grasslands.

Decomposers are also found in food webs. These are organisms (bacteria and fungi) that break down dead plant and animal material. This releases nutrients back into the soil or water.

Summary Questions

1 Match the following definitions to their meanings.

food chain	diagram showing linked food chains
food web	animal that is eaten
predator	animal that eats another animal
prey	diagram showing the transfer of energy between organisms

(3 marks)

2 Use the food web on this page to answer the questions below.

a Name a herbivore. (1 mark)
b Name a producer. (1 mark)
c State what the giraffe eats. (1 mark)
d Draw a food chain that has four levels. (2 marks)

3 Explain why most food chains have a maximum of four levels. (4 marks)

3.2 Disruption to food chains and webs

Learning objectives

After this topic, you will be able to:

- describe what is meant by the interdependence of organisms
- suggest and justify how the change in a population of one organism affects the population of another within a food web
- describe how toxic materials can accumulate in a food chain.

Reactivate your knowledge

1 What is a food web?
2 What is the first type of organism found in a food web?
3 What happens during pollination?

▲ **Figure 1** This bee is pollinating an apple tree in an orchard.

Some flowering plants rely on bees for pollination. Bees depend on flowers as they feed on their nectar to survive. Bees and flowers are said to be interdependent – they each depend on the other for survival (Figure 1).

Interdependence is the way in which living organisms depend on each other to survive, grow, and reproduce.

Decreasing bee populations in some areas is causing concern. If less pollination occurs, fewer crop plants may be produced, meaning human food supplies could decrease.

A Give an example of interdependence.

Interdependence in food webs

The number of animals or plants of the same type that live in the same area is called a **population**. In a food web, the populations of organisms are constantly changing. The population size of one type of organism has a direct effect on the population size of another type of organism.

The food web in Figure 2 shows the feeding relationships of organisms living in a field.

There are many food chains within this web. Some organisms, like the rabbit, have just one predator. Its predator is a fox. If the number of rabbits decreased due to a disease, the number of foxes would also decrease as they would have less to eat.

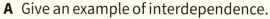

▲ **Figure 2** The organisms in this food web are interdependent – they depend on each other for survival.

Reactivate your knowledge answers
1 A series of linked food chains 2 Producer 3 Pollen is transferred from the anther to the stigma

Producer population

Grass is the producer. If there were no grass, there would be no food for the snails, caterpillars, or rabbits. These organisms would die (unless they travelled to another area). All the other animals in the food web would also die as their food source has gone. If the population of the producer falls then the populations of the consumers also fall.

> **B** State what happens to the populations of consumers if the population of the producer decreases.

Consumer population

If the snail population decreased, the thrush population would also decrease. This may reduce the population of hawks. However, the hawk population would not decrease if they could gain enough energy from eating more frogs and voles. If this happened the population of frogs and voles would decrease.

What is bioaccumulation?

It is not only energy that is transferred along a food chain. Some chemicals can also be passed on. One example is **insecticides** (Figure 3). These are chemicals that some farmers use to kill insects that eat their crops. Some insecticides are washed into rivers and end up in the sea.

4 One polar bear eats a lot of seals and so the insecticide accumulates into dangerous levels in the polar bear's body. This makes the bear ill and can cause death.

◄ **Figure 3** This section of a food chain shows how an insecticide can accumulate to dangerous levels.

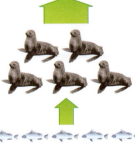

3 Each seal eats several fish so the levels of chemical accumulate (build up) in their body. This is called **bioaccumulation**.

2 Fish absorb small amounts of the insecticide directly into their bodies from the water, where it is stored.

1 Insecticide enters the sea.

> **C** Describe what is meant by bioaccumulation.

Interpreting food webs

In small groups, discuss what would happen to the other organisms in the food web in Figure 2 if disease reduced the population of frogs.

Key words

interdependence, population, insecticides, bioaccumulation

Summary Questions

1 Copy and complete the following sentences.

Organisms depend on each other for _____, _____ , and mates.

If two organisms both depend on each other for something, this is called _____.

Toxic chemicals can build up in organisms through a food chain. This is known as _____.

(4 marks)

2 Describe what is meant by the interdependence of organisms. (2 marks)

3 Using the food web in Figure 2:

a Suggest and explain what would happen to the population of rabbits if all the foxes died. (2 marks)

b Suggest and explain what would happen to the populations in the food web if all the voles died.

(4 marks)

Learning objectives

After this topic, you will be able to:

- define the terms habitat, community, and ecosystem
- describe how different organisms co-exist within an ecosystem.

Reactivate your knowledge

1 What is a population?
2 Name two things organisms depend on each other for.
3 What is the role of decomposers?

Link ↗

You can learn more about the relationships between different organisms in B2 3.4 *Competition* and B2 3.5 *Adapting to change*.

Sampling 🧪

Scientists cannot study every organism in an ecosystem so they take samples. Quadrats are used to sample plants (Figure 2).

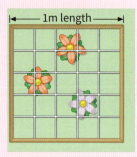

▲ **Figure 2** A quadrat.

After studying a number of sites in an area of garden, a scientist measured a mean value of 3 daisies per m². The garden is 400 m². Estimate the population size of daisies in this garden.

In a coral reef, there are many types of fish that live together (Figure 1). They can do this because they all require slightly different things from the reef and they each perform different roles.

◀ **Figure 1** Many species of fish live together in the coral reef.

What is an ecosystem?

An **ecosystem** is the name given to the plants and animals that are found in a particular location, and the area in which they live. These plants and animals depend on each other to survive.

The organisms in an ecosystem are known as a **community**. The area they live in is called a **habitat**. The conditions found in a habitat are known as the **environment**. These include the air, soil, and water.

For example, in a pond ecosystem:

- habitat – pond
- community – water plants, microorganisms, insects, fish, and fish-eating birds.

The plants and animals in a community and a habitat co-exist. This means that they live in the same place at the same time.

A Identify the habitat from this list: forest, heron, grass.

Reactivate your knowledge answers

1 Number of a particular type of plant/animal in an area 2 Food/shelter/mates/pollination 3 Break down dead plant and animal material

Co-existing in an ecosystem

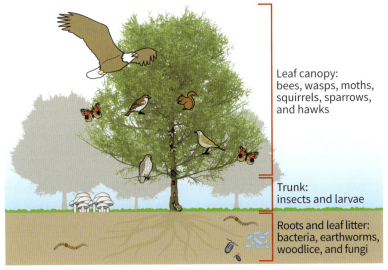

Leaf canopy:
bees, wasps, moths,
squirrels, sparrows,
and hawks

Trunk:
insects and larvae

Roots and leaf litter:
bacteria, earthworms,
woodlice, and fungi

▲ **Figure 3** An oak tree ecosystem.

Figure 3 shows an oak tree ecosystem. There are lots of living organisms that live in, or close to, the tree, but not every organism lives in the same part of the tree:

- Roots and leaf litter – decomposers, woodlice, and earthworms live at the base of the tree. They break down old leaves, releasing nutrients that the tree can absorb and use for new growth.
- Trunk – the tree trunk provides food or shelter for a number of insects and caterpillars.
- Tree canopy – many organisms live amongst the branches and leaves of the tree. For example, bees gather pollen and nectar when the tree is in blossom. Fungi may grow on the leaves. Squirrels gather acorns and moths lay their eggs. Small birds, such as sparrows, eat the moth larvae. Hawks feed on the sparrows.

> **B** Name three members of the oak tree ecosystem community.

What is a niche?

Each of the organisms living in the oak tree ecosystem has its own **niche**. A niche is a particular place or role that an organism has within an ecosystem. For example, they may live in a particular part of the tree or have a particular food source.

Sparrows and squirrels both live in the tree canopy but they do not compete for food. Squirrels feed on acorns, while sparrows feed on moth larvae and caterpillars. The sparrows and squirrels have similar but slightly different niches.

> **C** Describe how the niche of a sparrow and the niche of a squirrel differ.

Link

You will find out more about sampling in B3 4.4 *Investigating competition*.

Summary Questions

1 Match the words below to their definitions.

ecosystem	plants and animals found in a particular habitat
community	place where a plant or animal lives
habitat	living organisms in a particular area, and the habitat they live in

(2 marks)

2 Describe how bees and birds can both live within the canopy of a tree. (2 marks)

3 Explain why different organisms within the oak tree ecosystem have different niches. (4 marks)

Learning objectives

After this topic, you will be able to:

- explain the resources that plants and animals compete for
- describe the interaction between predator and prey populations.

Reactivate your knowledge

1   What is a predator?
2   What is a prey organism?
3   What does interdependence mean?

▲ **Figure 1** Birds competing for food.

If you have ever put food out for birds, you might see the birds 'fighting' over the food (Figure 1). Often, smaller species are scared off by larger birds. In the wild, all animals have to compete for resources.

What do animals compete for?

In a habitat there is a limited supply of resources, such as food, water, and space. To survive, animals compete with each other to get enough of these resources. This is known as **competition**.

Animals compete for:

1   food
2   water
3   space – to hunt and for shelter
4   mates – to reproduce.

> **A** State four resources that animals compete for.

What do plants compete for?

Plants also compete for resources in their environment. Plants compete for:

1   light
2   water
3   space
4   minerals – plants do not compete for food, as they produce their own through photosynthesis.

> **B** State four resources that plants compete for.

Key words

competition, predator, prey, population

Predator–prey graphs

Foxes are predators that eat rabbits. Sketch a line graph showing how the fox and rabbit populations change over time.

Reactivate your knowledge answers

1 An animal that eats another animal 2 An animal that gets eaten by another animal 3 When one organism depends on another to survive

Who are the best competitors?

When competing with other animals for food, the best **predators** will be fast, strong, and quick to spot their **prey**. These abilities allow them to sense their prey quickly and react before others, making sure that they get the food. Spotting their prey may require good eyesight or hearing.

Predator–prey relationships

Animals have to adapt to changes in their food supply. Only the best competitors will survive to reproduce.

When a predator feeds on just one type of prey, there is an interdependence between the predator **population** and the prey population. This means that changes in the population of one animal directly affect the population of the other. When plotted on a graph, this relationship shows a clear pattern (Figure 2).

> **C** State what the predator population is dependent on the prey population for.

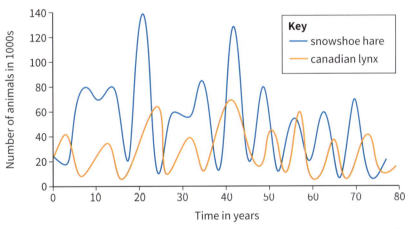

▲ **Figure 2** Predator–prey graph showing the interdependence of the lynx and the hare.

- When the prey population (hare) increases, the predators (lynx) have more to eat. The lynx survive longer and reproduce more.
- This increases the number of predators.
- The growing predator population eats more prey. The prey numbers fall.
- Eventually there is not enough food for all the predators, so their numbers decrease.
- There are now fewer lynx feeding on the hares. The hare population increases, and the cycle starts again.

3.5 Adapting to change

Learning objectives

After this topic, you will be able to:

- describe how organisms are adapted to their environment
- describe how organisms adapt to environmental changes.

Reactivate your knowledge

1 What do animals compete for?
2 What do plants compete for?
3 What is an adaptation?

▲ **Figure 1** A cheetah is **camouflaged** against its background. This makes it difficult for prey organisms to spot.

Cheetahs are the fastest land animals in the world (Figure 1). This incredible speed makes the cheetah a very successful predator. Like many other predators, they also have sharp claws and teeth. These adaptations enable the cheetah to be successful, and so survive.

How can animals live in a desert?

The desert is one of the harshest habitats to live in as food and water are scarce. Temperatures are also extremely hot during the day. Most desert animals are small and hide away in burrows to avoid the daytime heat. Only a few large mammals, such as camels and oryx, can survive. They travel long distances to find food, and can survive for long periods of time without drinking.

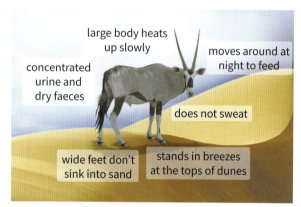

large body heats up slowly

moves around at night to feed

concentrated urine and dry faeces

does not sweat

wide feet don't sink into sand

stands in breezes at the tops of dunes

▲ **Figure 2** Adaptations of an oryx.

> **A** State two ways in which an oryx minimises water loss.

How can plants live in a desert?

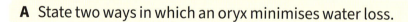

Plants in the desert have a number of adaptations to enable them to survive with very little water. These include:

- a waxy layer that covers the plant – this reduces water evaporating from the plant
- stems that can store water
- widespread roots – to collect water from a large area
- spines instead of leaves – this gives a smaller surface area to reduce water loss. Spines also prevent the plant from being eaten.

▲ **Figure 3** Cacti are very well adapted to surviving in a desert.

Reactivate your knowledge answers
1 Food, water, space, mates 2 Light, water, space, minerals 3 Special features (that allow an organism to survive in its environment)

B Describe how cacti are adapted to maximise the absorption of water.

How do organisms cope with environmental change?

Plants and animals can lose their habitat through fire or climate change. Food supplies may also be reduced by disease. Sudden changes result in increased **competition** for survival. The organisms best adapted to the change will survive and reproduce, increasing the population of that species. Organisms that are not very well adapted will have to move to another habitat, or die.

How do trees cope with the seasons?

Plants and animals have to cope with changes in their environment. For example, deciduous trees look different in each season. They grow rapidly during the spring when the weather is wet and warm but lose their leaves in winter. This saves energy. The fallen leaves provide a layer of warmth and protection around the base of the tree. The tree can reuse the nutrients from these leaves too.

How do animals cope with the seasons?

Animals have a number of ways of coping with cold winter temperatures, such as:

- **hibernation** – animals like bears find somewhere warm to sleep through the winter
- **migration** – animals like birds move somewhere warmer, or somewhere with more food
- growing thicker fur – animals like sheep are kept warm by their thick coat.

C State three ways that different animals are adapted to the winter.

The snowshoe hare grows fur of different colours in different seasons (Figure 4). This increases its chances of survival as it makes it harder for a predator to see it.

▲ **Figure 4** In the summer, the snowshoe hare grows reddish-brown fur to blend in with the rocks and earth. In the winter, it grows white fur to blend in with the snow.

Key words

predator, adaptation, camouflage, competition, hibernation, migration

Summary Questions

1 Copy and complete the following sentences.

Adaptations are _____ that help an organism to survive.

For example, animals that blend in with their habitat are said to be _____.

This increases their chances of _____ as they are less likely to be seen. (3 marks)

2 Describe **three** ways that a cactus is adapted to prevent water loss. (3 marks)

3 Explain how deciduous trees cope with environmental changes. (4 marks)

In this chapter you have looked at feeding relationships within food chains and how this can lead to a build up of toxic materials within organisms. You studied the interdependence of organisms by looking at population changes. You also interpreted graphs showing predator–prey interactions.

You looked in detail at the adaptations of a number of organisms that help them to be successful competitors and survive in harsh and changing environments. This included sampling ecosystems to identify the organisms present and the environmental conditions in which they live.

Metacognition and self-reflection task

Biology contains lots of key terms that you need to know and use. Make a list of 10 important terms in this chapter such as habitat and adaptation. Write a definition for each one and where possible add an example. Are there some terms and definitions that you find harder to remember than others? What will help you to remember them?

Journey through B2

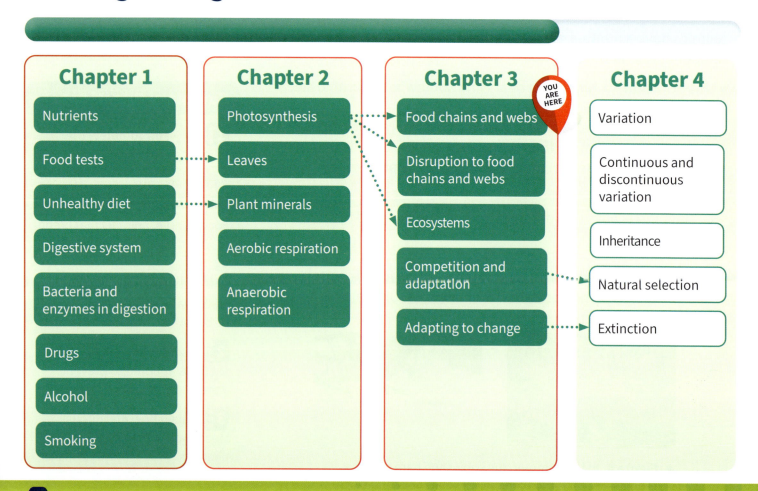

Chapter 1
- Nutrients
- Food tests
- Unhealthy diet
- Digestive system
- Bacteria and enzymes in digestion
- Drugs
- Alcohol
- Smoking

Chapter 2
- Photosynthesis
- Leaves
- Plant minerals
- Aerobic respiration
- Anaerobic respiration

Chapter 3
- Food chains and webs
- Disruption to food chains and webs
- Ecosystems
- Competition and adaptation
- Adapting to change

YOU ARE HERE

Chapter 4
- Variation
- Continuous and discontinuous variation
- Inheritance
- Natural selection
- Extinction

Chapter 3 Summary Questions

1 Figure 1 shows a polar bear. It has lots of adaptations to survive in its habitat.

▲ Figure 1

a Name the habitat in which the polar bear lives. (1 mark)
b Match the adaptation to how it helps the polar bear to survive.

white fur	insulation
thick fur	camouflage
large feet	to catch and eat prey
sharp claws and teeth	to stop the bear sinking into snow (4 marks)

(5 marks)

2 A student studied the small insects living in a log pile.

a State the resource that the insects use the logs for. (1 mark)
b Apart from your answer to part **a**, state **one** other resource that all animals need for survival. (1 mark)
c State **one** resource that plants compete for that animals don't compete for. (1 mark)

(3 marks)

3

a Rearrange the following organisms into a food chain: **owl, mouse, corn** (1 mark)
b Name the producer. (1 mark)
c Describe the difference in how energy is transferred to producers and consumers. (2 marks)
d Explain what would happen to the number of mice if a disease killed all of the owls. (2 marks)

(6 marks)

4 Figure 2 shows the feeding relationships between organisms in a garden.

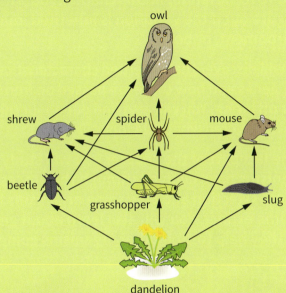

▲ Figure 2

a State and explain what would happen to the spider population if all the owls were removed from the area. (2 marks)
b State and explain what would happen to the grasshopper population if all the beetles died. (2 marks)
c Mice and shrews are very similar organisms. Explain why they can both successfully survive in the same habitat. (2 marks)
d A toxic chemical was used to kill all the dandelions. Explain how this could eventually result in the death of the owls. (3 marks)

(9 marks)

5 DDT is an insecticide that was once used to kill insects. It is no longer used, as it killed many fish-eating birds. The fish fed on plankton, which absorbed the insecticide from rivers. Draw a food chain to show this and explain how the insecticide killed the birds but not the fish.

(6 marks)

6 Using named examples, explain how animals are adapted to environmental changes **(6 marks)**

4 Inheritance

In biology, differences between organisms in a species are due to variation. In this chapter you will learn how to figure out if the variation is inherited, due to the environment, or both.

You will discover that inherited characteristics are due to your genes and how these are passed on from parents to their offspring. You will also find out about the scientists who discovered what DNA looks like.

In the last part of the chapter you will study how organisms have evolved through the process of natural selection and why some organisms have become extinct. You will also learn about gene banks and they help to stop other organisms going extinct.

Reactivate your knowledge

1 Use a photo or look at a classmate to identify the features they have inherited from a parent.

2 Draw a diagram to explain the process of fertilisation.

3 Describe one way in which a fossil can form.

You already know

The nucleus contains genetic material that is needed to make new cells.

During fertilisation genetic information from the egg and sperm are combined.

Living things have changed over time.

Fossils provide evidence of organisms that lived millions of years ago.

 How to plot a bar chart.

 How to work scientifically to: display practical results graphically.

Journey through B2

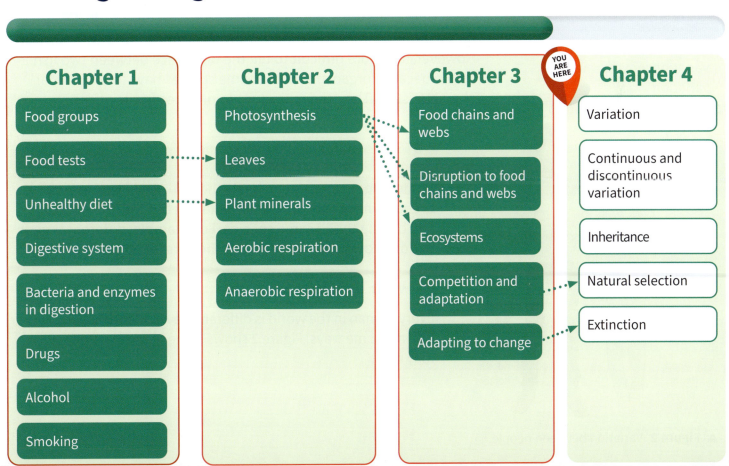

Chapter 1	Chapter 2	Chapter 3	Chapter 4
Food groups	Photosynthesis	Food chains and webs	Variation
Food tests	Leaves	Disruption to food chains and webs	Continuous and discontinuous variation
Unhealthy diet	Plant minerals	Ecosystems	Inheritance
Digestive system	Aerobic respiration	Competition and adaptation	Natural selection
Bacteria and enzymes in digestion	Anaerobic respiration	Adapting to change	Extinction
Drugs			
Alcohol			
Smoking			

YOU ARE HERE

Learning objectives

After this topic, you will be able to:

- define the term variation
- use examples to describe the difference between inherited and environmental variation.

Reactivate your knowledge

1 What process produces new offspring?
2 What are the male sex cells?
3 What are the female sex cells?

If you imagine your friends and family, you will picture people who look quite different from each other. For example, people may vary in height and have different colour hair. They have different characteristics.

How do organisms vary?

Differences in characteristics are known as **variation**.

> **A** State three ways that dogs vary.

It is easy to tell the difference between a dog and a fish. For example, a fish has fins and gills; a dog has four legs and is covered in fur. This is because these organisms belong to different **species**. Different species have lots of different characteristics.

However, it is more difficult to tell the difference between two fish. This is because organisms of the same species have lots of similar characteristics. They can reproduce to produce fertile offspring.

> **B** State what is meant by a species.

Sometimes a species can be further grouped into types or breeds. These may look quite different but the individuals still belong to the same species. For example, different breeds of dog show great variation but they are all dogs (Figure 1).

How do humans vary?

Every human in the world is different – even identical twins differ in some ways. Figure 2 shows some of the ways people may vary.

▲ **Figure 1** There is a lot of variation between types of dog.

Key words

variation, species, inherited variation, environmental variation

short — tall

blue eyes — brown eyes

lighter skin — darker skin

blood group A — blood group AB

speaks English — speaks Italian

good tennis player — rides a horse

▲ **Figure 2** Variation between people.

What causes variation?

Some variation is from characteristics the people have inherited from their parents, such as their eye colour. This is known as **inherited variation** (Figure 3).

Children usually share some characteristics with their mother and some with their father. They are not identical to either of their parents, as they get a mixture of their parents' features when the genetic material in the sperm and egg combine. Some examples of inherited variation are blood group and eye colour.

lobed ear

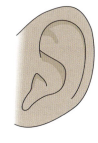
lobeless ear

◄ **Figure 3** Whether you have lobed or lobeless ears depends on the genetic material you inherit.

C Give three examples of inherited variation.

Variation caused by your surroundings and what happens to you is called **environmental variation**. For example, your characteristics can be affected by factors such as your diet, education, and lifestyle (Figure 4). Some examples of environmental variation are piercings and scars.

◄ **Figure 4** Dyed hair is an example of environmental variation.

D Give three examples of environmental variation.

Many characteristics are affected by both inherited and environmental variation. For example, you might inherit the characteristic to be tall from your father. However, if you eat a poor diet your rate of growth may be reduced. Skin colour is also inherited, but can change due to exposure to the Sun.

Spelling key terms

There are a lot of new scientific words in this chapter. Can you spell them all correctly? Look carefully at the spelling of the following words for two minutes: species, variation, inherited, environmental. Cover the words and ask a partner to test your spelling.

Summary Questions

1 Copy and complete the following sentences.

The organisms in a _____ share many of the same _____.
Differences in characteristics within a species are known as _____. Variation can be a result of _____ or _____ factors.
(5 marks)

2 Variation can be environmental or inherited.

a Copy and complete the table using the words below.

**body mass intelligence tattoo
blood group eye colour scar**

Environmental variation		
Inherited variation		
Both		

(3 marks)

b Describe why hairstyle is an example of environmental variation. (2 marks)

3 Explain why identical twins are the best people to study if you want to find out how the environment influences characteristics. (3 marks)

Learning objectives

After this topic, you will be able to:

- describe the difference between continuous and discontinuous variation
- represent variation within a species using graphs.

Key words

discontinuous variation, continuous variation

If you look around your classroom at the other students, you will see that some students share the same eye colour but very few are exactly the same height. This is because there are different types of variation.

What is discontinuous variation?

Characteristics that can only result in certain values show **discontinuous variation**. For example, eye colour shows discontinuous variation. There are a fixed number of possible values.

Another characteristic that shows discontinuous variation is your blood group.

> **A** Give three examples of characteristics that show discontinuous variation.

Which graph?

Which type of graph – a bar chart or histogram – would you use for the sets of data below?

a Members of your class who have lobed or lobeless ears.
b The length of feet of each of your teachers.
c The height of a group of seedlings, planted for a germination experiment.
d The number of strawberries per plant, from a sample of 25 plants.

What is continuous variation?

A characteristic that can take any value within a range is said to show **continuous variation**. For example, the height of the population ranges from the shortest person in the world to the tallest person. Everyone else's height can be any value in between. This is an example of continuous variation.

Other characteristics that show continuous variation are your body mass and arm span.

> **B** Give three examples of characteristics that show continuous variation.

Patterns of variation

To study variation, scientists take measurements of different characteristics. To come up with conclusions, they need to collect measurements from large numbers of the population. These data are then plotted on a graph so that patterns can be easily spotted.

How do you plot discontinuous variation?

Characteristics that show discontinuous variation should be plotted on a bar chart (Figure 1). For example, a person can only have one of four blood groups – A, B, AB, or O. These are the only values that a blood group can be, so you should plot a graph with four bars.

Characteristics that occur only as a result of inherited variation normally show discontinuous variation.

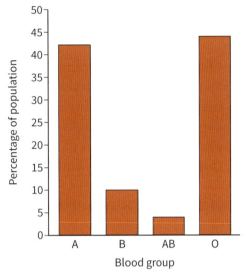

▲ **Figure 1** Discontinuous data are always plotted on a bar chart.

> **C** State the type of graph you should use to plot eye colour.

How do you plot continuous variation?

Characteristics that show continuous variation should be plotted on a histogram. A histogram is a chart that presents data in groups and is therefore plotted without gaps between the bars (Figure 2).

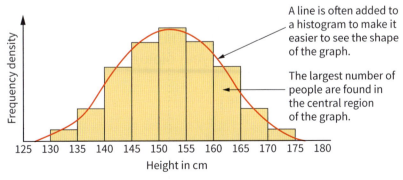

A line is often added to a histogram to make it easier to see the shape of the graph.

The largest number of people are found in the central region of the graph.

▲ **Figure 2** Continuous data are always plotted on a histogram.

Within a population, characteristics that show continuous variation will display a range of measurements from one extreme to another.

Characteristics that occur as a result of both environmental and inherited variation usually show continuous variation.

Summary Questions

1 Copy and complete the following sentences.

Characteristics that can only result in certain values show _____ variation. Characteristics that can have any value within a range show _____ variation.

A characteristic such as eye colour should be displayed using a _____.
Characteristics showing continuous variation, such as body mass, should be shown using a _____.   (4 marks)

2 Classify each of these characteristics into continuous variation and discontinuous variation.

hair colour, maximum sprinting speed, shoe size, average leaf size

(4 marks)

3 a Look at the graph of the variation in heights in Figure 2.

Describe the pattern that this variation shows.   (3 marks)

b Explain whether this variation is a result of environmental factors, inherited factors, or both.
(3 marks)

Learning objectives

After this topic, you will be able to:

- define the terms DNA, chromosome, and gene
- describe how characteristics are inherited
- describe how scientists worked together to develop the DNA model.

Reactivate your knowledge

1 What cell component contains genetic material?
2 What happens during fertilisation?
3 What type of variation is shown in characteristics gained from your parents?

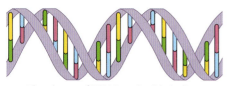

The shape of DNA is a double helix – a bit like a twisted ladder.

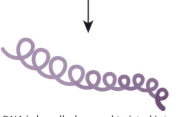

DNA is bundled up and twisted into long strands called chromosomes.

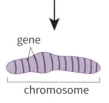

A gene is a section of the chromosome that holds information to produce a characteristic.

▲ **Figure 1** How DNA is arranged in the nucleus.

When people are biologically related to each other they have some of the same characteristics. Children often look like their biological parents due to inherited characteristics. Biological brothers and sisters do not look completely the same, as they each inherit a different mixture of characteristics, even when they have the same parents.

How do you inherit characteristics?

You inherit characteristics from your biological parents through genetic material stored in the **nucleus** of your cells. This material is a chemical called **DNA** (deoxyribonucleic acid). DNA contains all the information needed to make an organism.

> **A** State what DNA is.

Chromosomes

Inside the nucleus, your DNA is arranged into long strands called **chromosomes** (Figure 1). Different species have a different number of chromosomes in their nucleus. Humans have 46 chromosomes; cats have 38 chromosomes.

You inherit half of your chromosomes from your biological mother and half from your biological father. This is why you share some of your characteristics with each of your biological parents.

> **B** State what a chromosome is.

Genes

Each chromosome is divided into sections of DNA. The sections that hold the information to produce a characteristic are called **genes**. For example, one gene contains the information that sets your eye colour, while a different gene sets your hair colour. Each chromosome contains thousands of genes.

Teamwork

The scientists who discovered the structure of DNA did so by working together. Communication is very important so that scientists can share their ideas and carry out investigations.

Describe how scientists worked together to develop the DNA model.

Reactivate your knowledge answers
1 Nucleus 2 Egg and sperm nuclei join together 3 Inherited variation

C State what a gene is.

How is genetic material inherited?

Inside the nucleus of your cells, the 46 chromosomes are arranged into 23 pairs. One copy of the chromosome of each pair comes from your biological mother, and the other comes from your biological father.

Egg and sperm cells are the only cells to contain 23 chromosomes. They only have one copy of each chromosome. During fertilisation, the egg and sperm cells join together. When their nuclei join, their chromosomes pair up, producing an embryo with 46 chromosomes.

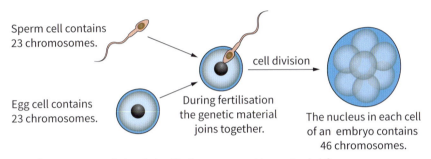

Sperm cell contains 23 chromosomes.

Egg cell contains 23 chromosomes.

cell division

During fertilisation the genetic material joins together.

The nucleus in each cell of an embryo contains 46 chromosomes.

▲ **Figure 2** You inherit half of your genetic material from your biological mother, and half from your biological father.

D State the number of chromosomes present in a normal human body cell.

Discovering DNA

Four scientists worked together to produce a model of the structure of DNA.

In the early 1950s, two scientists, Rosalind Franklin and Maurice Wilkins, used X-rays to investigate the structure of DNA. The image they produced is shown in Figure 3.

James Watson and Francis Crick, scientists working at another university, were also studying DNA. When they saw this image, it told them that DNA had a helical shape. Through further investigations, Watson and Crick worked out that the structure of DNA is like a twisted ladder. This is known as a double helix.

In 1962, Crick and Watson, along with Wilkins, won the Nobel Prize for Medicine for their discovery. Franklin died in 1958; some people say that, at the time, her role in this famous discovery wasn't recognised.

Key words

nucleus, DNA, chromosome, gene

▲ **Figure 3** The first image of DNA produced using X-rays.

Summary Questions

1 Copy and complete the following sentences.

_____ is the chemical containing the information to make an organism. A _____ is a long strand of DNA. A _____ is a section of DNA that holds the information for a characteristic.

(3 marks)

2 a Arrange these objects in order of size, starting with the smallest.

**cell   chromosome   gene
DNA   nucleus**

(2 marks)

b Describe how characteristics are inherited in humans.

(4 marks)

3 Explain why biological siblings appear similar, but not the same.   (4 marks)

4.4 Natural selection

Learning objectives

After this topic, you will be able to:

- describe the role of the fossil record as evidence for evolution
- describe the process of natural selection
- describe how new species evolve through the process of natural selection.

Reactivate your knowledge

1 How do we know that dinosaurs used to exist?
2 What are adaptations?
3 Why are many animals camouflaged?

Key words

adaptation, species, evolution, fossil, natural selection, gene

Link

You will study some more examples of natural selection in B3 4.5 *Natural selection and antibiotic resistant bacteria*

Have you heard the phrase 'survival of the fittest'? It means that organisms that are best adapted to a situation will survive, and those that are not will die. This is how scientists think that all organisms on Earth have developed.

What is evolution?

Scientists have shown that the **species** we see on Earth today have gradually developed over millions of years. This process is called **evolution**.

Evolution started with unicellular organisms. These organisms, similar to bacteria, lived in water more than three billion years ago. Over time they evolved to become multicellular organisms.

Eventually, this process resulted in organisms that could live on land and in the air.

> **A** State what is meant by evolution.

The **fossil** record provides most of the evidence for evolution. Fossils are the remains, or traces (such as footprints), of plants or animals that lived many years ago. They have been preserved by natural processes (Figure 1).

▲ **Figure 1** The fossil record provides evidence of species that no longer exist, such as dinosaurs.

Reactivate your knowledge answers
1 Through fossils 2 Characteristics that enable an organism to survive 3 To blend in with their environment so they can't be seen

B Describe what a fossil is.

How do organisms evolve?

Species evolve through the process of **natural selection** (Figure 2). The species changes slowly over time, to become better adapted to its environment. The process takes many years (sometimes millions) as it happens over a large number of generations.

C Describe the process of natural selection.

Peppered moths

Living organisms are continually evolving to adapt to their environment. Evolution usually happens slowly over many years. However, dramatic changes in the environment of a species can result in evolution happening quickly. Peppered moths evolved in this way during the 19th century.

Before the Industrial Revolution, most peppered moths in Britain were pale coloured. This was helpful to the moths, as they blended in with tree bark. A few peppered moths were dark coloured. This was a disadvantage, as they were easily seen by birds, and eaten (Figure 3). The pale moths were more likely to survive and reproduce, so most of the peppered moth population was pale coloured.

After the Industrial Revolution, many trees were covered in soot, turning the bark black. This meant that the dark moths were camouflaged, and the pale ones were easier for birds to spot and eat (Figure 4). More dark peppered moths survived and reproduced than pale moths. After several years, the population of dark peppered moths in towns and cities grew much larger than the population of pale peppered moths.

▲ **Figure 3** Before the Industrial Revolution, pale peppered moths were better adapted.

▲ **Figure 4** After the Industrial Revolution, dark peppered moths were better adapted.

Natural selection

Organisms in a species show variation – this is caused by differences in their **genes**.

⬇

The organisms with the characteristics that are best adapted to the environment survive and reproduce. Less well-adapted organisms die. This process is known as 'survival of the fittest'.

⬇

Genes from successful organisms are passed to the offspring in the next generation. This means the offspring are likely to possess the characteristics that made their parents successful.

⬇

This process is then repeated many times. Over a period of time this can lead to the development of a new species.

▲ **Figure 2** The process of natural selection.

Summary Questions

1 Copy and complete the following sentences.

All living organisms have _____ from a common ancestor. This process has taken _____ of years. _____ provide evidence for evolution. These are the _____ of plants or animals that died long ago. (4 marks)

2 Describe the process of natural selection. (4 marks)

3 Explain how peppered moths evolved as a result of the Industrial Revolution. (4 marks)

Learning objectives
After this topic, you will be able to:
- describe some factors that may lead to extinction
- describe how gene banks can be used to prevent the extinction of a species.

Reactivate your knowledge
1 What is a fossil?
2 What is the name of the process by which species evolve?
3 Name three things that animals compete for.

Key words
species, extinct, fossil, biodiversity, endangered, gene bank

Can you think of any species that no longer live on Earth? You might think of dinosaurs, which lived millions of years ago. However, there are many other animal and plant species that have also died out.

What does extinction mean?

If a **species** is not adapted to its environment, it will not survive. Organisms will die before reproducing and eventually the species will become **extinct**. A species becomes extinct when there are no more individuals of that species left anywhere in the world. An extinct species is gone forever; no new organisms can be created.

A State what is meant by the word extinct.

How do we know other species existed?

The **fossil** record shows that many species have become extinct. For example, you may have seen the fossils of ammonites (Figure 1). These animals existed at around the same time as the dinosaurs. They had spiral shells and could be up to 2 m wide.

▲ **Figure 1** Ammonites are animals that lived in the sea.

How do organisms become extinct?

There are a number of factors that can cause a species to become extinct, including:

- changes to the organism's environment
- destruction of habitat
- outbreak of a new disease
- introduction of new predators and competitors.

B State three causes of extinction.

▲ **Figure 2** The dodo was a large, flightless bird.

Extinction occurs naturally. For example, most scientists believe that dinosaurs became extinct due to a dramatic change in the

Reactivate your knowledge answers
1 Remains, or traces, of plants or animals 2 Natural selection 3 Space/shelter/mates/food/water

Earth's climate, after a meteor hit the Earth. Dinosaurs could not adapt to these changes in their environment and died out.

Humans can make extinction more likely. For example, the dodo lived on Mauritius, which was an uninhabited island (Figure 2). It had no natural predators. In the 17th century, people arrived on the island, and dodos were hunted for food. Rats that came on the ships also ate the dodos' eggs. In less than a century, the dodo became extinct.

Climate change has resulted in many organisms losing their habitat. For example, the size of the polar ice caps is shrinking. If a species that lives in these habitats cannot adapt successfully, or find somewhere else to live, it could become extinct.

When a species becomes extinct, **biodiversity** is reduced. Biodiversity is the range of organisms living in an area.

> **C** Name two organisms that have become extinct.

How can we prevent extinction?

Species of plants and animals that have only a small population in the world are said to be **endangered** (Figure 3).

Scientists are trying to help prevent these species becoming extinct, and therefore maintain biodiversity, through breeding in zoos and setting up nature reserves, for example.

Gene banks are also being used (Figure 4). They store genetic samples from different species, which can be used for research or to produce new individuals in the future

There are a number of different types of gene bank. These include:

- seed banks – store dried plant seeds at low temperatures
- tissue banks – store buds and other plant cells from plants
- cryobanks – store seeds, pollen, embryos, and sperm and egg cells at very low temperatures, normally in liquid nitrogen.

◀ **Figure 4** A seed bank.

> **D** Name three biological materials stored in a gene bank.

Extinction

Find out about an organism that has become extinct. Write a newspaper article that describes how and why the organism became extinct.

▲ **Figure 3** The black rhino has become endangered due to poachers killing them for their horns.

Summary Questions

1 Copy and complete the following sentences.

A species becomes _____ when there are no more individuals of that species left _____ in the world.

Changes in a species' _____ or the introduction of new _____ can cause a species to become extinct.

Gene banks store genetic samples from organisms, which can be used for _____ and to create new individuals.

(5 marks)

2 Describe the role of gene banks in preventing extinction.

(3 marks)

3 Explain how changes to a species' environment can lead to extinction. (4 marks)

In this chapter you have looked at differences between organisms in a species, and figured out whether the variation is inherited, due to the environment, or both. You then categorised characteristics as showing discontinuous or continuous variation.

You discovered that inherited characteristics are due to your genes and how these are passed on from parents to their offspring. You also found out about the scientists who discovered what DNA looks like.

In the last part of the chapter you studied how organisms have evolved through the process of natural selection. This included finding out why some organisms have become extinct and how gene banks can help to stop other organisms going extinct.

Metacognition and self-reflection task

Flashcards are a great way to summarise important facts. Making your own cards will help you to remember the information in this chapter. It's also a really useful skill that you will use all the way through your science lessons. Make one for each spread. Get a partner to test you on the flashcards a week later. Were some easier to recall than others?

Journey through B2

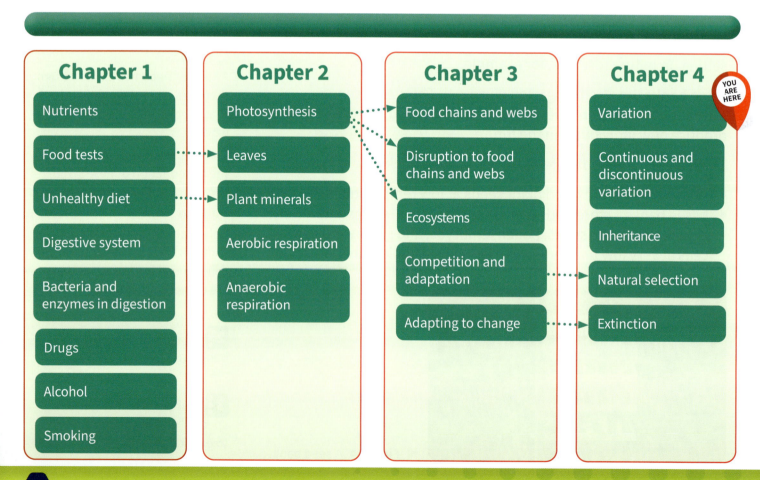

Chapter 1	Chapter 2	Chapter 3	Chapter 4
Nutrients	Photosynthesis	Food chains and webs	Variation
Food tests	Leaves	Disruption to food chains and webs	Continuous and discontinuous variation
Unhealthy diet	Plant minerals	Ecosystems	
Digestive system	Aerobic respiration	Competition and adaptation	Inheritance
Bacteria and enzymes in digestion	Anaerobic respiration	Adapting to change	Natural selection
Drugs			Extinction
Alcohol			
Smoking			

YOU ARE HERE

Chapter 4 Summary Questions

1 DNA is the chemical which stores all the information needed to make an organism.

▲ **Figure 1**

a State where DNA is found inside the cell (1 mark)

b Identify two scientists from the list below that worked together to develop the model of the DNA molecule.
Hook Watson Franklin Darwin Pasteur (2 marks)
(3 marks)

2 Charlie was investigating variation within his class. He decided to investigate the differences in body mass between students.

a State what is meant by variation. (1 mark)

b Name the piece of equipment Charlie should use to measure body mass. (1 mark)

c Body mass is an example of continuous data. State what this means. (1 mark)

d Name the type of graph Charlie should use to display his results. (1 mark)
(4 marks)

3 Characteristics are passed on from parents to their children through genetic material.

a Name the chemical which makes up genetic material. (1 mark)

b Describe the difference between a gene and a chromosome. (2 marks)

c Describe how genetic material is passed from parents to their children. (4 marks)
(7 marks)

4 Dinosaurs were animals that lived on Earth millions of years ago.

a State **one** piece of evidence that proves dinosaurs existed. (1 mark)

b State and explain **two** reasons that could cause an organism to become extinct. (4 marks)

c Describe the role of gene banks in helping to prevent extinction. (3 marks)
(8 marks)

5 The graph below shows a person's ability to roll their tongue.

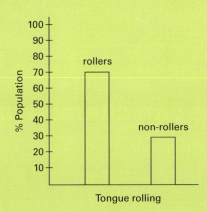

▲ **Figure 2**

a State the percentage of the population that can roll their tongue (1 mark)

b State and explain whether this characteristic shows continuous or discontinuous variation (2 marks)

c The ability to roll your tongue is determined by your genes. State one human characteristic which is determined by environmental variation (1 mark)
(4 marks)

6 Explain the process of natural selection and the role it plays in the evolution of species.
(6 marks)

7 Explain how many characteristics are affected by both the environment and through inheritance.
(6 marks)

Welcome

Chemistry is the study of matter, the stuff that everything is made of. You will learn about the atoms that make up all the different types of matter in you, on Earth, and in the Universe. You will find out how atoms give substances their properties, and how they rearrange to make new substances. You will also discover how chemistry explains the climate crisis and helps us to tackle its challenges.

2 chemistry

Where can chemistry take you?

The skills and knowledge you learn in science help to prepare you for all sorts of roles you might enjoy in the future.

Nutritionist

Retail manager

Environment worker

Sculptor/Artist

Beautician

Farmer

Mechanic

Forensic scientist

Chemistry and the world

The Earth's crust, oceans, and atmosphere provide all the resources we need. Chemistry gets metals from rock, salt from the sea, and gases needed for living organisms. Chemistry helps to make important mixtures, too, like vaccines, toothpaste, and paint. Chemistry skills help you to work out what's true and what's not. Is there evidence to support claims about a product or treatment? How can you find out, and tell others?

BIG QUESTIONS

How do we get the materials we need?
Chemists use separation techniques and chemical reactions to extract metals from rocks, to make bricks from clay, and to produce fabrics from plants or oil.

Can you drink seawater?
Seawater is made up of salt and water so you can't drink it. You must separate out the water by using two processes – evaporation and condensation.

How can we tackle the climate crisis?
If we could add less carbon dioxide to the air than plants and the oceans remove from it, global heating (and the climate crisis) would end.

Journey through C2

YOU ARE HERE

Chapter 1
- Three elements
- Physical properties of metals and non-metals
- Chemical properties of metals and non-metals
- Groups and periods
- The elements of Group 1
- The elements of Group 7
- The elements of Group 0

Chapter 2
- Pure substances
- Mixtures
- Solutions
- Solubility
- Filtration
- Evaporation and distillation
- Chromatography

Chapter 3
- Metals and acids
- Metals and oxygen
- The reactivity series
- Metal displacement reactions
- Extracting metals
- Ceramics
- Polymers
- Composites

Chapter 4
- The Earth and its atmosphere
- Sedimentary rocks
- Igneous and metamorphic rocks
- The rock cycle
- The carbon cycle
- Global heating
- Climate change

1 The Periodic Table

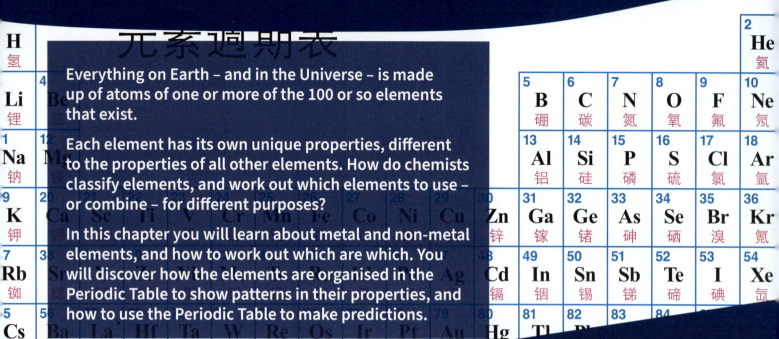

元素週期表

Everything on Earth – and in the Universe – is made up of atoms of one or more of the 100 or so elements that exist.

Each element has its own unique properties, different to the properties of all other elements. How do chemists classify elements, and work out which elements to use – or combine – for different purposes?

In this chapter you will learn about metal and non-metal elements, and how to work out which are which. You will discover how the elements are organised in the Periodic Table to show patterns in their properties, and how to use the Periodic Table to make predictions.

Reactivate your knowledge

1 Gold is a metal element. Describe its properties.

2 Write a list of 10 elements.

3 Predict which has the higher melting point – oxygen or gold.

4 Four solutions have these pH values:
A pH3, B pH6, C pH7, D pH10
Write the letters of the two acids.

You already know

An element is a substance that cannot be broken down into other substances. It has one type of atom.

There are about 100 elements.

Melting point is the temperature at which a substance changes state from solid to liquid.

Acids are substances with pH lower than 7 and bases are substances that neutralise acids.

 How to draw a bar chart using your maths skills.

 How to work scientifically to: describe patterns on bar charts.

Journey through C2

YOU ARE HERE

Chapter 1	Chapter 2	Chapter 3	Chapter 4
Three elements	Pure substances	Metals and acids	The Earth and its atmosphere
Physical properties of metals and non-metals	Mixtures	Metals and oxygen	Sedimentary rocks
Chemical properties of metals and non-metals	Solutions	The reactivity series	Igneous and metamorphic rocks
Groups and periods	Solubility	Metal displacement reactions	The rock cycle
The elements of Group 1	Filtration	Extracting metals	The carbon cycle
The elements of Group 7	Evaporation and distillation	Ceramics	Global heating
The elements of Group 0	Chromatography	Polymers	Climate change
		Composites	

1.1 Three elements

Learning objectives

After this topic, you will be able to:

- describe the properties of three elements
- explain how the uses of three elements are determined by their properties.

Reactivate your knowledge

1 What is an element?
2 How many elements are there: about 10, about 100, or about 1000?
3 Explain what the word *property* means in science.

Figure 1 shows the Museum of Fire in Poland. Its walls are covered in shiny copper. Copper is an element.

▲ **Figure 1** The Museum of Fire.

▲ **Figure 2** A solar farm.

▲ **Figure 3** Copper cables.

How is copper useful?

The architects chose copper for the museum because of its properties. Copper is a **metal**. It has an orange-brown colour and, like most metals, it is shiny. Copper is easy to hammer into thin sheets.

Copper is an excellent conductor of electricity. In a solar farm, long copper cables connect the solar panels (Figures 2 and 3). Every year, energy companies install more and more solar farms. This means that, every year, they need more and more copper.

A Explain why copper is used to make electric cables.

Reactivate your knowledge answers

1 A substance that cannot be broken down into other substances - one type of atom 2 100 3 Quality of a substance or material that describes its appearance or how it behaves

What is sulfur?

Figure 4 shows a pile of the element sulfur. People have known about sulfur for thousands of years. The ancient Egyptians used it to treat swollen eyelids, and in China it was used in gunpowder. Today, sulfur is mostly used to make fertilisers.

Sulfur is a **non-metal** element. It is not shiny, and does not conduct electricity. It is brittle, so breaks easily if it falls.

B Compare the properties of the elements copper and sulfur.

What is germanium?

If you have internet in your home, how fast is it? If you have superfast broadband, light carries data along fibre optic cables to your street. The glass in the cables includes germanium, which can change the direction of light more than almost any other substance. Figure 5 shows a fibre optic cable.

▲ **Figure 5** The glass in fibre optic cables includes the element germanium.

▲ **Figure 6** A piece of germanium.

Figure 6 shows a piece of germanium. Germanium is an element. It is shiny like copper, but brittle like sulfur.

C Describe one difference between germanium and sulfur.

▲ **Figure 4** This sulfur was produced alongside oil in Kazakhstan.

Element video

Make a short video clip to tell other students about the properties and uses of one of these elements: copper, sulfur, or germanium.

Key words

metal, non-metal

Summary Questions

1 Sort these properties into two lists – properties of copper and properties of sulfur.

Properties: good conductor of electricity, brittle, shiny, does not conduct electricity, easy to hammer into thin sheets, good conductor of thermal energy.

(5 marks)

2 Describe one use for each of the elements, copper and germanium. For each use, explain why the properties of the element make it suitable for this use. (4 marks)

3 Compare the properties of copper, sulfur, and germanium.

(4 marks)

1.2 Physical properties of metals and non-metals

Learning objectives

After this topic, you will be able to:

- use the Periodic Table to determine whether a given element is a metal or non-metal
- write the meaning of *physical properties*
- describe the physical properties of typical metal and non-metal elements.

Reactivate your knowledge

1 List three metal elements and one non-metal element.
2 Write the meaning of *melting point*.
3 The chemical symbol of copper is Cu. Explain what chemical symbols are.

▲ **Figure 1** 'Thoroughbred Racehorse', a sculpture by J.K. Brown.

Sculptor J.K. Brown made the horse in Figure 1 from pieces of scrap metal. How can you tell that it is metal?

How are elements organised?

Copper, sulfur, and germanium are elements. Altogether, about 100 elements exist naturally. Each element has its own properties, so it would be difficult to remember them all.

Luckily, there are patterns in the properties of elements. Russian chemist Dmitri Mendeleev used these patterns to create the Periodic Table. The modern Periodic Table lists all the known elements. It groups together elements with similar properties. Figure 2 shows the Periodic Table.

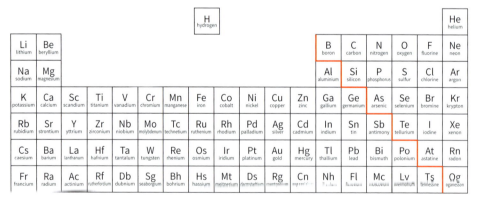

▲ **Figure 2** The Periodic Table. This version does not include every element.

▲ **Figure 3** Silver is a metal.

A Find the elements copper, sulfur, and germanium in the Periodic Table.

Reactivate your knowledge answers

1 For example: metals - copper, silver, gold; non-metal - sulfur 2 Temperature at which a substance changes from the solid to the liquid state 3 The one or two letter code for an element

Metal or non-metal?

There are several ways of sorting elements. One classification has two categories – metals and non-metals. In the Periodic Table, metals are on the left of the stepped line in Figure 2. Non-metals are on the right. Figure 3 shows a metal – silver. Figure 4 shows a non-metal – sulfur.

> **B** Find molybdenum on the Periodic Table and predict whether it is a metal or a non-metal.

How can you tell whether an element is a metal or a non-metal? You can look at its properties. Table 1 shows some properties of metal and non-metal elements.

Properties of a typical metal (when solid)	Properties of a typical non-metal (when solid)
good conductor of electricity	poor conductor of electricity
good conductor of thermal energy	poor conductor of thermal energy
shiny	dull
high density	low density
malleable (you can hammer it into different shapes)	brittle (breaks easily)
ductile (you can pull it into wires)	brittle
sonorous (makes a ringing sound when hit)	not sonorous

▲ **Table 1** Properties of metal and non-metal elements.

Most metals have high melting points. They are usually solid at 20 °C. Many non-metals have low boiling points. For example, oxygen and chlorine are in the gas state at 20 °C.

Melting and boiling points, and the properties in Table 1, are **physical properties**. They describe properties you can observe or measure without changing the material.

> **C** Describe six physical properties of a typical non-metal.

Do all elements fit the pattern?

Most elements are easy to classify as metals or non-metals. But the system is not perfect. Mercury is a metal, but is in the liquid state at 20 °C. One form of the non-metal element carbon, graphite, is a good conductor of electricity.

The elements near the stepped line in the Periodic Table, like germanium and silicon, are **metalloids**. Their properties are between those of metals and non-metals. Most metalloids are shiny. They are semiconductors of electricity.

▲ **Figure 4** Sulfur is a non-metal.

> ### Link ↗
>
> C2 3.1–3.5 describe metal properties in detail.

> ### Key words 🔑
>
> physical property, metalloid

Summary Questions

1 Copy and complete the following sentence.

The physical **properties/reactions** of a substance are properties that you can observe and measure **with/without** changing the material. (2 marks)

2 Sort these elements into two lists: metals and non-metals. Use the Periodic Table in Figure 2 to help.

Elements: chlorine, copper, magnesium, oxygen, sulfur, zinc. (6 marks)

3 Compare the physical properties of metals and non-metals. (6 marks)

Learning objectives

After this topic, you will be able to:

- write the meaning of *chemical properties*
- describe the chemical properties of metals and non-metals.

Reactivate your knowledge

1 Write the meaning of *compound*.
2 Name the two elements whose atoms are in sulfur dioxide.
3 Copy and complete: The pH of an acidic solution is less than _____.

Hot, acidic water bubbles from the ground, and fumes of acidic gases choke the air. Welcome to the Danakil Desert (Figure 1).

▲ **Figure 1** The Danakil Desert.

One of the acidic gases in the Danakil Desert is sulfur dioxide. Carbon dioxide, hydrogen chloride, and hydrogen sulfide are also part of the corrosive mixture.

How do non-metals react with oxygen?

Many non-metal elements react with oxygen. The products are oxides. For example:

$$\text{sulfur} + \text{oxygen} \longrightarrow \text{sulfur dioxide}$$

$$\text{carbon} + \text{oxygen} \longrightarrow \text{carbon dioxide}$$

Most non-metal oxides are gases at 20 °C. They dissolve in water to form acidic solutions, with a pH of less than 7.

Sulfur dioxide and nitrogen dioxide are acidic gases. They are formed when fossil fuels burn in car engines. The products of

▲ **Figure 2** Acid rain damages trees.

Reactivate your knowledge answers
1 A substance made up of atoms of two or more elements, chemically joined 2 Sulfur, oxygen 3 7

the burning reactions dissolve in rain, making it acidic. **Acid rain** damages trees, as in Figure 2. Acid rain also makes lakes acidic.

> **A** Predict whether the pH of nitrogen dioxide is less than 7 or greater than 7. Explain your answer.

How do metals react with oxygen?

Many metals react with oxygen. The products are oxides. For example:

$$\text{magnesium} + \text{oxygen} \longrightarrow \text{magnesium oxide}$$

$$\text{calcium} + \text{oxygen} \longrightarrow \text{calcium oxide}$$

Most metal oxides are solid at 20 °C. Many metal oxides are basic. This means that, if they dissolve in water, they form alkaline solutions, with pH greater than 7. Figure 3 shows a metal oxide.

◀ **Figure 3** Magnesium oxide is basic. It is solid at room temperature.

> **B** An oxide of element X dissolves in water to make a solution of pH 5. Predict whether element X is a metal or non-metal.

What are chemical properties?

There is a pattern in the chemical reactions of elements with oxygen:

- most non-metals react with oxygen to make acidic oxides
- most metals react with oxygen to make basic oxides.

The chemical reactions of elements with oxygen are examples of **chemical properties**. The chemical properties of a substance describe its chemical reactions.

> **C** Describe one chemical property of a typical metal and one physical property of a typical metal.

Metal, non-metal, or metalloid?

Decide whether each element below is a metal or non-metal, or whether it might be a metalloid. Give reasons for your decisions.

	Melting point in °C	Oxide
element A	1085	basic
element B	−102	acidic
element C	938	can act as both an acid and a base

Link

C2 3.1–3.5 describe metal properties in detail.

Key words

acid rain, chemical property

Summary Questions

1 Sort these properties into two lists – properties of metal oxides and properties of non-metal oxides.

Properties: acidic, basic, gas at 20 °C, solid at 20 °C. (4 marks)

2 Write the meaning of *chemical properties*. (1 mark)

3 A teacher reacts sodium with oxygen, and then sulfur with oxygen. Compare the products of the two reactions. (2 marks)

Learning objectives

After this topic, you will be able to:

- determine the group and period numbers of elements
- from data describe patterns in the elements' properties in groups or periods
- use data to predict the properties of another element in a group or period.

▲ **Figure 1** Palladium is a metal element. It is used in catalytic converters in cars, surgical instruments, and some flutes.

Key words

group, period

Palladium is a metal. What can you predict about its properties?

Figure 1 shows that palladium is shiny. You might have predicted that it is a good conductor of thermal energy and of electricity. If you find palladium in the Periodic Table, you can make even better predictions.

What are groups?

In the Periodic Table, the vertical columns are called **groups**. Figure 2 shows some groups of the Periodic Table. For example, the elements beryllium (Be) and magnesium (Mg) are in Group 2.

The elements in a group have similar physical and chemical properties. Going down a group, there are patterns in properties.

1	2												3	4	5	6	7	0
			H															He
Li	Be												B	C	N	O	F	Ne
Na	Mg												Al	Si	P	S	Cl	Ar
K	Ca	Sc	Ti	V	Cr	Mn	Fe	Co	Ni	Cu	Zn	Ga	Ge	As	Se	Br	Kr
Rb	Sr	Y	Zr	Nb	Mo	Tc	Ru	Rh	Pd	Ag	Cd	In	Sn	Sb	Te	I	Xe
Cs	Ba	La	Hf	Ta	W	Re	Os	Ir	Pt	Au	Hg	Tl	Pb	Bi	Po	At	Rn

group number

▲ **Figure 2** Some groups of the Periodic Table.

A The chemical symbol of tin is Sn. Give the group number of tin.

Tables 1, 2, and 3 show data for elements near palladium in the Periodic Table. Each table shows the elements in one group.

Element	Melting point in °C	Element	Melting point in °C	Element	Melting point in °C
iron	1535	cobalt	1492	nickel	1453
ruthenium	2500	rhodium	1970	palladium	
osmium	3000	iridium	2440	platinum	1769

▲ **Tables 1, 2, and 3** Melting points of elements in three groups of the Periodic Table.

Sophie studies the data. She makes this prediction:

For the groups headed by iron and cobalt, melting point increases from top to bottom. The nickel group is likely to show the same pattern. So I predict that the melting point of palladium is between 1453 °C and 1769 °C.

A data book gives the melting point of palladium as 1550 °C. Sophie's prediction is correct.

> **B** Describe the pattern in melting points of the elements in Table 1.

What are periods?

The horizontal rows of the Periodic Table are called **periods** (Figure 3).

Period 1	H																He
Period 2	Li	Be											B	C	N	O	F	Ne
Period 3	Na	Mg											Al	Si	P	S	Cl	Ar
Period 4	K	Ca	Sc	Ti	V	Cr	Mn	Fe	Co	Ni	Cu	Zn	Ga	Ge	As	Se	Br	Kr
Period 5	Rb	Sr	Y	Zr	Nb	Mo	Tc	Ru	Rh	Pd	Ag	Cd	In	Sn	Sb	Te	I	Xe
Period 6	Cs	Ba	La	Hf	Ta	W	Re	Os	Ir	Pt	Au	Hg	Tl	Pb	Bi	Po	At	Rn

▲ **Figure 3** Some periods of the Periodic Table.

Going across a period, there are patterns in the properties of the elements. Figures 4 and 5 show some of these patterns.

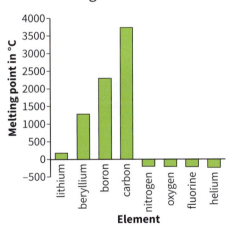

▲ **Figure 4** The melting points of Period 2 elements.

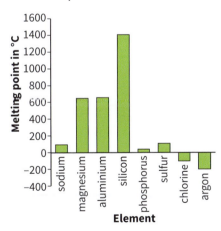

▲ **Figure 5** The melting points of Period 3 elements.

Amara describes the patterns shown by Figure 4.

For Period 2, the melting point increases from left to right for the first four elements. The others have low melting points.

> **C** The chemical symbol of silver is Ag. Give its period number.

Predictable patterns?

Table 4 shows the sizes of atoms of some Group 1 elements. Draw a bar chart to display these data.

Group 1 element	Relative atomic radius
lithium	15
sodium	18
potassium	23
rubidium	24

▲ **Table 4** Sizes of Group 1 element atoms.

Summary Questions

1 Copy and complete the following sentences.

The vertical columns of the Periodic Table are **groups/periods**. The horizontal rows are **groups/periods**. (2 marks)

2 Table 5 gives the densities of three elements in the same group of the Periodic Table. Describe the pattern in density, from top to bottom of the group. (2 marks)

Element	Density in g/cm³
cobalt	8.9
rhodium	12.4
iridium	22.5

▲ **Table 5**

3 Compare the patterns shown in Figures 4 and 5. (2 marks)

1.5 The elements of Group 1

Learning objectives

After this topic, you will be able to:

- describe the physical properties of the Group 1 elements
- using data, describe patterns in the melting and boiling points of the Group 1 elements
- use the pattern in the reactions of the Group 1 elements with water to predict the reaction of another Group 1 element with water.

Reactivate your knowledge

1. State whether the elements on the left of the Periodic Table are metals or non-metals.
2. List three physical properties of a typical metal.
3. Give one chemical property of a typical metal.

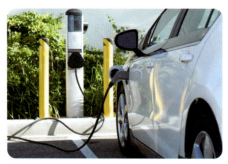

▲ **Figure 1** An electric car.

Figure 1 shows an electric car. It is powered by a lithium battery. Lithium is an element in Group 1, on the left of the Periodic Table.

Figure 2 shows the position of **Group 1** in the Periodic Table, also known as the alkali metals.

Group 1 – the alkali metals
H
He
Li Be
B C N O F Ne
Na Mg
Al Si P S Cl Ar
K Ca Sc Ti V Cr Mn Fe Co Ni Cu Zn Ga Ge As Se Br Kr
Rb Sr Y Zr Nb Mo Tc Ru Rh Pd Ag Cd In Sn Sb Te I Xe
Cs Ba La Hf Ta W Re Os Ir Pt Au Hg Tl Pb Bi Po At Rn
Fr Ra Ac Rf Db Sg Bh Hs Mt Ds Rg

▲ **Figure 2** The Group 1 elements.

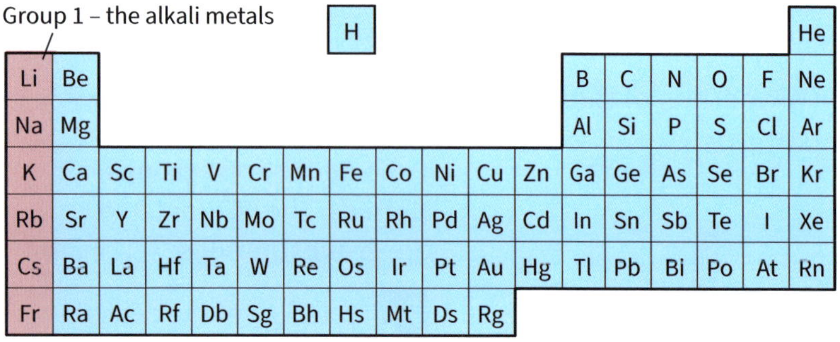

Are Group 1 elements like other metals?

In many ways, the Group 1 elements are like other metals:

- They are good conductors of electricity and thermal energy.
- They are shiny when freshly cut.

In some ways, Group 1 elements are different to other metals. Table 1 shows that Group 1 elements have lower melting points than typical metals, such as copper and platinum. The Group 1 elements are also softer than most other metals, and have lower densities.

Density in g/cm³
1.8
1.6
1.4
1.2
1.0
0.8
0.6
0.4
0.2
0
lithium
sodium
potassium
rubidium
Element

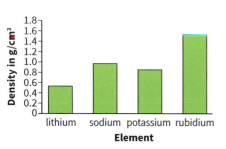

▲ **Figure 3** Densities of Group 1 elements.

Element	Is the element in Group 1?	Melting point in °C
lithium	yes	180
sodium	yes	98
potassium	yes	64
rubidium	yes	39
copper	no	1083
platinum	no	1796

▲ **Table 1** Melting points of Group 1 elements and other metals.

A Describe one difference between Group 1 elements and other metal elements.

Reactivate your knowledge answers

1 Metals **2** Three from: high melting and boiling points, good conductor of electricity/thermal energy, shiny, high density, malleable, ductile, sonorous **3** Reacts with oxygen to make a sold, basic oxide

Are there patterns in Group 1 properties?

The Group 1 elements show patterns in their physical and chemical properties.

Physical properties

The data in the first four rows of Table 1 show that melting point decreases from top to bottom of Group 1. The data in Table 2 show that boiling point also decreases from top to bottom of the group.

Element	Boiling point in °C
lithium	1330
sodium	890
potassium	774
rubidium	688

▲ **Table 2** Boiling points of Group 1 elements.

> **B** Describe the pattern in boiling points from top to bottom of Group 1.

Chemical properties

The Group 1 elements are very **reactive**. This means that they easily take part in chemical reactions. The Group 1 elements have exciting chemical reactions with water. The reactions make hydrogen gas and an alkaline solution. For example:

lithium + water ⟶ lithium hydroxide + hydrogen

There is a pattern in the reactions. They all make hydrogen gas. Figures 4 and 5 show that the reactions get more vigorous from top to bottom of Group 1.

▲ **Figure 4** Lithium, at the top of Group 1, reacts vigorously with water.

▲ **Figure 5** The reaction of potassium with water is very vigorous.

> **C** Predict the gas product in the reaction of rubidium with water.

Which conclusion?

The bar chart in Figure 3 shows densities for Group 1 elements. Describe the pattern.

Summary Questions

1 Copy and complete the following sentences.

The Group 1 elements **conduct/ do not conduct** electricity. They have **high/low** densities. The Group 1 elements are **softer/ harder** than most other metals.
(3 marks)

2 Table 3 gives hardness values for some Group 1 elements. The bigger the value, the harder the element.

Element	Mohs hardness
lithium	0.6
sodium	0.5
potassium	
rubidium	0.3
caesium	0.2

▲ **Table 3**

a Plot the hardness values on a bar chart. (6 marks)
b Describe the pattern in hardness. (2 marks)
c Predict the hardness of potassium. Explain your prediction. (2 marks)

3 Predict the gas product of the reaction of caesium with water. Justify your answer.
(2 marks)

Learning objectives

After this topic, you will be able to:

- describe the physical properties of the Group 7 elements
- using data, describe patterns in the melting and boiling points of the Group 7 elements
- use a pattern in chemical reactions of Group 7 elements to make predictions.

Reactivate your knowledge

1 State whether the elements on the right of the Periodic Table are metals or non-metals.
2 List two physical properties of a typical non-metal.
3 Write the names of the elements with these chemical symbols – F, Cl, Br, I. Use the Periodic Table on page 90 to help you.

Key words

Group 7, halogen

Have you ever smelt chlorine in tap water? Chlorine and its compounds do a vital job. Tiny amounts destroy deadly bacteria, making water safe to drink and swim in.

Are Group 7 elements like other non-metals?

Chlorine is in **Group 7** of the Periodic Table. Figure 1 shows that the other elements of the group are fluorine, bromine, iodine, and astatine. The Group 7 elements are also called **halogens**.

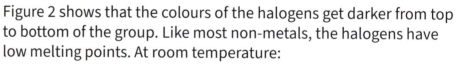

▲ **Figure 1** Group 7 is towards the right of the Periodic Table.

Figure 2 shows that the colours of the halogens get darker from top to bottom of the group. Like most non-metals, the halogens have low melting points. At room temperature:

- chlorine is a pale green gas
- bromine is a dark red liquid. Some of the liquid may evaporate as an orange gas.
- iodine is a brittle grey solid. Some of the solid may sublime as a purple gas.

▲ **Figure 2** Chlorine, bromine, and iodine.

A Compare the colours and states of chlorine and iodine at room temperature.

Reactivate your knowledge answers

1 Non-metals 2 Two from: low melting and boiling points, poor conductor of electricity/thermal energy, dull in solid state, low density in solid state, brittle, not sonorous 3 Fluorine, chlorine, bromine, iodine

Are there patterns in Group 7 properties?

Physical properties

Element	Melting point in °C	Boiling point in °C	State at room temperature
fluorine	−220	−188	gas
chlorine	−101	−35	gas
bromine	−7	59	liquid
iodine	114	184	solid

▲ **Table 1** Melting and boiling point data for the Group 7 elements.

In Group 7, melting point increases from top to bottom of the group.

> **B** Describe the pattern in boiling points for the Group 7 elements.

Chemical properties

The Group 7 elements are reactive. Their chemical reactions are similar. For example, all the Group 7 elements react with iron. The word equations below summarise the reactions:

$$iron + chlorine \longrightarrow iron\ chloride$$

$$iron + bromine \longrightarrow iron\ bromide$$

$$iron + iodine \longrightarrow iron\ iodide$$

Figure 3 shows that the reaction of chlorine with iron is very vigorous. The reactions get less vigorous going down the group. This is different to Group 1, in which reactions get more vigorous from top to bottom.

> **C** Predict the product of the chemical reaction of iron with fluorine.

▲ **Figure 3** Iron reacts vigorously with chlorine.

Better bar charts

Look at the boiling point data in Table 1. Plot a bar chart of these data. Swap bar charts with a partner. Can you suggest improvements?

Summary Questions

1 Copy and complete the following sentences.

The Group 7 elements are also called the _____. They are on the _____ of the stepped line. This means they are _____. Iron reacts with chlorine to make iron _____. The chemical reactions of the halogens with Iron get _____ vigorous from top to bottom.

(5 marks)

2 Describe the colours and states at room temperature of chlorine, bromine, and iodine.

(6 marks)

3 Compare the pattern in melting points of the Group 7 elements with the pattern in melting points of the Group 1 elements. Use data from Table 1 on this page and Table 1 on page 96.

(4 marks)

Learning objectives

After this topic, you will be able to:

- describe the physical properties of the Group 0 elements
- from data, describe patterns in melting and boiling points of the Group 0 elements
- explain how the properties of the Group 0 elements make them suitable for their uses.

Reactivate your knowledge

1 State whether metals or non-metals have higher boiling points, in general.
2 Write the chemical symbols of these elements – helium, neon, argon, krypton, xenon. Use the Periodic Table on page 92 to help you.

▲ **Figure 1** Double glazing.

Key words

Group 0, noble gas, unreactive

What do double glazing, bar-code scanners, and helium balloons have in common? (Figures 1 to 3).

▲ **Figure 2** Bar code scanner.

▲ **Figure 3** Helium balloons.

They all make use of elements in the same group of the Periodic Table, **Group 0**. Group 0 includes helium, neon, argon, krypton, xenon, and radon. The elements of Group 0 are also called the **noble gases**.

Figure 4 shows that Group 0 is on the right of the Periodic Table.

Group 0 – the noble gases

																		He
Li	Be											B	C	N	O	F	Ne
Na	Mg											Al	Si	P	S	Cl	Ar
K	Ca	Sc	Ti	V	Cr	Mn	Fe	Co	Ni	Cu	Zn	Ga	Ge	As	Se	Br	Kr
Rb	Sr	Y	Zr	Nb	Mo	Tc	Ru	Rh	Pd	Ag	Cd	In	Sn	Sb	Te	I	Xe
Cs	Ba	La	Hf	Ta	W	Re	Os	Ir	Pt	Au	Hg	Tl	Pb	Bi	Po	At	Rn
Fr	Ra	Ac	Rf	Db	Sg	Bh	Hs	Mt	Ds	Rg							

(H is shown at the top above the main table)

▲ **Figure 4** Group 0 is on the right of the Periodic Table.

Element	Boiling point in °C
helium	−269
neon	−246
argon	−186
krypton	−152
xenon	−108

▲ **Table 1** The boiling points of the noble gases.

Are there patterns in Group 0 properties?

Physical properties

The noble gases have low melting and boiling points, like many other non-metals. They are colourless gases at room temperature. Table 1 shows their boiling points.

A Describe the pattern in boiling points for the Group 0 elements.

Chemical properties

The noble gases take part in very few chemical reactions. Scientists say they are **unreactive**. From top to bottom of the group, the noble gases get slightly more reactive. For example:

- helium is at the top of Group 0. As far as we know, it never takes part in chemical reactions.
- xenon is at the bottom of Group 0. It is very unreactive. However, it does form compounds with fluorine and oxygen.

B Write the meaning of the word *unreactive*.

Why are the Group 0 elements useful?

The properties of the noble gases make them suitable for their uses. For example, helium has a lower density than air. This is why it is used in helium balloons (Figure 3).

Figures 5 to 7 show other uses of the noble gases.

▲ **Figure 5** Argon is a better thermal insulator than air, so it is used in the gap between the two panes of glass in double glazing.

▲ **Figure 6** The noble gases glow brightly when high-voltage electricity passes through them. This property explains why neon is used in advertising signs.

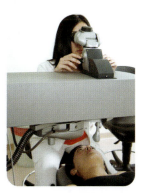

▲ **Figure 7** The eye surgeon is using a krypton laser to repair a damaged retina, at the back of the eye.

C Explain why argon gas is used in double glazing.

Where do noble gases come from?

All the noble gases exist in the atmosphere, mixed with other gases. Companies separate them from the air. Helium is also found mixed with natural gas under the ground or under the sea. It is expensive to separate helium from the mixture.

Summary Questions

1 Copy and complete the following sentences.

The Group 0 elements are **metals/non-metals**. They are **brightly coloured/colourless**. They have **low/high** boiling points, so they are in the **solid/liquid/gas** state at room temperature. They are **very reactive/unreactive**.   (5 marks)

2 Explain why helium is used to fill balloons.   (1 mark)

3 Table 2 shows the melting points of the noble gases. Describe the pattern, and predict the melting point of argon.

Element	Melting point in °C
helium	−270
neon	−249
argon	
krypton	−157
xenon	−112

▲ **Table 2**

(2 marks)

In this chapter, you have developed your knowledge of the elements that make up everything on Earth and in the Universe.

You have learnt how chemists classify elements as metals or non-metals, according to their properties. You have discovered how the elements are organised in the Periodic Table to show patterns in their properties, and how to use the Periodic Table to make property predictions.

Metacognition and self-reflection task

Making and sorting cards is a good way of practising how to classify substances or properties. Start with 12 cards. Write a different property of metals on six separate cards. Write properties of non-metal elements on the other six cards. Do **not** use the word *metal* or *non-metal* on the cards. Then shuffle the cards, and sort into two piles – one for non-metals, and the other for metals.

You can use the same strategy for elements in different groups in the Periodic Table. Write a different property of the Group 1 elements on four separate cards. Repeat for Groups 7 and 0. Then shuffle and sort the cards into three piles, one for each group.

Did you find some elements or groups harder to classify than others? These are the ones you need to practise.

Journey through C2

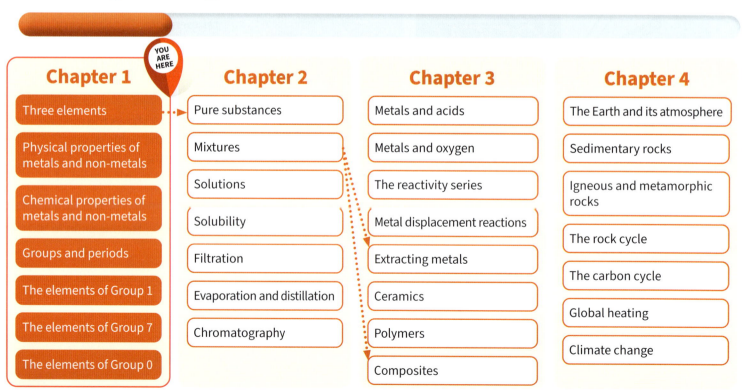

Chapter 1	Chapter 2	Chapter 3	Chapter 4
Three elements	Pure substances	Metals and acids	The Earth and its atmosphere
Physical properties of metals and non-metals	Mixtures	Metals and oxygen	Sedimentary rocks
Chemical properties of metals and non-metals	Solutions	The reactivity series	Igneous and metamorphic rocks
Groups and periods	Solubility	Metal displacement reactions	The rock cycle
The elements of Group 1	Filtration	Extracting metals	The carbon cycle
The elements of Group 7	Evaporation and distillation	Ceramics	Global heating
The elements of Group 0	Chromatography	Polymers	Climate change
		Composites	

Chapter 1 Summary Questions

1 The bar chart in Figure 1 shows the melting points of three elements in the same group of the Periodic Table. Titanium is at the top of the group, and hafnium is at the bottom of the group.

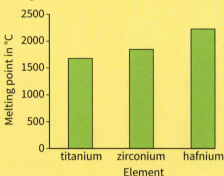

▲ **Figure 1**

a Describe the pattern shown in Figure 1. (2 marks)

b Use the bar chart to estimate the melting point of zirconium. (2 marks)

(4 marks)

2 Two elements, X and Y, have the properties shown in Table 1.

Element	Melting point	Appearance in solid state	Reaction with oxygen
X	low	dull	reacts to make acidic oxide
Y	high	shiny	reacts to make basic oxide

▲ **Table 1**

a Give one physical property of element X. (1 mark)

b Suggest whether element X is a metal or a non-metal. Justify your answer. (2 marks)

c One of the elements in Table 1 is a good conductor of electricity. Predict whether it is X or Y. (1 mark)

(4 marks)

3 Katya watches as her teacher adds a small piece of sodium to water. She makes these observations:
The sodium moves around on the surface of the water.
Bubbles are formed.
After the reaction finished, the teacher added Universal Indicator to the solution. The indicator went purple.

a Explain what the bubbles show. (1 mark)

b Explain why the indicator went purple. (1 mark)

c Write a word equation for the reaction of sodium with water. (3 marks)

d Potassium also reacts with water.

i Describe one way in which this reaction is similar to the reaction of sodium with water. (1 mark)

ii Describe one way in which this reaction is different to the reaction of sodium with water. (1 mark)

e Describe the trend in the reactions of the first three Group 1 elements (lithium, sodium, and potassium) with water. (1 mark)

(8 marks)

4 Table 3 gives the relative size of the atoms of the Period 2 elements. Describe the trend shown in the table. (1 mark)

Element	Relative size
sodium	16
magnesium	14
aluminium	13
silicon	12
phosphorous	11
sulfur	10
chlorine	10

▲ **Table 2**

5 Group 7 elements are non-metals.

a Name two elements in Group 7. (2 marks)

b Give **two** properties of the Group 7 elements. (2 marks)

c Table 2 gives most of the melting and boiling points of four Group 7 elements.

Element	Melting point in °C	Boiling point in °C
fluorine	−220	−118
chlorine		−35
bromine	−7	59
iodine	114	184

▲ **Table 3**

i Name the element in Group 7 that is liquid at 20 °C. (1 mark)

ii Describe the trend in boiling points in Group 7. (1 mark)

iii Use the trend in melting points to predict the melting point of chlorine. (1 mark)

(7 marks)

Separation techniques

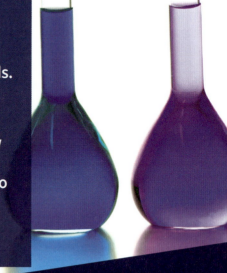

What do you drink in the mornings? Hot drinks, milk, and fruit juice are all mixtures. The different things that are in them are not joined together, they are just mixed up. Tap water is another mixture, of water and dissolved compounds. But vaccines, aquariums, and engine cooling systems need pure water. How do chemists make water pure?

In this chapter, you will learn what mixtures are, and how mixtures are like – and unlike – compounds. You will find out how particles mix to make solutions, as well as how to separate solutions and make pure water. Finally, you will use chromatography to separate and identify substances in solution.

Reactivate your knowledge

1 Describe how to separate sand from a mixture of sand and water.

2 Draw a diagram to show some particles in a grain of sugar. Show each particle as a circle.

3 Draw a diagram to show some particles in liquid water. Show each particle as a circle.

4 Describe how particles leave a liquid by evaporation.

You already know

Some substances dissolve in water to make a solution.

You can use evaporation to obtain a dissolved substance from its solution.

You can use filtering to obtain an undissolved solid from its solution.

Condensing is the change of state from gas to liquid.

 How to subtract masses using your maths skills.

 How to work scientifically to: describe what a line graph shows.

Journey through C2

Chapter 1	Chapter 2	Chapter 3	Chapter 4
Three elements	Pure substances	Metals and acids	The Earth and its atmosphere
Physical properties of metals and non-metals	Mixtures	Metals and oxygen	Sedimentary rocks
Chemical properties of metals and non-metals	Solutions	The reactivity series	Igneous and metamorphic rocks
Groups and periods	Solubility	Metal displacement reactions	The rock cycle
The elements of Group 1	Filtration	Extracting metals	The carbon cycle
The elements of Group 7	Evaporation and distillation	Ceramics	Global heating
The elements of Group 0	Chromatography	Polymers	Climate change
		Composites	

YOU ARE HERE

2.1 Pure substances

Learning objectives

After this topic, you will be able to:

- write the meaning of *pure* in science
- use a temperature-time graph to decide if a melting substance is pure.

Reactivate your knowledge

1 What is a substance?
2 What is a molecule?
3 Name the apparatus used to measure temperature.

▲ **Figure 1** Pure water contains water molecules only. Not to scale.

Key words

pure, impure

▲ **Figure 3** Scientists do not say that juice is pure.

The man in Figure 2 is having a vaccination. The vaccine contains an active ingredient, to stop him getting ill. It also contains water.

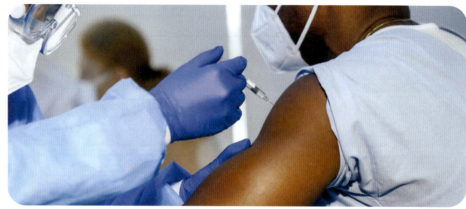

▲ **Figure 2** Having a vaccine.

What is a pure substance?

In science, a **pure** substance is one substance only. All of its particles are the same. Some pure substances are elements, and some are compounds. There is nothing mixed with a pure substance.

Vaccine companies use pure water in their vaccines. Pure water contains water molecules only, as shown in Figure 1. The vaccine company does not use tap water, because tap water is not pure. Tap water has other substances mixed with it.

A Explain why tap water is not pure.

The word *pure* has different meanings in science and in everyday life. In everyday life, a pure substance is one that has not been processed, like the juice in Figure 3. Scientists do not say that juice is pure. This is because juice contains more than one substance, including water and fructose (sugar).

B Explain why scientists do not say that juice is pure.

Reactivate your knowledge answers
1 A material that is not a mixture 2 A group of two or more atoms, strongly joined together 3 Thermometer

How can you identify pure substances?

A pure substance has a fixed melting point. Shilpa has two samples of stearic acid, X and Y. One sample is pure. The other sample is **impure**, which means that different substances are mixed with it.

Shilpa sets up the apparatus in Figure 4 to find out which sample is pure.

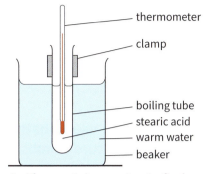

▲ **Figure 4** Apparatus to find out if stearic acid is pure.

Shilpa heats sample X. She records the temperature every minute. She does the same for sample Y. She plots the graphs in Figure 5 and 6.

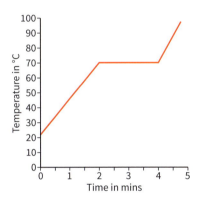
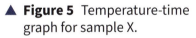

▲ **Figure 5** Temperature-time graph for sample X.

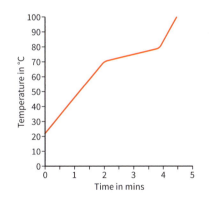

▲ **Figure 6** Temperature-time graph for sample Y.

Figure 5 shows that sample X has a fixed melting point. Its temperature stays at 70 °C until all the solid has melted. Sample X is pure.

Figure 6 shows that sample Y melts between 70 °C and 80 °C. It does not have a fixed melting point. Sample Y is impure.

> **C** Explain how the graph in Figure 6 shows that sample Y is impure.

Link

You learnt about temperature-time graphs for boiling in C1 1.5 *Boiling*.

Interpreting graphs

Work out why Shilpa drew line graphs in Figures 5 and 6, and why she labelled the axes as she did. Discuss your answers with a partner.

Summary Questions

1 Choose the best meaning of the word pure in science from the list below. (1 mark)

A One substance only, with identical particles.
B A natural substance.
C An element or compound.

2 Tim heats a sample. He plots the temperature every minute. Use the graph in Figure 7 to decide whether the sample is a pure substance or a mixture of substances. Explain your decision. (2 marks)

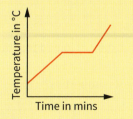

▲ **Figure 7** Tim's graph.

3 Compare the meanings of the word pure in science and in everyday life. (2 marks)

Learning objectives

After this topic, you will be able to:

- write the meaning of *mixture* in science
- compare mixtures and compounds.

▲ **Figure 1** Bath bombs.

Have you ever used a bath bomb, like those in Figure 1? A bath bomb is a mixture of substances. In water, substances in the mixture take part in chemical reactions. The chemical reactions make bubbles of carbon dioxide gas.

A **mixture** contains two or more substances. The substances may be elements or compounds. In a mixture, the particles of the different substances are not joined together. They are just mixed up. There are millions of different mixtures.

> **A** Write the definition for a mixture.

How are mixtures and compounds different?

Figure 3 shows a mixture of two elements, iron and sulfur. The elements are not joined together. You can see yellow sulfur powder and shiny grey iron. You can use a magnet to separate the mixture. The iron sticks to the magnet, leaving sulfur powder behind.

▲ **Figure 2** A compound, iron sulfide.

Figure 2 shows one dark-grey substance. The substance is a compound, iron sulfide. In the compound, iron and sulfur atoms are joined together. You cannot separate them with a magnet.

▲ **Figure 3** A mixture of two elements, iron and sulfur.

Table 1 shows how mixtures and compounds are different.

	Mixture of elements	Compound
Are its substances joined together?	No.	Yes – atoms of its elements are joined together strongly.
What are its properties?	The substances in the mixture keep their own properties.	A compound may have different properties to those of its elements.
Is it easy to separate?	Yes, usually.	No – you need to do chemical reactions to split a compound into its elements.
How much of each substance is in it?	You can change the amounts of substances.	The relative amounts of each element cannot change.

▲ **Table 1** The differences between mixtures and compounds.

B Describe two differences between mixtures and compounds.

More mixtures

Most materials are mixtures. Some exist naturally:

- Most rocks are mixtures of compounds.
- Seawater is a mixture of water, sodium chloride, and other compounds.
- Air is a mixture of elements (such as nitrogen, oxygen, argon) and compounds (such as carbon dioxide).

Chemists make mixtures that are suitable for different uses. They work out the best amounts of each substance to add to the mixture.

The Oxford AstraZeneca COVID-19 vaccine is a mixture. The mixture, shown in Figure 4, includes:

- a harmless virus with genes that make the spike protein on the coronavirus
- a natural acid, to keep the pH constant
- magnesium chloride, sodium chloride (salt), and sucrose (sugar). These stabilise the DNA in the vaccine
- pure water.

C Explain why sodium chloride is included in some vaccines.

Paint (Figure 5) is another useful mixture. It includes a pigment to provide colour, a binder to attach the paint to an object, and a solvent to help the paint spread out.

▲ **Figure 5** Paints are mixtures.

Key word

mixture

Link

You learnt about compounds in C1 2.3 *Compounds*.

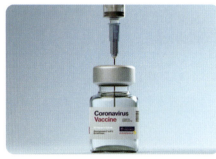

▲ **Figure 4** Vaccines, like this Oxford AstraZeneca COVID-19 vaccine, are mixtures.

Summary Questions

1 Copy the sentences that are true. Write corrected versions of the two sentences that are false.

a A mixture is made up of different substances that are joined together.
b You cannot change the amounts of substances in a mixture.
c The substances in a mixture keep their own properties.
(3 marks)

2 Write a few sentences to compare mixtures and compounds. (4 marks)

3 Give two examples of useful mixtures, and explain why each is useful. (4 marks)

Learning objectives

After this topic, you will be able to:

- write the meanings of *solution*, *solute*, *solvent*, and *dissolve*
- use the particle model to explain dissolving
- predict the mass of a solution made from given masses of solute and solvent.

Reactivate your knowledge

1 What is a mixture?
2 How are the particles arranged in a solid?
3 How do the particles move in a liquid?

Key words

solution, solute, solvent, dissolve

If you add sugar to water and stir, the sugar dissolves to make a solution. A solution is usually a mixture of a liquid with a solid or gas. All parts of a solution are the same. You cannot see the separate substances.

In a **solution**, the substance that dissolves is the **solute**. The liquid it dissolves in is the **solvent**. The complete mixing of a solute with a solvent is called **dissolving**.

> **A** Name the solute in a solution of sugar in water.

Does a solute disappear when it dissolves?

You cannot see white sugar in a solution. But if you taste the solution, you know the sugar is there. Of course, you must not taste things in the laboratory. Are there other ways of detecting the solute in a solution?

Some solutions are coloured. Coffee solution is brown, and copper sulfate solution is blue. The colours show that the solute is there.

▲ **Figure 1** The mass of solution on the left is the same as the total mass of brown sugar and water on the right.

You can also use evidence from mass measurements, as shown in Figure 1:

- The mass of $200 \, cm^3$ of pure water is $200 \, g$.
- The mass of a solution made when $5 \, g$ of sugar dissolves in $200 \, g$ of water is $(200 \, g + 5 \, g) = 205 \, g$.

> **B** Calculate the mass of solution made when $3 \, g$ of salt dissolves in $90 \, g$ of water.

Solution masses

Sarah dissolves $3 \, g$ of copper sulfate in $100 \, g$ of water. Calculate the mass of the solution.

How can we explain dissolving?

Figures 2 and 3 show some particles in solid sugar and in water. When sugar dissolves, its particles separate from each other.

Reactivate your knowledge answers

1 Contains two or more substances, whose particles are not joined together 2 Regular pattern 3 Move around, sliding over each other

Water particles surround the separate sugar particles (Figure 4). The sugar particles mix randomly with the water, and all the particles move around, sliding over each other. The overall volume does not change.

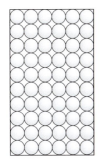

▲ **Figure 2** Particles in solid sugar. Not to scale.

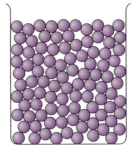

▲ **Figure 3** Particles in liquid water. Not to scale.

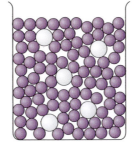

▲ **Figure 4** Particles in sugar solution. Not to scale.

You can use rice and beans to model particles in a solution. In Figure 5, rice grains represent water particles. Beans represent sugar particles.

> **C** Describe the arrangement and movement of particles in a solution.

▲ **Figure 5** Rice and beans can model a sugar solution.

Is water the only solvent?

Nail varnish does not dissolve in water. That's why it does not come off in the shower. But nail varnish does dissolve in a solvent called propanone. The nail varnish remover in Figure 6 is mainly propanone.

▲ **Figure 6** Nail varnish remover contains a solvent called propanone.

Link ↗

You learnt about concentrated and dilute solutions in C1 4.1 *Acids and alkalis.*

Modelling dissolving

With a partner, plan how to use rice and beans, or other objects, to explain dissolving to primary-school children. Use diagrams and notes to show what you will do and say.

Summary Questions

1 Copy and complete the following sentences.

When salt dissolves in water, a **solvent/solute/solution** forms. Salt is the **solvent/solute/solution** and water is the **solvent/solute/solution**. In the solution, **water/salt** particles surround the **water/salt** particles. (5 marks)

2 Use the particle model to explain what happens when sugar dissolves in water. (4 marks)

3 A student dissolves 4 g of salt in water, making 75 g of solution. Calculate the mass of water in the solution. (2 marks)

Learning objectives

After this topic, you will be able to:

- write the meaning of *solubility*
- plot a solubility graph from data in a table
- describe how solubility changes with temperature for a named substance, given data.

Reactivate your knowledge

1 What is a solution?
2 What is a solute?
3 What are the units of mass and temperature?

▲ **Figure 1** Adding sugar to tea.

Substance	Solubility at 20 °C in g/100 g of water
Sucrose (sugar)	202
Sodium chloride (salt)	36

▲ **Table 1** Solubility of sugar and salt.

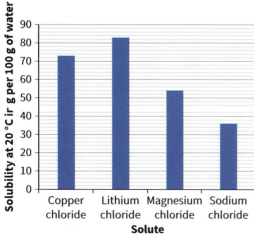

▲ **Figure 2** The solubilities of four substances.

Imagine a glass of water, or a cup of tea (Figure 1). Which dissolves better in the water, sugar or salt? How could you find out?

At room temperature, you can dissolve more than 200 g of sugar in 100 g of water. That's more than 40 teaspoons. But if you add even more sugar to the solution, it just falls to the bottom. It does not dissolve. You have made a **saturated solution**.

A saturated solution contains the maximum mass of a solute that will dissolve at that temperature. There is always some undissolved solute in the container.

You can make a saturated solution of salt (sodium chloride) by adding more than 36 g of salt to 100 g of water.

What is solubility?

The mass of solute that dissolves in 100 g of water to make a saturated solution is the **solubility** of the solute. Every substance has its own solubility. Table 1 gives solubility values for sugar and salt.

A Give the solubility of salt at 20 °C.

Table 1 shows that more sugar than salt can dissolve in 100 g of water. Sugar is more **soluble** than salt. The greater the mass of a substance you can dissolve in 100 g of water, the more soluble the substance.

Figure 2 shows the solubilities of four more substances at 20 °C.

B Name the most and least soluble substances in Figure 2.

Some substances cannot dissolve in water. They are **insoluble**. Chalk (calcium carbonate) and sand are insoluble in water.

Reactivate your knowledge answers

1 A mixture of a liquid with a solid or gas, in which all parts of the mixture are the same **2** The substance that dissolves in a solvent **3** Mass – grams (g) or kilograms (kg); temperature – degrees celcius (°C)

How does temperature affect solubility?

Think again about dissolving sugar. Can you dissolve more sugar in hot water, or in cold water?

The data in Table 2 show that the higher the temperature, the greater the mass of sugar that dissolves.

Temperature in °C	Solubility of sugar in g/100 g of water
20	202
40	236
60	289
80	365
100	476

▲ **Table 2** The solubility of sugar at different temperatures.

Most substances get more soluble as temperature increases. But the increase is greater for some substances than for others. Compare the solubility values of sugar at 20 °C and at 100 °C (Table 2) to those of salt (Table 3).

Temperature in °C	Solubility of salt in g/100 g of water
20	36
100	39

▲ **Table 3** The solubility of salt at different temperatures.

> **C** Describe how the solubility of salt changes as temperature increases.

Grappling with graphs

Figure 3 shows how the solubilities of six solutes change with temperature. With a partner, take turns to choose a line on the graph and describe what it shows.

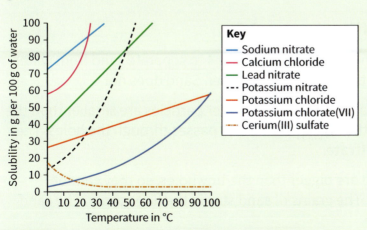

Key
— Sodium nitrate
— Calcium chloride
— Lead nitrate
--- Potassium nitrate
— Potassium chloride
— Potassium chlorate(VII)
-·- Cerium(III) sulfate

▲ **Figure 3** Graph to show how the solubilities of six solutes change with temperature.

Key words

saturated solution, solubility, soluble, insoluble

Summary Questions

1 Write four sentences from the sentence starters and enders below.

Sentence starters
An insoluble substance …
A soluble substance…
Solubility …

Sentence enders
…does not dissolve.
…dissolves in a solvent.
…is the mass of substance that dissolves in 100 g of water.
…increases with temperature, for most solutes.   (4 marks)

2 Plot the values in the table on a line graph, and draw the line or curve of best fit. Describe the relationship shown.

Temperature in °C	Solubility of zinc bromide in g per 100 g of water
20	446
40	590
60	616
80	647
100	669

(4 marks)

3 Compare how the solubilities of lead nitrate and cerium(III) sulfate change with temperature. Use data from Figure 3.   (4 marks)

Learning objectives

After this topic, you will be able to:

- name the types of mixtures that can be separated by filtration
- explain how filtration works
- explain some uses of filtration.

Reactivate your knowledge

1 Name a useful mixture that scientists make.
2 What does *insoluble* mean?
3 What are the three states of matter?

▲ **Figure 1** Filtration separates an insoluble solid from a liquid, for example, sand and water.

▲ **Figure 2** Filtration separates small pieces of solid from gases. For example, the filter in a face mask removes coronavirus particles from breathed-out air.

▲ **Figure 3** Filtration separates an insoluble solid from a solution, for example, coffee solution from ground-up coffee beans.

Scientists work out how to make useful mixtures, such as vaccines and paint. Scientists also work out how to separate mixtures.

One method of separation is filtration. **Filtration**, or **filtering**, separates several types of mixtures, as shown in Figures 1, 2, and 3.

Filtration *cannot* separate a dissolved solid from its solution.

> **A** Name two types of mixture that can be separated by filtration.

How does filtering work?

You can use the apparatus in Figure 4 to separate sand from water. Water passes through the filter paper. Sand does not.

Filter paper has tiny holes in it. Water particles are smaller than the tiny holes. In the liquid state, water passes through the holes. The water is the **filtrate**.

Grains of sand are bigger than the tiny holes, so they cannot pass through. The grains of sand stay in the filter paper. The sand is the **residue**.

filter paper
residue (sand)
filter funnel
clamp

conical flask

filtrate (water)

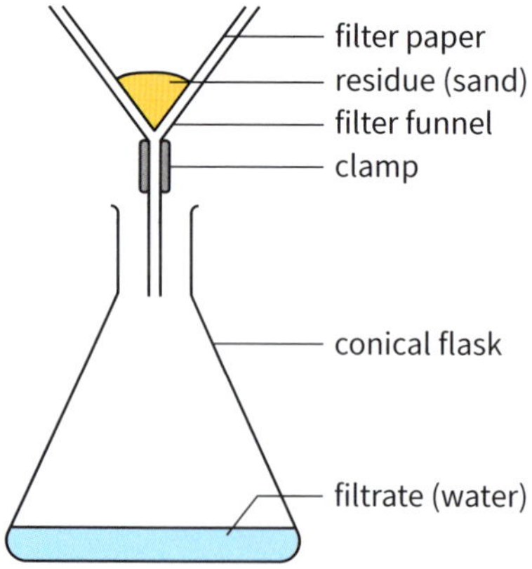

▲ **Figure 4** Apparatus to filter a mixture of sand and water.

B Martha filters a mixture of glitter and water. Name the filtrate and the residue.

How is filtration useful?

You have seen that filtration is useful in face masks and coffee making. Figures 5 and 6 show two more uses of filtration.

◀ **Figure 5** The yellow part is an oil filter in a car engine. The filter contains cotton or wood fibre. The fibre traps solid bits of dirt. Liquid oil passes through gaps between the fibres. The dirt would damage the engine if it stayed in the oil.

C List two uses of filtration.

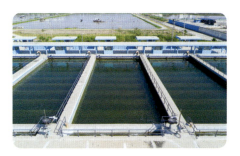

▲ **Figure 6** Sand filters help make water safe to drink. In a rapid sand filter, dirty water flows downwards, through sand. Bits of dirt get stuck in the sand.

Separating a solution from an insoluble solid

If you have a mixture of sand and salt, you can separate the sand like this:

- Add water to the mixture.
- Stir. The salt dissolves. The sand does not.
- Pour the mixture into a filter paper funnel. Salt solution passes through the paper. The residue is sand.

Solubility puzzle

Naomi pours 100 g of water into four beakers. She adds 100 g of a different compound to each beaker, and stirs to dissolve. She filters each mixture, and measures the mass of undissolved solid that remains. She records the data in Table 1. Use the data to work out the most and least soluble substances.

Name of substance	Mass of substance added to 100 g of water in g	Mass of residue after filtering in g
Calcium chloride	100	25
Calcium hydrogencarbonate	100	84
Calcium bromide	100	0
Calcium iodide	100	33

▲ **Table 1** Data for solubility experiment.

Summary Questions

1 Use the phrases below to finish labelling Figure 7.

liquid filtrate, insoluble residue

 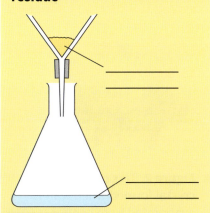

▲ **Figure 7** (2 marks)

2 Explain how filtration cleans engine oil in a car engine. (2 marks)

3 Name three types of mixture that can be separated by filtration, and give an example of each type. (6 marks)

Learning objectives

After this topic, you will be able to:

- use the particle model to explain evaporation
- describe how to use distillation to separate the solvent from a solution.
- determine whether to use evaporation or distillation to separate a substance from a solution.

Reactivate your knowledge

1. What is a solution?
2. Name the start and end states for evaporation.
3. Name the change of state when a gas becomes liquid.

▲ **Figure 1** Obtaining salt from seawater in Taiwan.

For many centuries, people have obtained salt from seawater (Figure 1). How do they do this?

Seawater is a solution of salts (mainly sodium chloride) in water. Salt workers make shallow ponds of seawater. When the Sun transfers energy to the seawater, water evaporates but salt does not. When all the water particles have evaporated from a seawater pond, solid salt remains.

A Describe how to separate salt from seawater.

Key word

evaporation, distillation

▲ **Figure 2** This copper sulfate crystal formed when water evaporated from copper sulfate solution.

How is evaporation useful?

Evaporation is useful for obtaining salt. Figures 2, 3, and 4 show three more uses of evaporation.

▲ **Figure 3** Evaporation makes some glues dry. The solvent evaporates. A sticky substance remains, joining the surfaces.

▲ **Figure 4** Electric cars have lithium batteries. Under the ground in South America are millions of litres of dissolved lithium compounds. Companies pump the solution to the surface. Here, water evaporates. Solid lithium compounds remain.

Link

You learnt about making crystals from solution in C1 4.4 *Making salts*.

B Give three uses of evaporation.

Reactivate your knowledge answers

1 A mixture of a liquid with a solid or gas, in which all parts of the mixture are the same **2** Liquid, gas **3** Condensing

What is distillation?

Imagine you are alone on a desert island. There is nothing to drink. How could you get drinking water from the sea?

Salt has a much higher boiling point than water. You can use this difference in properties to separate the two substances by distillation. **Distillation** uses boiling and condensing to obtain a solvent from a solution.

In the laboratory, you can use the distillation apparatus in Figure 5 to obtain water (the solvent) from a salt solution.

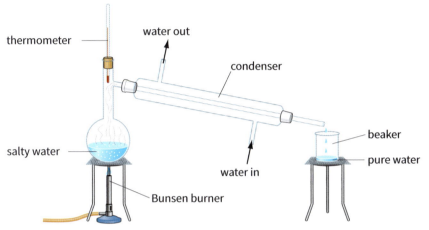

▲ **Figure 5** Distillation apparatus.

Distillation works like this:

- On heating, water in the salt solution boils, forming steam. Salt does not boil, because its boiling point is much higher.
- Steam leaves the solution.
- Steam travels through the condenser, and cools down.
- The steam condenses to liquid water.
- Pure liquid water drips into the beaker.

Saudi Arabia has little rain, and no permanent rivers. The country uses distillation to obtain some of its drinking water from seawater. You can also use distillation to separate water from inky water.

C Name the two changes of state involved in distillation.

Evaporation or distillation?

If you need the solute from a solution, use evaporation. If you need the solvent from a solution, use distillation.

Ancient distillation

Jabir ibn Hayyan lived in Persia almost 2000 years ago. He developed some of the earliest distillation apparatus, the alembic (Figure 6). Discuss with a partner how the alembic might work. Then write a description of your ideas.

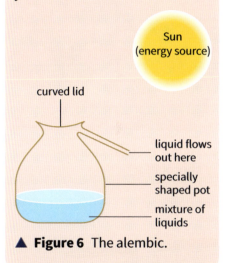

▲ **Figure 6** The alembic.

Summary Questions

1 Describe how to separate salt from salt solution. (2 marks)

2 Describe how distillation works. Use the words *evaporates* and *condenses* in your answer. (4 marks)

3 State whether to use evaporation or distillation to obtain the substances below from their mixtures. Give a reason for each decision.

a copper chloride crystals from copper chloride solution
b propanone, the solvent in nail varnish remover
c ethanol, the solvent in some types of glue (3 marks)

Learning objectives

After this topic, you will be able to:

- describe how to use chromatography to separate the substances in a mixture
- use evidence from chromatography to identify unknown substances in mixtures.

Reactivate your knowledge

1 What is a solvent?
2 What is dissolving?
3 What is a mixture?

▲ **Figure 1** Sugar-coated chocolates.

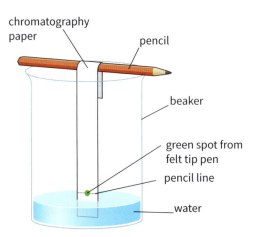

▲ **Figure 2** Chromatography apparatus.

Key words

chromatography, chromatogram

Link

You can learn more about nutrients in B2 1.1 Nutrients

Do you like sugar-coated chocolates? Which of the colours in Figure 1 tastes best?

The coloured crunchy coatings contain mixtures of dyes. You can use **chromatography** to separate the dyes and find out which dyes are in which colours. Chromatography works when the substances in a mixture are soluble in the same solvent.

> **A** State what chromatography does.

How does chromatography work?

To find out which dyes are in a green felt-tip pen, set up the apparatus in Figure 2. Water moves up the paper. As it passes the green spot, the dyes mix with the water. The mixture moves upwards.

Some dyes in the mixture mix with water better than others. All the dyes are attracted to the paper, but some are attracted more strongly than others.

In one minute, a dye that is attracted more strongly to the water than to the paper moves further than a dye that is attracted more strongly to the paper. This means that the dyes separate. The separated dyes make a **chromatogram**.

In Figure 3, the blue dye has moved further than the yellow dye. This might be because the blue dye mixes better with the water than the yellow dye. Or it might be because the yellow dye is attracted more strongly to the paper.

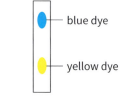

▲ **Figure 3** Chromatogram of green felt-tip pen ink.

> **B** Give the number of dyes in the green felt-tip pen ink in Figure 3.

How is chromatography useful?

Aidan grinds up a spinach leaf in a pestle and mortar. He puts a spot of spinach juice near the bottom of some chromatography paper. He dips the paper in a solvent.

The solvent travels up the paper, taking spinach juice with it. This makes the chromatogram in Figure 4. The chromatogram shows the pigments (colours) in spinach. Each pigment is a different nutrient.

▲ **Figure 4** Spinach leaf chromatogram.

> **C** Give the colour of the nutrient that moved furthest in Figure 4.

Cassava is an important food in Nigeria, and many other countries. Scientists used chromatography to compare the amounts of vitamin A in different sorts of cassava. Children may lose their sight if they do not consume enough vitamin A.

The scientists found that dark-green cassava leaves have more vitamin A than light-green leaves. Yellow cassava roots have more vitamin A than white roots. They advise people to cook dark-green leaves (Figure 5) and yellow roots (Figure 6).

▲ **Figure 5** Cooked cassava leaves.

▲ **Figure 6** Yellow cassava roots.

Clever chromatography

Make notes about three uses of chromatography. Organise your notes in a logical order. Then write a few paragraphs describing how chromatography is useful. Ask a partner to check your writing.

Summary Questions

1 Label the chromatography apparatus in Figure 7.

▲ **Figure 7** Chromatography apparatus. **(6 marks)**

2 Look at the chromatogram in Figure 8. It was made from the leaves of different plants. Write down which plant the unknown sample is from. Explain your choice.

▲ **Figure 8** Chromatogram of leaves. **(1 mark)**

3 Use the particle model to explain why some substances travel further than others in chromatography. **(2 marks)**

119

In this chapter, you have learnt what mixtures are, and how mixtures are like – and unlike – compounds. You have found out about different types of mixtures, including how particles mix to make solutions.

You have used different techniques to separate mixtures, including filtration to separate an undissolved solid from a liquid, and evaporation to separate a dissolved solid from its solvent. You have used distillation to obtain a solvent – such as pure water – from its solution, as well as chromatography to separate and identify mixtures of substances in solution.

Metacognition and self-reflection task

It is helpful to make a table to summarise and compare information. Draw a table with three columns and five rows. Write these three column headings: A – type of mixture; B – separation technique; C – example. Then complete the table to show how to separate these types of mixture: 1 – undissolved solid from its liquid; 2 – dissolved solid from its solvent; 3 – solvent from its solution; 4 – mixture of substances that are soluble in the same solvent.

Journey through C2

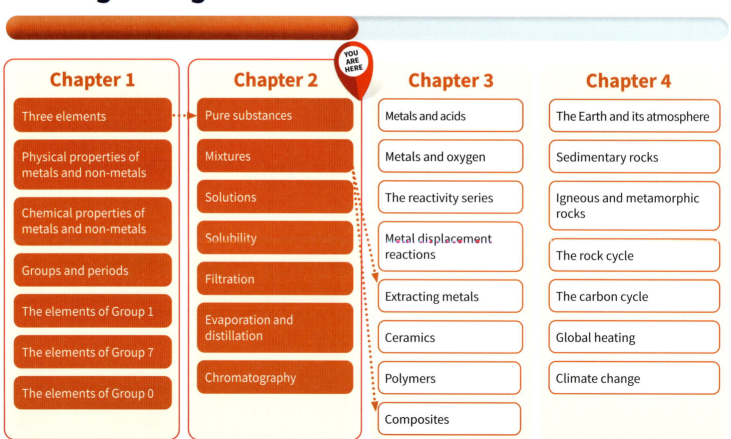

Chapter 1	Chapter 2	Chapter 3	Chapter 4
Three elements	Pure substances	Metals and acids	The Earth and its atmosphere
Physical properties of metals and non-metals	Mixtures	Metals and oxygen	Sedimentary rocks
Chemical properties of metals and non-metals	Solutions	The reactivity series	Igneous and metamorphic rocks
Groups and periods	Solubility	Metal displacement reactions	The rock cycle
The elements of Group 1	Filtration	Extracting metals	The carbon cycle
The elements of Group 7	Evaporation and distillation	Ceramics	Global heating
The elements of Group 0	Chromatography	Polymers	Climate change
		Composites	

YOU ARE HERE

Chapter 2 Summary Questions

1 Sarah has a square cut from an unknown leaf. She wants to know if the leaf is from a spinach plant or a nettle plant. She has the apparatus in Figure 1.

▲ **Figure 1**

The stages below describe what to do. They are in the wrong order. Write the letters in the best order.

A Pour solvent into the bottom of the beaker. Stand the paper in the beaker.
B Use a pestle and mortar to extract liquid from three leaves – the unknown leaf, a spinach leaf, and a cassava leaf.
C Wait as the solvent moves up the paper.
D Draw a pencil line on the chromatography paper.
E Take out the paper. Compare the patterns.
F Put one spot of liquid from each leaf on the pencil line.
(4 marks)

2 Kai wants to make a golf ball float in water. He has the apparatus in Figure 2.

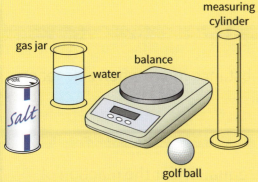

▲ **Figure 2**

Kai dissolves different masses of salt in 100 g of water. He records whether the ball floats. His results are in Table 1.

Mass of salt dissolved in 100 g of water in g	Does the golf ball float?
5	no
10	no
15	no
20	yes
25	yes

▲ **Table 1**

a Name the independent variable. (1 mark}
b Name the dependent variable. (1 mark)
c Suggest one control variable. (1 mark)
d Calculate the total mass of solution made when Kai adds 10 g of salt to the water. (2 marks)
e Use data from Table 1 to give the smallest mass of salt needed to make the ball float. (1 mark)
f Predict the mass of salt that Kai would need to add to 200 g of water to make the ball float. Explain your prediction. (2 marks)
(8 marks)

3 Table 2 shows the solubilities of sodium nitrate at different temperatures.

Temperature in °C	Mass of sodium nitrate that dissolves in 100 g of water in g
0	73
10	81
20	88
30	95
40	102
50	
60	122
70	
80	133
90	
100	160

▲ **Table 2**

a Plot the data on a line graph. Label the x-axis 'temperature, in °C' and label the y-axis 'maximum mass of sodium nitrate that dissolves in 100 g of water, in g'. (5 marks)
b Draw the line of best fit on the graph. (1 mark)
c Describe the pattern on the graph. (2 marks)
(8 marks)

Look around you. Which objects are made from metal, plastic, or glass?

There are hundreds of useful materials. Chemists classify materials into groups, like metals and ceramics. What are the properties of these materials, and how do their properties make them useful?

In this chapter, you will learn about the properties of metals, ceramics, polymers, and composites. You will also study patterns in the properties of metals, and use these patterns to work out how to obtain different metals from the Earth or sea.

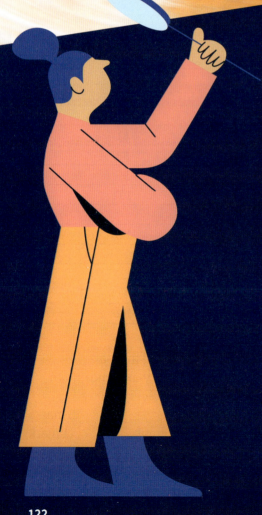

Reactivate your knowledge

1 Write down a property of brick, and explain how this property makes it useful for building houses.

2 Name the substance made when zinc reacts with oxygen.

3 Write a word equation for the reaction of zinc with hydrochloric acid to make zinc chloride and hydrogen.

4 Suggest how to separate magnetic iron oxide from its mixture with sand.

You already know

The uses of materials depend on their properties.

Some metals react with oxygen to make oxides, and some react with acids to make salts.

How to write word equations to show chemical reactions simply.

It may be easy to separate the substances in a mixture, but you need chemical reactions to split a compound into its elements.

 How to use percentages in calculations.

 How to work scientifically to: look for patterns in properties.

Journey through C2

Chapter 1	Chapter 2	YOU ARE HERE Chapter 3	Chapter 4
Three elements	Pure substances	Metals and acids	The Earth and its atmosphere
Physical properties of metals and non-metals	Mixtures	Metals and oxygen	Sedimentary rocks
Chemical properties of metals and non-metals	Solutions	The reactivity series	Igneous and metamorphic rocks
Groups and periods	Solubility	Metal displacement reactions	The rock cycle
The elements of group 1	Filtration	Extracting metals	The carbon cycle
The elements of group 7	Evaporation and distillation	Ceramics	Global heating
The elements of group 0	Chromatography	Polymers	Climate change
		Composites	

3.1 Metals and acids

Learning objectives

After this topic, you will be able to:

- predict the products of the reaction of a metal with acid
- write a word equation for the reaction of a metal with acid.

Reactivate your knowledge

1. Where are metals in the Periodic Table?
2. List three physical properties of a typical metal.
3. What is a salt?

▲ **Figure 1** This hyena is ill.

Zookeepers were worried. The hyena in Figure 1 was ill. Its foot was swollen. It refused to eat. What was wrong?

Vets used X-rays to solve the mystery. The hyena had swallowed 20 zinc coins. In its stomach, zinc reacted with hydrochloric acid. The reaction made zinc chloride. Zinc chloride dissolves in water. It mixes with blood and travels around the body. This causes zinc poisoning.

How do other metals react with hydrochloric acid?

As you know, metals have similar physical properties. They are shiny, and conduct electricity. Metals also have patterns in their chemical properties, including their reactions with acids.

Anna pours dilute hydrochloric acid into a test tube. She adds magnesium ribbon. The mixture bubbles. The magnesium ribbon gets smaller, and a colourless solution remains. There has been a chemical reaction:

magnesium + hydrochloric acid ⟶ magnesium chloride + hydrogen

Anna repeats the experiment with different metals (Figure 2). Zinc bubbles steadily in acid. Iron and lead react more slowly.

Key words

metal, acid

Link

You can learn more about the chemical properties of metals in C2 3.2 *Metals and oxygen* and C2 3.3 *The reactivity series*.

Sulfuric similarities?

Plan an experiment to answer this question: Do metals that react vigorously with hydrochloric acid also react vigorously with sulfuric acid?

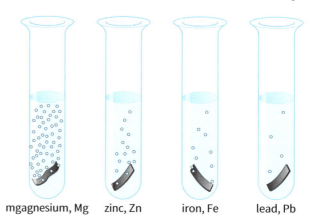

mgagnesium, Mg   zinc, Zn   iron, Fe   lead, Pb

▲ **Figure 2** Metals reacting with hydrochloric acid.

Reactivate your knowledge answers

1 Left of the stepped line 2 For example, shiny when cut, good conductor of electricity, good conductor of thermal energy
3 A compound that forms when an acid reacts with a metal element or metal-containing compound

All the reactions make a salt (for example, zinc chloride) and hydrogen gas:

zinc + hydrochloric acid ⟶ zinc chloride + hydrogen

iron + hydrochloric acid ⟶ iron chloride + hydrogen

> **A** Name the two products of the reaction of iron and hydrochloric acid.

Figure 4 shows how the particles are rearranged in the reaction of zinc and hydrochloric acid. The acid has separate hydrogen and chloride particles, mixed with water. The products are zinc chloride solution and hydrogen gas.

▲ **Figure 3** Gold does not react with dilute acids.

Key
- ⬤ zinc particle
- ● chloride particle
- ○ hydrogen particle

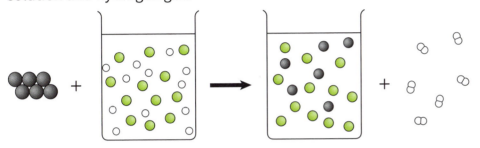

▲ **Figure 4** The rearrangement of particles when zinc reacts with hydrochloric acid. Water particles in the solutions are not shown. *Not to scale.*

> **B** Look at Figure 4. Give the number of hydrogen atoms in a hydrogen molecule.

Some metals do not react with dilute acids. Figure 3 shows that nothing happens if you add gold to hydrochloric acid.

Which salt?

As you know, if a metal reacts with hydrochloric acid, it makes a salt called a chloride. You saw in C1 4.4 *Making salts* that different acids make different salts:

- Sulfuric acid makes sulfates, for example:

  magnesium + sulfuric acid ⟶ magnesium sulfate + hydrogen

- Nitric acid makes nitrates, for example:

  zinc + nitric acid ⟶ zinc nitrate + hydrogen

> **C** Write a word equation for the reaction of zinc and sulfuric acid. The products are zinc sulfate and hydrogen.

Summary Questions

1 Copy and complete the following sentences.

Some metals react with hydrochloric acid. The products are **a salt/an alkali** and **oxygen/ hydrogen** gas. Iron reacts more vigorously than **magnesium/ zinc/lead** and less vigorously than **magnesium/lead/copper**. Some metals, for example, **zinc/gold/magnesium**, do not react with dilute acids. (5 marks)

2 Calcium reacts with hydrochloric acid to make calcium nitrate and hydrogen. Write a word equation for the reaction. (3 marks)

3 Predict the products of the reaction of calcium with nitric acid, and write a word equation for the reaction. (4 marks)

3.2 Metals and oxygen

Learning objectives

After this topic, you will be able to:

- predict the products of the reaction of a metal with oxygen
- write a word equation for the reaction of a metal with oxygen
- compare the patterns in the reactivity of metals with acids and with oxygen.

Reactivate your knowledge

1 What are chemical properties?
2 What does *reactive* mean?
3 Which metal reacts more vigorously with acids – magnesium or iron?

Key word

unreactive

Have you ever burned magnesium in the lab? What did you see? Magnesium burns vigorously. It reacts with oxygen from the air. The product is magnesium oxide.

$$\text{magnesium} + \text{oxygen} \longrightarrow \text{magnesium oxide}$$

Magnesium reacts with oxygen even when you do not heat it. If you leave magnesium in the air, its surface atoms react with oxygen. This forms a thin layer of magnesium oxide.

> **A** Name the product of the reaction of magnesium and oxygen.

How do other metals react with oxygen?

As you know, when a metal reacts with oxygen, the product is an oxide. But there are differences in the reactions of metals with oxygen.

If you sprinkle zinc powder into a Bunsen flame, you see bright white sparks. Zinc oxide forms:

$$\text{zinc} + \text{oxygen} \longrightarrow \text{zinc oxide}$$

Figure 1 shows a similar reaction with iron filings. The product is iron oxide.

Copper does not burn in a Bunsen flame. Instead, it forms black copper oxide on its surface:

$$\text{copper} + \text{oxygen} \longrightarrow \text{copper oxide}$$

▲ **Figure 1** Iron filings burn in air.

> **B** Write a word equation for the reaction of iron with oxygen.

Reactivate your knowledge answers

1 Properties that describe the chemical reactions of a substance 2 Easily take part in chemical reactions 3 Magnesium

Gold does not burn. Its surface atoms do not react with oxygen. This explains why gold is always shiny.

Gold makes connectors in high quality audio equipment (Figure 2). Two properties of gold make it suitable:

- Gold conducts electricity well (a physical property).
- Gold does not react with oxygen (a chemical property).

▲ **Figure 2** Gold makes high quality connectors in audio equipment.

How do reactions with acids and oxygen compare?

Magnesium reacts vigorously with dilute acids. It also burns in oxygen. This means that magnesium is a reactive metal. Gold does not react with dilute acids, or with oxygen, or with other substances. Gold is **unreactive**.

There is a pattern. Metals that react vigorously with dilute acids also react vigorously with oxygen. Metals that do not react with dilute acids do not react with oxygen. Table 1 summarises the reactions of some metals with dilute acids and oxygen.

Metal	Reaction with dilute acid	Reaction with oxygen
magnesium	reacts very vigorously	burns vigorously
zinc	reacts steadily	burns less vigorously
iron	reacts steadily	burns
lead	reacts slowly	do not burn; when heated form a later of oxide on surface
copper	no reaction	
gold		no reaction

▲ **Table 1** The reactions of some metals with dilute acids and oxygen.

C Sodium reacts very vigorously with dilute acid. Predict how vigorously it reacts with oxygen.

Link

You learnt about some other reactive metals in C2 1.5 *The elements of Group 1*.

Fair test?

Jamila wants to list four metals in order of how vigorously they react with oxygen. She has magnesium ribbon, an iron nail, zinc filings, and a piece of copper pipe. She also has a Bunsen burner and tongs. With a partner, discuss how Jamila can compare the burning reactions. How could she improve her investigation?

Summary Questions

1 Copy and complete the following sentences.

Some metals burn vigorously in air, for example, _____. The products are metal _____. Some metals form an oxide layer on their surface when heated, for example, _____. Some metals, for example _____, do not react with oxygen.   (4 marks)

2 Zinc reacts with oxygen to make zinc oxide. Write a word equation for the reaction.
                    (3 marks)

3 Lithium reacts very vigorously with dilute hydrochloric acid. Predict how vigorously it reacts with oxygen, and the product of the reaction. Explain your answers.   (4 marks)

Learning objectives

After this topic, you will be able to:

- predict the products of the reaction of a metal with water
- write a word equation for the reaction of a metal with water
- use the reactivity series to predict how vigorously metals react with acids, oxygen, and water.

Reactivate your knowledge

1 Name a reactive metal and an unreactive metal.
2 What is the product of the reaction of zinc and oxygen?
3 Name three metals in Group 1 of the Periodic Table.

▲ **Figure 1** Copper water pipes do not react with water.

Key word

reactivity series

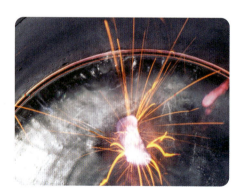

▲ **Figure 3** Potassium reacts vigorously with water.

Look at the metals around you. Do they react with water? Stainless steel taps do not. Also gold jewelery does not, and neither do the copper pipes in Figure 1.

Some metals do react with water. Figure 2 shows the reaction of calcium with water. There is vigorous bubbling, and the lumps of calcium get smaller. The bubbles contain one of the products – hydrogen gas. The other product is calcium hydroxide:

$$\text{calcium} + \text{water} \longrightarrow \text{calcium hydroxide} + \text{hydrogen}$$

A Name the products of the reaction of calcium with water.

▲ **Figure 2** Calcium reacts vigorously with water.

How do other metals react with water?

As you know, the Group 1 metals also react vigorously with water. Figure 3 shows that there is a flame when potassium reacts with water. Sodium and lithium react slightly less vigorously.

Reactivate your knowledge answers

1 Reactive metal – for example: potassium, sodium, lithium, calcium, magnesium; unreactive metal – for example: gold, copper
2 Zinc oxide 3 Three from: lithium, sodium, potassium, rubidium, caesium

There is a pattern in the Group 1 metal reactions with water. They all make soluble hydroxides and bubbles of hydrogen gas:

potassium + water ⟶ potassium hydroxide + hydrogen

> **B** Lithium reacts with water to make lithium hydroxide and hydrogen. Write a word equation for the reaction.

How do metals react with steam?

Magnesium reacts slowly with cold water. This shows that magnesium is less reactive than potassium, sodium, lithium, and calcium. But magnesium reacts quickly with steam (Figure 5).

magnesium + water ⟶ magnesium oxide + hydrogen

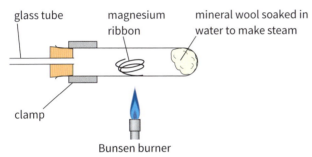

▲ **Figure 5** Apparatus for the reaction of magnesium with steam.

Zinc and iron also react with steam. The products are hydrogen, and a metal oxide.

Copper and gold are unreactive. They do not react with cold water or steam, just as they do not react with dilute acids and oxygen.

What is the reactivity series?

The patterns of metal reactions with acids, oxygen, and water are similar. The **reactivity series** (Figure 4) describes these patterns. It lists the metals in order of how vigorously they react with other substances. The metals at the top have very vigorous reactions. Going down the list, the metals get less reactive.

> **C** Use the reactivity series in Figure 4 to predict which of these metals reacts most vigorously with oxygen – calcium, iron, or zinc.

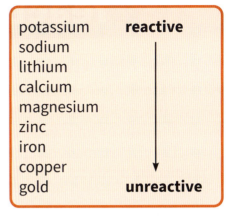

potassium	**reactive**
sodium	
lithium	
calcium	
magnesium	
zinc	
iron	
copper	
gold	**unreactive**

▲ **Figure 4** The reactivity series.

Summary Questions

1 Sodium reacts with water to make sodium hydroxide and hydrogen. Write the letter of the correct word equation for this reaction. (1 mark)

A sodium + water ⟶
            sodium hydroxide

B sodium hydroxide + hydrogen
            ⟶ sodium + water

C sodium + water ⟶
    sodium hydroxide + hydrogen

2 Predict the two products of the reaction of lithium and water. (2 marks)

3 Use the evidence in Table 1 to predict the position of nickel in the reactivity series. Explain your prediction. (2 marks)

Metal	Observations after leaving metal in water and air for one week	Observations on adding dilute hydrochloric acid
nickel	no change	bubbles form slowly
iron	makes red-brown flaky substance	bubbles form slowly
lead	no change	no change

▲ **Table 1**

Learning objectives

After this topic, you will be able to:

- write the meaning of *displacement reaction*
- identify pairs of substances that do, and do not, react in displacement reactions
- predict the products of displacement reactions.

Reactivate your knowledge

1 What is the reactivity series?
2 Calcium is reactive. Is it near the top or bottom of the reactivity series?
3 In a word equation, what does the arrow mean?

magnesium
aluminium
zinc
iron
lead
copper
gold

▲ **Figure 1** Part of the reactivity series.

Key words

displace, displacement

Planning paragraphs

Make notes for a piece of writing to explain displacement reactions. Decide how to divide the information into paragraphs. Plan what to include in each paragraph. Then write your paragraphs. Swap with a partner. Can you suggest improvements?

What does Figure 2 show? The object is a copper heat sink in a computer. It transfers thermal energy away from the computer processor, to prevent it from overheating.

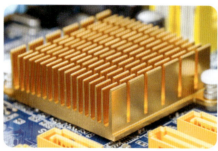

▲ **Figure 2** A copper heat sink in a computer.

▲ **Figure 3** This rock contains copper compounds.

Copper comes from rock that contains copper compounds (Figure 3). Scientists use chemical reactions to get copper from rock.

Here's how:

- Add sulfuric acid to the rock. Copper sulfate solution forms.
- Add waste iron to the copper sulfate solution. There is a chemical reaction. One of the products is copper:

$$\text{iron} + \text{copper sulfate} \longrightarrow \text{iron sulfate} + \text{copper}$$

The reactivity series (Figure 1) shows that iron is more reactive than copper. Iron **displaces** copper from its compound, copper sulfate. The reaction is a **displacement** reaction. In a displacement reaction, a more reactive element displaces, or pushes out, a less reactive element from its compound.

A State what a displacement reaction is.

Reactivate your knowledge answers
1 A list of metals in order of how vigorously they react with other substances 2 Top 3 Reacts to make

Other displacement reactions

Ben adds magnesium to copper sulfate solution. Magnesium is more reactive than copper. So magnesium displaces copper from its compound.

magnesium + copper sulfate ⟶ magnesium sulfate + copper

If you add copper to magnesium sulfate solution, there is no reaction. Copper is less reactive than magnesium. So copper cannot displace magnesium from its compounds.

> **B** Explain why copper cannot displace magnesium from magnesium sulfate solution.

Do oxides take part in displacement reactions?

Aluminium is more reactive than iron. It displaces iron from its compounds. For example:

aluminium + iron oxide ⟶ aluminium oxide + iron

This is the thermite reaction, shown in Figure 4. It involves mixing aluminium and iron oxide powders, and heating them strongly. The reaction is exothermic. It gets so hot that iron forms in the liquid state.

Other metal–metal oxide pairs react. The metal on its own must be more reactive than the metal in the compound. For example:

zinc + copper oxide ⟶ zinc oxide + copper

Zinc has displaced copper from copper oxide. Figure 5 shows how the particles rearrange and join together differently in the reaction.

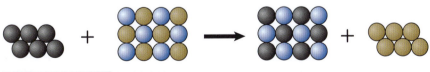

Key
- ⬤ zinc particle
- ⬤ copper particle
- ⬤ oxygen particle

▲ **Figure 5** The reaction of zinc with copper oxide makes zinc oxide and copper. *Not to scale.*

Copper does not react with zinc oxide. This is because zinc is less reactive than iron.

Link ↗

In C2 4.8 *Recycling*, you will learn about metal recycling.

▲ **Figure 4** The thermite reaction.

Summary Questions

1 Use the reactivity series in Figure 1 to identify which metal is more reactive – zinc or lead.
(1 mark)

2 Predict which of these pairs of substances react in displacement reactions.
a zinc and copper sulfate solution
b iron and zinc chloride solution
c aluminium powder and copper oxide powder
d iron filings and lead oxide powder
(3 marks)

3 Write word equations for the displacement reactions of:
a zinc and copper chloride solution
b zinc and lead oxide
c magnesium and iron chloride solution.
(6 marks)

3.5 Extracting metals

Learning objectives

After this topic, you will be able to:

- describe the steps to extract a metal from its ore
- name metals that are extracted by heating their ores with carbon
- calculate the mass of metal in an ore.

Reactivate your knowledge

1 What is a displacement reaction?
2 Which is more reactive, iron or zinc? (see Figure 3).
3 List three physical properties of metals.

Key word

ore

Figure 1 shows a train in Uzbekistan. What is it made from?

▲ **Figure 1** This train is made from steel and other materials.

The train is made from steel. Steel is mainly iron. But where does iron come from? You cannot find iron on its own in the Earth's crust.

What is an ore?

In the Earth's crust, iron is joined to other elements, in compounds. In many of these compounds, iron is joined to oxygen. These are iron oxides.

▲ **Figure 2** Hematite, one type of iron ore.

Most iron oxide is mixed with other compounds in rock. A rock that you can extract a metal from – and that has enough of the metal to make it worth extracting – is an **ore**. For example:

- iron ore (Figure 2) is a mixture of iron oxide and other compounds
- aluminium ore is a mixture of aluminium oxide and other compounds.

Reactivate your knowledge answers

1 A chemical reaction in which a more reactive element displaces, or pushes out, a less reactive element from its compound
2 Zinc   3 For example – good conductor of electricity, good conductor of thermal energy, malleable, ductile

How much metal is in an ore?

Different ores contain different amounts of metal. A company may extract iron from ores that are between 16% and 70% iron.

To calculate the mass of metal in an ore, you need to know the mass of ore and the percentage of metal in the ore.

One lump of ore in Figure 2 has a mass of 600 g. The ore is 50% iron.

mass of iron = percentage of iron in ore × mass of ore
= 50% × 600 kg
= 300 kg

> **A** Calculate the mass of iron in 20 kg of ore that is 25% iron.

How are metals extracted from ores?

There are two main steps in extracting iron from its ore:

1 Separate iron oxide from the compounds it is mixed with.

2 Use chemical reactions to extract iron from iron oxide.

The chemical reactions involve heating iron oxide with carbon.

> **B** State which step above (**1** or **2**) is a physical change.

Which metal oxides react with carbon?

Carbon is a non-metal. But we can place it in the reactivity series, between aluminium and zinc (Figure 3).

Carbon displaces any metal that is below it in the reactivity series. For example, on heating, carbon displaces copper from copper oxide:

copper oxide + carbon ⟶ copper + carbon dioxide

> **C** Name four metals that can be displaced from their compounds by carbon.

Can carbon extract any metal from its compounds?

You cannot use carbon to get aluminium from aluminium oxide, because aluminium is more reactive than carbon.

Gold is so unreactive that it is found as an element not in a compound. The gold just needs separating from the substances it is mixed with.

Ore waste

Calculate the masses of waste from 1 tonne (1000 kg) of each of these ores: an ore that is 50% iron, an ore that is 16% iron, and an ore that is 70% iron.

aluminium
magnesium
carbon
zinc
iron
lead
copper

▲ **Figure 3** Part of the reactivity series, including carbon.

Summary Questions

1 Give the two steps needed to extract a metal from its ore.
(1 mark)

2 An ore contains 6% copper. Calculate the mass of copper in 400 kg of this ore. (2 marks)

3 Magnesium is not extracted from its ore by heating with carbon. Explain why. (2 marks)

3.6 Ceramics

Learning objectives
After this topic, you will be able to:
- describe the properties of ceramics
- explain why the properties of ceramics make them suitable for their uses.

Reactivate your knowledge
1 What are materials?
2 A substance has a melting point of 3000°C. What is its state at 20°C?
3 Give the meaning of *physical properties*.

▲ **Figure 1** Toilets are made from pottery, which is a ceramic.

Figure 1 shows a toilet. What are toilets made from?

Toilets are made from pottery. Pottery is an example of a **ceramic** material. Figures 2, 3, and 7 also show objects made from ceramic materials – brick, earthenware, and china. A ceramic is a hard, brittle material that is made by firing a material, such as clay, at a high temperature.

> **A** Write down what a ceramic material is.

▲ **Figure 2** Bricks are made by heating clay. Chemical reactions occur, which harden the clay.

▲ **Figure 3** The pot is made from earthenware, which – like all ceramics – is brittle.

What are the properties of ceramics?

All ceramic materials have similar physical properties. They are:

- hard – you can only scratch them with harder materials
- brittle – they break easily (Figure 3)
- stiff – they are difficult to bend
- solid at room temperature, with very high melting points
- strong when forces press on them
- easy to break when pulled
- electrical insulators.

Ceramics also have similar chemical properties to each other. They do not react with water, acids, or alkalis.

Key word

ceramic

Reactivate your knowledge answers
1 The different types of stuff that things are made from 2 Solid 3 Properties that you can observe or measure without changing the material

B Give four physical properties and one chemical property of ceramics.

What makes ceramics useful?

Ceramics have many uses. Figures 4, 5, 6, and 7 show how their uses depend on their properties.

▲ **Figure 4** Bricks are strong when forces press on them. They are durable and attractive. This makes brick suitable for buildings.

▲ **Figure 5** Ceramics are electrical insulators. They do not react with water. This makes them useful for electrical power-line insulators.

▲ **Figure 6** Ceramics have high melting points. This makes them suitable for jet-engine turbine blades, which get very hot.

▲ **Figure 7** Ceramics do not react with water, acids, or alkalis. You can decorate them. This makes them useful for plates, bowls, cups, and jugs.

C Write down two uses of ceramics. Explain how their properties make them suitable for these uses.

What gives ceramics their properties?

In ceramic materials, millions and millions of atoms join together in one big structure. There are strong forces between the atoms.

This structure explains the properties of ceramic materials:

- You need a great amount of energy to break forces between atoms. This explains why ceramics have high melting points.
- The bonds between atoms are very strong. This is why ceramic materials are hard.

Summary Questions

1 Read the list of properties. From the list, write the properties of a typical ceramic.

List of properties:

hard, soft, bendy, brittle, electrical insulator, high melting point, electrical conductor

(4 marks)

2 Look at the data in the table. Decide which materials could be ceramics. Explain your choices.

Material	Relative hardness	Melting point in °C
A	2.0	321
B	9.0	3532
C	3.0	825
D	9.0	2930
E	5.8	2800

(2 marks)

3 Explain why ceramic materials have high melting points. (2 marks)

3.7 Polymers

Learning objective
After this topic, you will be able to:
- explain how polymer properties make them suitable for their uses.

Reactivate your knowledge
1 What is a molecule?
2 What is density?
3 Why do different materials have different uses?

▲ **Figure 1** This person is wearing a jumper.

▲ **Figure 2** Bicycle wheels have rubber tyres.

Plotting polymers ÷×

Every polymer has its own properties. Plot the density data in Table 1 on a bar chart. Show your chart to a partner. Ask them to check your scale, labels, and accuracy.

Polymer	Density in g/cm³
low-density poly(ethene)	0.92
high-density poly(ethene)	0.96
poly(vinyl chloride)	1.30
soft rubber	1.10

▲ **Table 1**

What do jumpers and tyres have in common (Figures 1 and 2)?

Jumpers and tyres are made from polymers. A **polymer** is a substance with very long molecules. Figure 3 shows that a polymer molecule has identical groups of atoms, repeated many times.

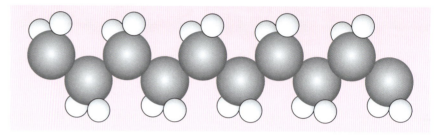

▲ **Figure 3** A small part of a molecule of a polymer called poly(ethene). The black spheres represent carbon atoms. The white spheres represent hydrogen atoms.

There are many polymers. Different polymers have different properties. Their properties make them suitable for their uses.

A State what a polymer is.

What makes natural polymers useful?

Plants and animals make **natural polymers**, including wool and rubber. Figures 4 and 5 explain why wool and rubber are suitable for their uses.

▲ **Figure 4** Sheep make wool. Wool fibres trap air between them. This means that wool traps thermal energy, making it useful for jumpers and socks.

▲ **Figure 5** Rubber trees produce rubber. Rubber is flexible, waterproof, and durable. These properties make it suitable for tyres.

Reactivate your knowledge answers
1 A group of two or more atoms, strongly bonded together 2 Density of a substance is its mass in a certain volume 3 Different metals have different properties, making them suitable for different uses

B Describe three properties of rubber.

What makes synthetic polymers useful?

Synthetic polymers do not occur naturally. They are made in labs and factories. There are hundreds of synthetic polymers, each with its own properties.

One polymer is poly(ethene), which is the scientific name for polythene. There are two types of poly(ethene), low-density and high-density.

- The molecules in low-density poly(ethene) (LDPE) slide over each other. This makes it flexible. LDPE is also strong. It is used for packaging.
- High-density poly(ethene) (HDPE) is also strong. It is harder than LDPE. Its surfaces can be very smooth. HDPE is used in some artificial knee joints (Figure 6), along with a metal.

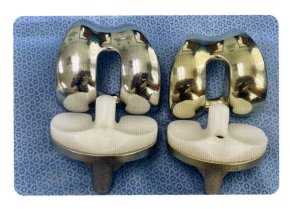

◀ **Figure 6** Some artificial knee joints include the polymer HDPE.

Both types of poly(ethene) do not wear away or break down (decay) naturally. This property is very important for artificial knee joints. But the same property makes it difficult to dispose of poly(ethene) objects, like bags (Figure 7).

◀ **Figure 7** Poly(ethene) does not decay naturally, so it can harm animals.

C State why high-density poly(ethene) (HDPE) is used in some artificial joints.

Summary Questions

1 Give two properties of low-density poly(ethene).
(2 marks)

2 The list gives some properties of a polymer called poly(styrene).

Choose a property from the list that explains why poly(styrene) is suitable for:

a packaging
b disposable cups for hot drinks.

Properties: low density; does not conduct electricity; poor conductor of thermal energy; white colour. (2 marks)

3 Table 2 gives data about two synthetic polymers. Use the data to compare the properties of the polymers.

Polymer	Strength when pulled in N/mm²	Relative hardness
poly(vinyl chloride) (PVC)	48	20
nylon	60	10

▲ **Table 2**

(3 marks)

3.8 Composites

Learning objectives

After this topic, you will be able to:

- explain the properties of some composites
- explain why the properties of composites make them suitable for their uses.

Reactivate your knowledge

1 What are properties?
2 What are ceramic materials?
3 What is a polymer?

Key word

composite, carbon fibre

▲ **Figure 1** The Burj Khalifa is the tallest building in the world.

The Burj Khalifa, Dubai, is the tallest building in the word (Figure 1). It is made from reinforced concrete. What is this material, and why is it so strong?

◀ **Figure 2** The builder pours concrete into the gaps between the steel rods. The concrete sets hard.

Reinforced concrete consists of steel bars with concrete around them (Figure 2). Concrete is not damaged when forces press on it. Steel is not damaged by stretching forces. Together, steel and concrete withstand high squashing forces and high stretching forces.

> **A** Name the two materials in reinforced concrete.

Reinforced concrete is a composite material. A **composite** is a mixture of materials. Each material has different properties. The composite has properties that are a combination of the properties of the materials that are in it.

Reactivate your knowledge answers

1 Properties describe what a substance looks like and how it behaves 2 Hard, brittle materials that are made by firing materials like clay at high temperatures 3 A substance with very long molecules, in which identical groups of atoms are repeated many times

Scientists experiment with different combinations of materials. They develop composites with the best properties for particular uses. At the moment, scientists are researching materials to replace concrete, since making concrete produces huge amounts of carbon dioxide gas. Carbon dioxide has been linked to climate change, so it is important that we try to reduce it.

B State what a composite material is.

Carbon-fibre-reinforced plastic

The bicycle in Figure 3 is made from **carbon-fibre**-reinforced plastic (CFRP). The composite consists of two materials:

- carbon fibres, which are thin tubes of carbon. The fibres are woven into a fabric.
- a glue-like polymer, which is moulded into different shapes when soft.

Many cyclists prefer CFRP bicycles to steel ones. This is because:

- CFRP has a lower density than steel, making lighter bicycles.
- CFRP does not rust.
- You can mould CFRP into any shape.

CFRP has some disadvantages. Bicycles made from CFRP are expensive. If crashed, they are badly damaged.

C Explain why carbon-fibre-reinforced plastic is suitable for bicycles.

▲ **Figure 3** This bike has a carbon-fibre-reinforced plastic mudguard.

Comparing composites

Ash makes three blocks of a composite material from mud and straw. They put different amounts of straw in each block. The mud dries.

Discuss how they could use the apparatus in Figure 3 to compare the strengths of the blocks. Write down the variables, and suggest how to make the investigation fair.

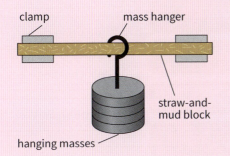
clamp   mass hanger

straw-and-mud block

hanging masses

◀ **Figure 4** Apparatus set-up to compare the strengths of blocks.

Summary Questions

1 Describe three properties of carbon-fibre-reinforced plastic. (3 marks)

2 Explain why reinforced concrete withstands both pushing and pulling forces. (2 marks)

3 Fibreglass is a composite material. It is made from a polymer called polyester resin, and glass fibres. Use the data in Table 1 to suggest why fibreglass is a better material for canoes than polyester resin alone. (1 mark)

Material	Strength when pulled in MPa	Strength when squashed in MPa
polyester resin	55	140
fibreglass	250	150

▲ **Table 1**

In this chapter, you learnt about patterns in the chemical properties of metals, and how to use the reactions of metals with acids, oxygen, and water to list metals in the reactivity series. You have found out about displacement reactions and used the reactivity series to predict whether a displacement reaction will occur. You have also learnt to use the reactivity series to work out how a metal is extracted from its ore.

Finally, you have studied the properties of three other groups of materials – ceramics, composites, and polymers – and considered how these properties make them suitable for their uses.

Metacognition and self-reflection task

It is useful to summarise information about a topic on one side of paper. Divide a piece of paper into four sections – one big, and three small. In the big section, summarise the evidence used to list metals in the reactivity series. Then add information to show how the reactivity series is useful. In each small section, summarise information about the properties and uses of one of these groups of materials – ceramics, polymers, and composites. Which parts did you find easier and which were more challenging?

Journey through C2

Chapter 1	Chapter 2	Chapter 3	Chapter 4
Three elements	Pure substances	Metals and acids	The Earth and its atmosphere
Physical properties of metals and non-metals	Mixtures	Metals and oxygen	Sedimentary rocks
Chemical properties of metals and non-metals	Solutions	The reactivity series	Igneous and metamorphic rocks
Groups and periods	Solubility	Metal displacement reactions	The rock cycle
The elements of Group 1	Filtration	Extracting metals	The carbon cycle
The elements of Group 7	Evaporation and distillation	Ceramics	Global heating
The elements of Group 0	Chromatography	Polymers	Climate change
		Composites	

YOU ARE HERE

Chapter 3 Summary Questions

1 The list shows some properties of materials.

List of properties
brittle
electrical insulator
flexible
hard
high melting point
low melting point
soft
stiff

Write down the properties of ceramics, choosing
from the list. **(5 marks)**

2 This question is about composite materials.

a Write down what a composite material is. **(1 mark)**
b Reinforced concrete is a composite.
Name the two materials in reinforced
concrete. **(2 marks)**
c Explain why reinforced concrete is suitable
as a building material. **(1 marks)**
(4 marks)

3 Anne adds some metals to water. Draw lines to
match each metal to an observation.

Metal	Observation
calcium	moves on surface of water and purple flame
copper	bubbles vigorously
potassium	no change

(2 marks)

4 Lamek compares the reactivity of iron, lead, and
zinc with hydrochloric acid.

a Write down **two** things he must do to compare
the reactions fairly. **(2 marks)**
b Write down **one** safety precaution Lamek
must take. Give a reason for this. **(2 marks)**
c Predict which metal will react most vigorously.
Give a reason for your choice. **(2 marks)**
d Name the gas formed when a metal reacts
with a dilute acid. **(1 mark)**
(7 marks)

5 Copy and complete the word equations.

a magnesium + oxygen → magnesium _____
b sodium + water → sodium hydroxide + _____
c zinc + hydrochloric acid → zinc _____ + hydrogen
d iron + _____ → iron oxide
e potassium + _____ → potassium hydroxide + hydrogen
f calcium + _____ acid → calcium chloride + hydrogen
g zinc + copper oxide → zinc oxide + _____
h magnesium + iron oxide → magnesium _____ + iron
(8 marks)

6 Marvin investigates displacement reactions. He
heats the pairs of substances in the list.
Pair W   iron and aluminium oxide
Pair X   iron and copper oxide
Pair Y   copper and magnesium oxide
Pair Z   iron and lead oxide
a Write down the letters of **two** pairs of substances
that react. Explain your choices. **(2 marks)**
b Write a word equation for one of the reactions
you choose in part **a**. **(3 marks)**
5 marks)

7 Nishma wants to investigate the reactions of metals
with dilute hydrochloric acid. She has the apparatus
shown in Figure 1.

dilute
hydrochloric acid
iron
zinc
magnesium

▲ **Figure 1**

a Nishma thinks about the variables in her investigation.
  i. Identify the variable she will change. **(1 mark)**
  ii. Identify two variables she must
     control. **(2 marks)**
  iii. Explain why she must control these
     variables. **(1 mark)**
b Write an outline plan for the investigation. **(3 marks)**
c Draw a results table for the investigation. **(2 marks)**
d Nishma decides to repeat the investigation
with a different dilute acid. Suggest why. **(1 mark)**
(10 marks)

Breathe in. You have inhaled a mixture of gases, including oxygen, nitrogen, and carbon dioxide. Where do these gases come from? The carbon dioxide molecules around you may have been made by a kitten, a spider, a tree, a car, your classmates – or perhaps even by a dinosaur.

This chapter explains how carbon atoms move between the atmosphere, the Earth, and the sea. It asks you to consider the impacts of increasing amounts of carbon dioxide in the air, including global heating and climate change. You will also find out how to classify rocks into groups, and learn how the material in rocks is recycled over millions of years.

Reactivate your knowledge

1   List three properties you can use to classify rocks into groups.

2   Name the states of matter a substance is in before and after it melts.

3   Predict which emits more radiation per second – the Sun or the surface of the Earth.

4   Write two word equations – one for photosynthesis, and one for respiration.

You already know

You can group rocks based on their appearance and properties.

Freezing is the change of state from liquid to solid.

Energy can be transferred from objects as a wave, called radiation. The hotter an object, the more energy it transfers by radiation.

Plants take in carbon dioxide from the air for photosynthesis. Plants and animals add carbon dioxide to the air through respiration.

 How to compare different temperatures using your maths skills.

 How to work scientifically to: describe patterns shown by line graphs.

Journey through C2

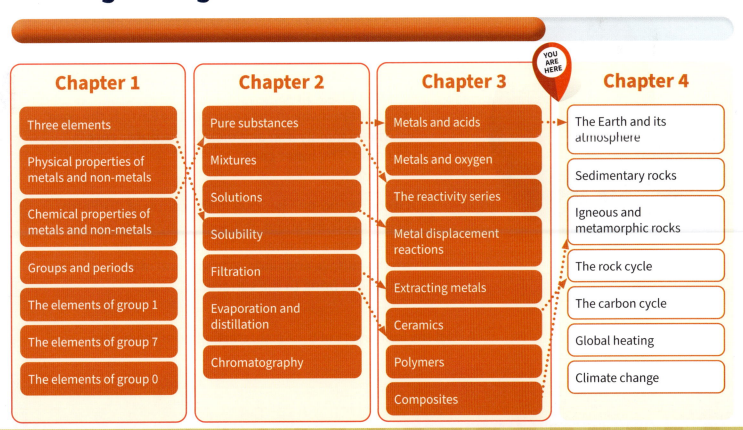

Chapter 1	Chapter 2	Chapter 3	Chapter 4
Three elements	Pure substances	Metals and acids	The Earth and its atmosphere
Physical properties of metals and non-metals	Mixtures	Metals and oxygen	Sedimentary rocks
Chemical properties of metals and non-metals	Solutions	The reactivity series	Igneous and metamorphic rocks
Groups and periods	Solubility	Metal displacement reactions	The rock cycle
The elements of group 1	Filtration	Extracting metals	The carbon cycle
The elements of group 7	Evaporation and distillation	Ceramics	Global heating
The elements of group 0	Chromatography	Polymers	Climate change
		Composites	

YOU ARE HERE

4.1 The Earth and its atmosphere

Learning objectives

After this topic, you will be able to:

- describe the layers of the Earth
- describe the composition of the atmosphere.

Reactivate your knowledge

1 Describe two properties of a substance in the solid state.
2 Describe two properties of a substance in the gas state.
3 What is an element?

What goes into a packet of crisps (Figure 1)?

The potatoes come from plants. The plants use water and nutrients from the soil with carbon dioxide from the air to grow. The salt comes from the sea, or from a mine. Aluminium for the bags comes from bauxite ore. The crisps are packed in nitrogen, which was separated from the air.

Everything for the packet of crisps – and everything we use – comes from the Earth, the air, or the oceans.

▲ **Figure 1** A packet of crisps.

What is the structure of the Earth?

The Earth is made up of four layers, shown in Figure 2.

- The outer layer is the rocky **crust**. Its depth varies between 8 km and 40 km.
- Beneath the crust is the **mantle**. This is mostly solid rock, but it can flow. Very slowly, hotter rock rises and cooler rock sinks.
- About halfway to the centre of the Earth is the **core**. This is mainly iron and nickel. The **outer core** is liquid. The **inner core** is solid.

Of course, no-one has dug to the centre of the Earth. Scientists learn about its structure by studying shock waves from earthquakes. They also examine rocks on the surface and under oceans, and materials that volcanoes bring to the surface.

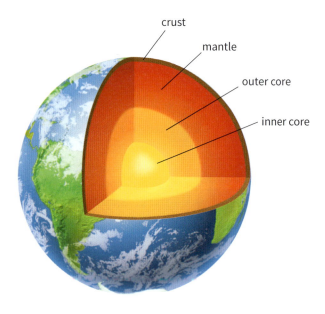

crust
mantle
outer core
inner core

▲ **Figure 2** The structure of the Earth.

A List the four layers of the Earth, starting from the centre.

What's in the crust?

Most rocks are mixtures of compounds. The pie chart in Figure 3 shows the elements that make up these compounds.

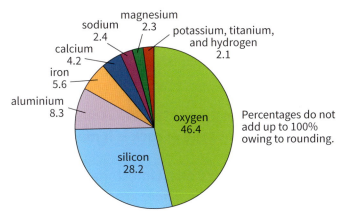

▲ **Figure 3** The most common elements in the Earth's crust, by mass.

> **B** List the six most common elements in the Earth's crust.

What is the atmosphere?

The **atmosphere** is a mixture of gases that surrounds the Earth. The part of the atmosphere nearest the Earth is the **troposphere**. This layer goes up to about 10 km above the surface of the Earth. Figure 4 shows that the troposphere is mainly a mixture of two elements, oxygen and nitrogen. There are smaller amounts of other substances, including argon and carbon dioxide.

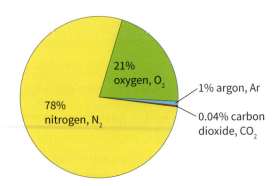

▲ **Figure 4** The most common substances in the Earth's atmosphere, by volume.

> **C** Name three elements and one compound in the Earth's atmosphere.

Questioning the crust

Use the pie charts in Figures 3 and 4 to write questions about the composition of the Earth's crust and the atmosphere. Swap with a partner, and answer each other's questions.

Key words

crust, mantle, core, outer core, inner core, atmosphere, troposphere

Link

You will learn more about carbon dioxide in the atmosphere in C2 4.5 *The carbon cycle*.

Summary Questions

1 Name the four layers of the Earth in order, starting from the outermost layer. (4 marks)

2 Copy and complete the following sentences.

The atmosphere is a mixture of substances in the _____ state. The atmosphere is 78% _____ gas, 21% _____ gas, about 1% _____ gas, and 0.04% _____ _____. (5 marks)

3 Compare the physical properties of the crust and the outer core. (3 marks)

4.2 Sedimentary rocks

Learning objectives

After this topic, you will be able to:

- explain two properties of sedimentary rocks
- describe steps in making sedimentary rocks
- explain how sedimentary rock properties make them suitable for their uses.

Reactivate your knowledge

1 What is the name of the Earth's outer layer?
2 Which layer is at the centre of the Earth?
3 If a material is soft, what can you easily do to it?

▲ **Figure 1** The sphinx of Giza in Egypt.

Link ↗

You can learn about the other rock groups in C2 4.3 *Igneous and metamorphic rocks*.

Key words 🔑

sedimentary, porous, weathering, sediment, erosion, transport, deposition, compaction, cementation

▲ **Figure 2** Biological weathering. As the tree roots grow, they break up the rock.

Figure 1 shows a statue in Egypt. Stonemasons carved it more than 4000 years ago. What type of rock is it made from?

The statue is made from limestone. Limestone belongs to a group of rocks called **sedimentary** rocks. There are two other groups of rock.

What are the properties of sedimentary rocks?

Sedimentary rocks are made up of separate grains. You can see these with a hand lens. There are gaps between the grains. Air or water can get into the gaps, so most sedimentary rocks are **porous**.

The forces between the grains are weak. This means that sedimentary rocks are easy to scratch. They are soft.

> **A** Describe two properties of sedimentary rocks.

How are sedimentary rocks made?

Sedimentary rocks are made from pieces of older rocks. The process has four stages.

Weathering

Weathering breaks up all types of rock into smaller pieces called **sediments**. There are different types of weathering:

- In freeze–thaw weathering, water gets into a crack in a rock. In cold weather, the water freezes, making ice. Ice takes up more space than liquid water. It pushes against the sides of the crack. When this happens many times, the rock breaks.
- Chemical weathering happens when acids in rain react with substances in the rock.
- Biological weathering happens when plants and animals break up rock (Figure 2).

Weathering makes sediments, but does not move them away from the original rock.

Reactivate your knowledge answers
1 Crust 2 Inner core 3 Scratch it

Erosion and transport

Next, sediments move away from the rock. Together, the breaking of rock into sediments and their movement away is called **erosion**.

Transport processes move sediments far from the original rock. Water, ice, wind, and gravity can all move sediments.

Deposition

Eventually, sediments stop moving. They settle in one place. This is **deposition**. Layers of different types of sediment may settle on top of each other.

Compaction or cementation

Over many years deposited sediments join together to make new rock. This happens by:

- **compaction** – the weight of sediments above squashes together the sediments below or
- **cementation** – another substance sticks the sediments together.

> **B** List four stages in making sedimentary rocks.

How are sedimentary rocks useful?

There are many types of sedimentary rock. They have different properties and uses. Figures 3 and 4 show that sandstone and limestone make good building materials. This is because they can withstand strong pushing forces.

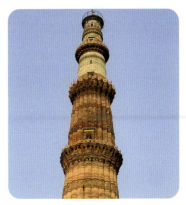

▲ **Figure 3** This sandstone minaret is in India.

▲ **Figure 4** Limestone is a strong and attractive building material.

> **C** Explain why limestone is a good building material.

Sedimentary sequence

With a partner, plan a talk to explain how sedimentary rocks are formed. Present it to another pair. Then listen to their talk. How did they make it interesting?

Summary Questions

1 Describe three properties of sedimentary rocks. (3 marks)

2 Write five correct sentences from the sentence starters and enders.

Sentence starters

Weathering…

Erosion…

Transport…

Deposition…

Compaction…

Sentence enders

…involves the weight of sediment above making sediments below stick together.

…moves sediments far away from the original rock.

…breaks rock into smaller pieces.

…breaks rock into smaller pieces and moves them from the original rock.

…is the settling of sediments. (5 marks)

3 Suggest one advantage and one disadvantage of making statues from limestone. (2 marks)

Igneous and metamorphic rocks

Learning objectives

After this topic, you will be able to:

- describe how igneous and metamorphic rocks are made
- explain the properties of igneous and metamorphic rocks
- explain how igneous and metamorphic rock properties make them suitable for their uses.

Reactivate your knowledge

1 Name two sedimentary rocks.
2 What does porous mean?
3 Name the before and after states for freezing.

▲ **Figure 1** It is easy to see the crystals in this igneous rock, granite.

Granite quarry

Rubislaw Quarry, near Aberdeen, is one of the biggest holes in Europe. Between 1740 and 1971 quarry workers dug 6 million tonnes of granite from the quarry. Calculate the mean mass of granite dug from the quarry each week.

▲ **Figure 3** Making a granite path.

Figure 2 shows the Giant's Causeway in Northern Ireland. It formed around 50 million years ago. What are its columns made from?

▲ **Figure 2** The Giant's Causeway.

The rock in the Giant's Causeway is basalt. Basalt is an **igneous** rock. Igneous rock forms when liquid rock cools and freezes.

Almost all types of igneous rock consist of crystals (Figure 1). There are no gaps between the crystals. This explains why igneous rocks are not porous.

How are igneous rocks useful?

Igneous rocks are hard. They are also **durable**, which means they are difficult to damage. These properties make igneous rocks suitable for paths and pavements (Figure 3).

A State three properties of most igneous rocks.

Reactivate your knowledge answers
1 For example: sandstone, limestone 2 For example, a rock that has gaps that air or water can get into
3 Before – liquid; after – solid

How are igneous rocks made?

Underground, liquid rock is called **magma**. As magma slowly cools and freezes, its particles have time to arrange themselves into big crystals. This forms igneous rock, such as granite.

Liquid rock cools more quickly under the sea, or on the surface of the Earth after a volcanic eruption (Figure 4). This forms igneous rock, such as basalt. There is not enough time for big crystals to form, so basalt crystals are smaller than granite crystals. You need a hand-lens to see them.

▲ **Figure 4** On the surface of the Earth, liquid rock is called **lava**. This lava will cool and freeze to form basalt.

What are metamorphic rocks?

Figures 5 and 6 show two **metamorphic** rocks, marble and gneiss.

▲ **Figure 5** Marble. ▲ **Figure 6** Gneiss.

Metamorphic rocks form when heat, high pressure, or both, change existing rock. For example:

- Marble starts out as limestone. Marble forms when limestone below the Earth's surface heats up. The limestone does not melt, but its particles rearrange.
- Slate starts out as a sedimentary rock called mudstone. Slate forms when high pressure underground squashes the mudstone. This squeezes out water, making layers of new crystals.

B Describe how slate forms from mudstone.

How are metamorphic rocks useful?

Metamorphic rocks are made up of crystals. They are not porous. Figures 7 and 8 show two useful metamorphic rocks.

▲ **Figure 7** A marble worktop. ▲ **Figure 8** Slate is not porous. It is made up of layers, so splits into thin sheets. It makes good roofing tiles.

C Explain why slate is suitable for roofing tiles.

Summary Questions

1 Copy and complete the following sentences.

When liquid rock cools and freezes, **igneous/metamorphic** rock forms. Granite and basalt are examples of **igneous/metamorphic** rocks. High pressure underground may change any rock type into **igneous/metamorphic** rock. Slate and marble are examples of **igneous/metamorphic** rocks. **Igneous and metamorphic** rocks are **porous/non-porous**. Igneous rocks are **hard/soft**.

(6 marks)

2 Explain why igneous rocks are suitable for paths. (3 marks)

3 Compare how igneous and metamorphic rocks are made. (4 marks)

Learning objectives

After this topic, you will be able to:

- use the rock cycle to explain how the material in rocks is recycled
- explain how uplift gives evidence for the rock cycle.

Reactivate your knowledge

1 What is weathering?
2 What is deposition?
3 What are metamorphic rocks?

▲ **Figure 1** A volcanic eruption.

Imagine you came back to Earth a million years after your death. How would the rocks around you be different?

All the time, rocks are changing. Weathering breaks down rock. Sediments make new rock. Volcanoes erupt (Figure 1), and their lava freezes. And, deep within the crust, heating and high pressure change rock of all types.

A Describe one way that rock changes over time.

What is the rock cycle?

Different rock types, and the processes that change one rock type into another, are linked in the **rock cycle** (Figure 2). The rock cycle shows how rocks change, and how their materials are recycled over millions of years.

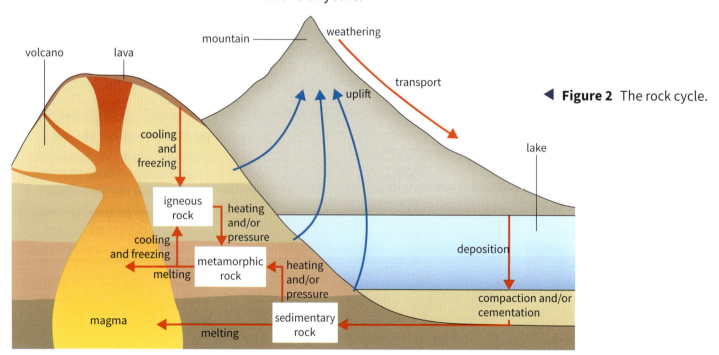

◄ **Figure 2** The rock cycle.

Reactivate your knowledge answers
1 The breaking up of rock of all types into sediments 2 The settling of sediments in one place 3 Rocks formed when thermal energy/heat or high pressure, or both, change existing rock

How does the rock cycle recycle materials?

There are many routes around the rock cycle. Here is one example:

- On the side of a mountain, water pours into a crack. Every night, the water freezes. The ice pushes against the sides of the crack. Sediments break free. Gravity transports them down the mountain.
- A stream flows over the sediments. It transports them to a lake. Sediments settle on the lake bed. Over many years, sediments join together. This makes sedimentary rock.
- Layers of rock build up. The lower layers heat up. Particles in these layers move, forming crystals. Metamorphic rock forms.
- Near the metamorphic rock, hot magma pushes upwards. The magma heats the rock. The rock melts, and becomes part of the magma.
- Magma moves upwards. It forces its way to the surface, and erupts from a volcano. The liquid rock cools and freezes. Igneous rock forms.

> **B** Name two processes by which igneous rock may change to become metamorphic rock.

What is uplift?

The Earth's crust moves constantly. When continents collide, huge forces from inside the Earth push rock upwards, and mountains can form. This is called **uplift**. Taiwan, near China, is moving upwards by 1 cm every year. Earthquakes often happen at the same time as uplift.

Uplift provides evidence for the rock cycle. It moves up rocks that were once buried. Figure 3 shows fossils of sea animals that were found on Mount Everest. The mountain is made from limestone that formed on the seafloor.

▲ **Figure 3** Fossils from Mount Everest.

> **C** Describe the process of uplift.

Summary Questions

1 Name the processes that may change…

a …metamorphic rock into magma. (1 mark)

b …magma into igneous rock. (2 marks)

c …layers of sediment into sedimentary rock. (2 marks)

2 Use an example to explain how uplift provides evidence for the rock cycle. (2 marks)

3 Use the rock cycle to explain how the material from a metamorphic rock may become part of a sedimentary rock and then part of an igneous rock. (6 marks)

4.5 The carbon cycle

Learning objectives

After this topic, you will be able to:

- explain why the concentration of carbon dioxide in the atmosphere did not change for many years
- describe how carbon atoms move from one store to another.

Reactivate your knowledge

1 What is the atmosphere?
2 What is the percentage of carbon dioxide in the atmosphere?
3 What are fossil fuels?

▲ **Figure 1** The air is a mixture of gases, including carbon dioxide.

Key words

respiration, combustion, photosynthesis, dissolving, carbon cycle, carbon store

▲ **Figure 2** Burning methane.

Link

You can learn more about how plants use carbon dioxide in B2 2.1 *Photosynthesis*.

Imagine you took 10 000 particles from the air (Figure 1). How many of them would be carbon dioxide molecules?

As you know, carbon dioxide makes up 0.04 % of the atmosphere. This means that four in 10 000 particles are carbon dioxide molecules.

But carbon dioxide is vital. Without it, plants cannot make their food. Without carbon dioxide, Earth would be too cold for life as we know it.

Carbon dioxide: into and out of the atmosphere

All the time, carbon dioxide enters and leaves the atmosphere.

These processes *add* carbon dioxide to the atmosphere:

- **Respiration** transfers energy from food, in both plants and animals. Carbon dioxide is a waste product of respiration.

$$\text{glucose} + \text{oxygen} \longrightarrow \text{carbon dioxide} + \text{water}$$

- **Combustion** Fossil fuels and wood make carbon dioxide during combustion (Figure 2). Fossil fuels include coal, petrol, and natural gas. Natural gas is mainly methane.

$$\text{methane} + \text{oxygen} \longrightarrow \text{carbon dioxide} + \text{water}$$

A Name one human activity that adds carbon dioxide to the atmosphere.

These processes *remove* carbon dioxide from the atmosphere:

- **Photosynthesis** Plants take carbon dioxide from the atmosphere, and use it to make glucose.

$$\text{carbon dioxide} + \text{water} \longrightarrow \text{glucose} + \text{oxygen}$$

Reactivate your knowledge answers

1 The mixture of gases that surrounds the Earth 2 0.04% 3 Fuels from under the ground or sea, such as coal and oil. They cannot be replaced once they have been used, so they will run out.

- **Dissolving** in the oceans.

$$\text{carbon dioxide} + \text{water} \longrightarrow \text{carbonic acid}$$

In the 1700s, the concentration of carbon dioxide in the atmosphere did not change. This is because carbon dioxide was added to the atmosphere – and removed from it – at the same rate.

> **B** Name the process by which plants (Figure 3) remove carbon dioxide from the atmosphere.

What is the carbon cycle?

The **carbon cycle** (Figure 4) shows how carbon atoms move between carbon dioxide in the atmosphere, and carbon compounds on Earth. The places where carbon and its compounds may remain for a long time are called **carbon stores**. Carbon stores include:

- the atmosphere
- oceans, with dissolved carbon dioxide
- sedimentary rocks, such as calcium carbonate
- fossil fuels, such as coal, oil, and natural gas
- plants and animals (Figure 3)
- soil.

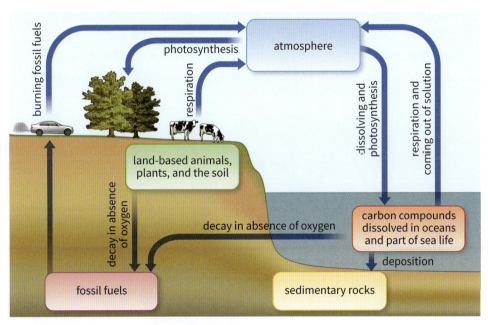

▲ **Figure 4** The carbon cycle.

> **C** Name the process that adds carbon dioxide to the oceans.

▲ **Figure 3** This yew tree has stored carbon compounds in its trunk for over 2000 years.

Summary Questions

1 Copy and complete the following sentences.

Carbon dioxide enters the atmosphere by **photosynthesis/respiration** and **dissolving/combustion**. It leaves the atmosphere by **photosynthesis/respiration** and **dissolving/combustion**. The atmosphere is a store of carbon. Other stores of carbon include soil, **igneous/sedimentary** rocks and fossil fuels such as **coal/wood**.
(6 marks)

2 Describe a route that a carbon atom might take around the carbon cycle. Include four carbon stores that the atom passes through, and give the names of the processes involved. (7 marks)

3 The processes of combustion and dissolving helped to keep the concentration of carbon dioxide in the atmosphere constant for many years. Compare these two processes. (4 marks)

4.6 Global heating

Learning objectives

After this topic, you will be able to:
- give the meaning of the greenhouse effect
- give the meaning of global heating
- describe how the concentration of carbon dioxide in the atmosphere has changed.

Key words

greenhouse effect, greenhouse gases, global warming, global heating

Imagine the Earth with no atmosphere. What would be different?

Without the atmosphere, the surface of the Earth would be about 30 °C colder than now. The average temperature would be around −18 °C. There would be no liquid water. There would be no life as we know it.

What is the greenhouse effect?

Some gases in the atmosphere keep the surface of the Earth warmer than it would otherwise be. Read on to find out how.

Look at Figure 1. It shows that the Sun heats the Earth's surface. The warm surface of the Earth emits thermal radiation. Some of this radiation goes into space. Some of the radiation is absorbed and stored by gases in the atmosphere. This keeps the Earth warmer than it would be if all the radiation went back into space.

Global graph

Work with a partner. Look at Figure 4 and take turns to describe how the concentration of carbon dioxide in the atmosphere changed from 1960 to 2020. Include at least three pieces of data in your descriptions.

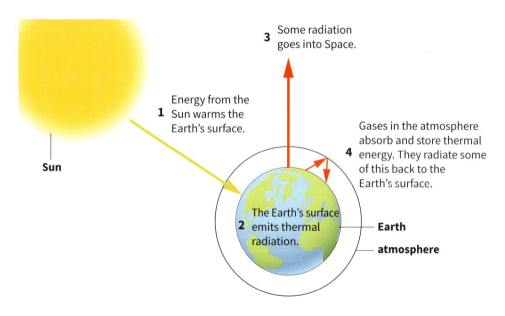

3 Some radiation goes into Space.

1 Energy from the Sun warms the Earth's surface.

Sun

4 Gases in the atmosphere absorb and store thermal energy. They radiate some of this back to the Earth's surface.

2 The Earth's surface emits thermal radiation.

Earth

atmosphere

▲ **Figure 1** The greenhouse effect. The diagram is simplified and not to scale.

The overall transfer of energy from the Sun to the thermal store of gases in the Earth's atmosphere is the **greenhouse effect**. Different gases store different amounts of energy. Carbon dioxide molecules and methane molecules store much more energy than oxygen or nitrogen molecules. This is why carbon dioxide and methane are called **greenhouse gases**.

A Give the meaning of the 'greenhouse effect'.

What is global heating?

Ever since thermometers were invented, scientists have measured and recorded air temperature. They calculated average air temperatures for each year. Figure 2 shows some of this data.

Figure 2 shows that the average air temperature has increased over time. The increase in air temperature at the surface of the Earth is called **global warming** or **global heating**.

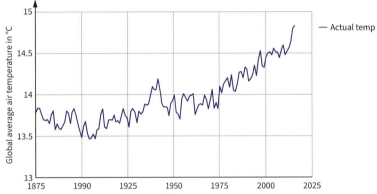

▲ **Figure 2** Global average air temperature since 1875.

B Give the meaning of 'global heating'.

What causes global heating?

In the 1950s, scientists wondered whether extra carbon dioxide in the atmosphere causes global heating. They set up the observatory in Figure 3 on a remote mountain in Hawaii. They measured the concentration of carbon dioxide in the air, and have collected data from the observatory ever since. Figure 4 shows some of their data.

▲ **Figure 3** Mauna Loa observatory.

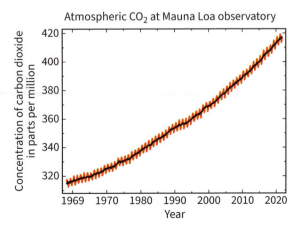

Atmospheric CO_2 at Mauna Loa observatory

▲ **Figure 4** The concentration of carbon dioxide in the atmosphere.

C Use Figure 4 to estimate the concentration of carbon dioxide in 2020.

Link

You can learn more about the causes and effects of global heating in C2 4.7 *Climate change*.

Summary Questions

1 Copy and complete the following sentences.

The transfer of energy from the Sun to the gases in the atmosphere is **global heating/ the greenhouse effect**. The increase in average air temperature is called **global heating/the greenhouse effect**. (2 marks)

2 Give two advantages of having carbon dioxide in the atmosphere. (2 marks)

3 Look at Figure 2. Describe how the average air temperature changed from 1875 to 2020. Include at least three pieces of data in your description. (5 marks)

Learning objectives

After this topic, you will be able to:

- explain why global heating happens
- describe some impacts of global warming
- describe how to prevent climate change.

Reactivate your knowledge

1. What is the greenhouse effect?
2. What is global heating?
3. Name two gases involved in global heating.

Key words

deforestation, climate change

What links the pictures in Figures 1 and 2?

▲ **Figure 1** A forest fire.

▲ **Figure 2** An aeroplane.

The pictures show human activities that add extra carbon dioxide to the atmosphere, including:

- burning fossil fuels to generate electricity, heat homes, and fuel cars and aeroplanes
- burning or cutting down forests to make space for crops or cattle. This is **deforestation**. Deforestation means that there are fewer trees to remove carbon dioxide from the atmosphere.

Farming animals also adds extra greenhouses gases, including methane and carbon dioxide.

A Describe two ways that people add extra carbon dioxide to the air.

Climate collaboration

With a partner, discuss how your school could help stop climate change.

Do human activities cause global heating?

For many years, the concentration of carbon dioxide in the atmosphere stayed the same. But since 1800 more carbon dioxide has been added to the atmosphere every year than is removed, so its concentration increased. The graphs in 4.6 *Global heating* show the increase since 1960.

Reactivate your knowledge answers

1 The overall transfer of energy to the thermal store of gases in the atmosphere 2 The increase in air temperature at the surface of the Earth 3 Carbon dioxide and methane

Scientists agree that carbon dioxide from human activities causes global heating. On their own, the similar shapes of the graphs in 4.6 *Global heating* can only show that there is a pattern. But evidence collected by thousands of scientists, including lab experiments showing that carbon dioxide and methane molecules trap thermal energy, show that greenhouse gases from human activity definitely cause global heating.

B Describe evidence for greenhouse gases causing global heating.

What are the impacts of global heating?

As a result of global heating, glaciers and polar ice melt. Melting ice makes sea levels rise. This causes flooding on low-lying coasts (Figure 4).

Global heating also changes local weather patterns. In some areas, rainfall increases, leading to flooding. Other areas suffer droughts and heatwaves, which make crops fail.

▲ **Figure 4** Flooding in a Caribbean town.

Long-term changes to weather patterns are called **climate change**. Climate change has led to the extinction of some plant and animal species. Climate change makes it harder for people to grow food.

C Give the meaning of climate change.

How can we stop climate change?

In November 2021, leaders from 120 countries met in Scotland at the COP26 climate change conference (Figure 3).

The leaders promised to work together to keep the increase in global average temperature below 1.5°C. They promised to stop deforestation, reduce methane emissions, and speed up the switch to electric vehicles. Richer countries promised to transfer money to compensate poorer countries for climate change damage.

Individual countries, cities, and people can also help to stop climate change.

▲ **Figure 3** At COP26, the Prime Minister of Barbados, Mia Mottley, said that global heating is a death sentence for people in Barbados and other poor countries with low-lying coasts. She said, "We do not want that death sentence and we have come here to say 'Try harder' because our people [and] the climate, need our actions now."

Summary Questions

1 Copy and complete the following sentences.

Humans add carbon dioxide to the atmosphere by burning **fossil fuels/hydrogen**. Extra carbon dioxide causes **deforestation/global heating**. Global heating causes **climate change/the greenhouse effect**.

(3 marks)

2 Describe three impacts of global heating. (3 marks)

3 Suggest three actions your village, town, or city could take to prevent climate change. Explain how each might work.

(6 marks)

4.8 Recycling

Learning objectives

After this topic, you will be able to:

- write the meaning of recycling
- explain how aluminium is recycled
- describe some advantages and disadvantages of recycling.

Reactivate your knowledge

1. Where do all the materials that we use come from originally?
2. What is an ore?
3. Name the before and after states for freezing.

▲ **Figure 1** You can recycle many materials.

Figure 1 shows some recycling boxes. What do you recycle?

You can recycle many types of material, including paper, metals, and plastics. But is it worth the effort?

Where do resources come from?

The materials that make everything we use come originally from the Earth's crust, atmosphere, or oceans. These resources will not last forever. The faster we extract them, the sooner they will run out.

Table 1 shows when the ores that we get some metals from may run out.

Element	Uses of element	When the main sources of the element in the Earth's crust will run out (estimated year)
aluminium	aeroplanes, overhead power lines, kitchen foil	2500
gold	jewellery, electrical connectors	2050
tin	food containers, solder	2035

▲ **Table 1** Estimates of when sources of four elements will run out.

A According to Table 1, when will tin ore run out?

What is recycling?

Recycling means collecting and processing used objects so that their materials can be used again. Examples include:

- recycling paper to make new paper
- recycling plastic bottles to make fleeces (Figure 2)
- recycling aluminium cans to make aluminium sheets to make more cans.

Recycling is different from reusing. Reusing an object means that you or someone else uses it again, either for its original purpose or for a different purpose.

▲ **Figure 2** Sarah's fleece is made from recycled plastic bottles.

Reactivate your knowledge answers

158

1 The Earth's crust, oceans, and the atmosphere **2** An ore that you can extract a metal from, and that contains enough of the metal to make it worth extracting **3** Before – liquid; after – solid

How is aluminium recycled?

Alex puts out some aluminium cans for recycling (Figure 3). A lorry takes them to a factory. At the factory, machines shred the cans and a furnace melts the shreds. The liquid aluminium is poured into a mould. Here, it cools and freezes to make an ingot (Figure 4). The ingot is heated to 600 °C to soften it. Rollers roll it into thin sheets, which make new cans.

▲ **Figure 3** Squashed aluminium cans.   ▲ **Figure 4** An aluminium ingot.

B Write the meaning of recycling.

Advantages and disadvantages

Recycling has many advantages:

- It means that natural resources, like metal ores, will last longer.
- It needs less energy than using new materials. Extracting 1 kg of aluminium from its ore needs around 255 MJ of energy. Only 15 MJ is needed to make 1 kg of recycled aluminium.
- It reduces waste and pollution.

There are some disadvantages to recycling. Some people do not like sorting their waste. Recycling lorries use fuel and make pollution.

C List three advantages of recycling.

Can you recycle everything?

Some materials are easier to recycle than others. Recycling plastics involves separating different plastics from each other, which is not easy (Figure 5).

▲ **Figure 5** Sorting plastic waste.

Link

You can learn more about metal ores in C2 3.5 *Extracting metals*.

Key word

recycling

Summary Questions

1 Write down the two statements below that are examples of recycling.

- collecting old glass bottles, melting the glass, and making new bottles
- wrapping your sandwiches in a bag from an online delivery
- collecting and melting poly(propene) bottle tops, and using them to make poly(propene) rope

(2 marks)

2 Describe how aluminium is recycled.   (7 marks)

3 Evaluate the advantages and disadvantages of recycling.

(6 marks)

In this chapter, you have learnt how carbon atoms move between the atmosphere, the Earth, and the sea. You have considered the impacts of increasing amounts of carbon dioxide in the air, including global heating and climate change.

You have also used the properties of rocks to classify them into groups, and learned how the material in rocks is recycled over millions of years.

Metacognition and self-reflection task

Making and labelling diagrams is an excellent way of consolidating knowledge. Start by sketching an outline diagram of the rock cycle, including the arrows. Use *C2 4.4 The rock cycle* to help you. Then close this book and label the arrows with the names of the processes that convert the material in rock from one type to another. Repeat the procedure for the carbon cycle. Do you understand how each process works?

Journey through C2

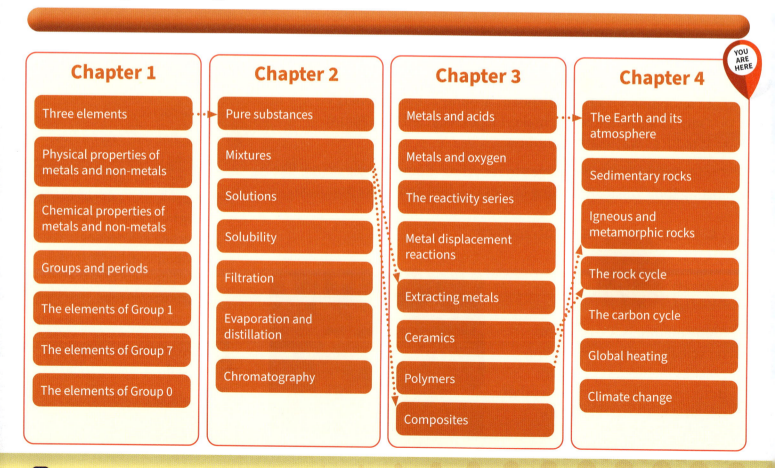

Chapter 1	Chapter 2	Chapter 3	Chapter 4
Three elements	Pure substances	Metals and acids	The Earth and its atmosphere
Physical properties of metals and non-metals	Mixtures	Metals and oxygen	Sedimentary rocks
Chemical properties of metals and non-metals	Solutions	The reactivity series	Igneous and metamorphic rocks
Groups and periods	Solubility	Metal displacement reactions	The rock cycle
The elements of Group 1	Filtration	Extracting metals	The carbon cycle
The elements of Group 7	Evaporation and distillation	Ceramics	Global heating
The elements of Group 0	Chromatography	Polymers	Climate change
		Composites	

YOU ARE HERE

Chapter 4 Summary Questions

1 Copy and complete the sentences below, using the following words:

igneous, metamorphic, sedimentary

Scientists classify rocks into three groups. Rocks that were formed when magma or lava cooled and froze are _____ rocks. Rocks formed by the action of heat pressure on existing rock are _____ rocks. Rocks formed from fragments of rock are _____ rocks.

(2 marks)

2 Copy and complete Figure 1 by adding the missing labels. **(2 marks)**

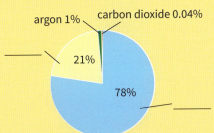

argon 1%   carbon dioxide 0.04%

_____   21%

78%

Gases in the atmosphere of the Earth.

▲ **Figure 1**

3 Figure 2 shows the structure of the Earth.

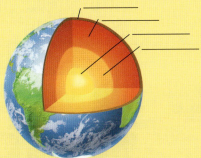

▲ **Figure 2**

a Copy Figure 2. Then use the words below to label it.

outer core, inner core, crust, mantle   (4 marks)

b Copy and complete Table 1.

Layer	Solid, liquid, or gas?
crust	
inner core	
mantle	
outer core	

▲ **Table 1**

(4 marks)

(8 marks)

4 Two students investigate some rocks. They write their results in Table 2.

Rock	Does it have grains or crystals?	Is it porous?
A	grains	yes
B	crystals	no
C	crystals	–

▲ **Table 2**

a Name a piece of equipment the students could use to decide whether the rock is made up of grains or crystals. **(1 mark)**

b Give the letter of the sedimentary rock. **(1 mark)**

c Predict whether or not rock C is porous. **(1 mark)**

d Give the letter of one rock that might be basalt. **(1 mark)**

e Give the letter of one rock that might be limestone. **(1 mark)**

f Give the letter of one rock whose formation involved deposition. **(1 mark)**

g Give the letter of one rock that may have been formed from magma. **(1 mark)**

(7 marks)

5 Figure 4 shows the rocks on a cliff face.

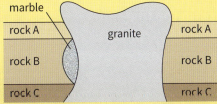

marble

rock A   granite   rock A

rock B   rock B

rock C   rock C

▲ **Figure 4**

a Rocks A, B, and C are sedimentary rocks. Write the letter of the layer of sedimentary rock that formed first. **(1 mark)**

b Write the letter of the youngest sedimentary rock. **(1 mark)**

c Granite is an igneous rock. Explain how the granite in the diagram was formed. **(2 marks)**

d Suggest why the granite sticks up above rock A. **(2 marks)**

e Marble is a metamorphic rock. Suggest **two** reasons why it formed only in the position shown on the diagram. **(2 marks)**

(8 marks)

Welcome

Physics is the study of the physical world. You will study how circuits work, learn about magnetism, and how electricity and magnetism are linked. You will compare fields of different types: gravitational, magnetic, and electric.

You will explore the concept of energy, how it is stored and transferred. You will relate your everyday experiences to models of energy transfer and work. You will also link ideas you have learned about forces to the motion of objects, pressure, and why some forces produce a turning force.

2 Physics

Where can physics take you?

Knowledge of physics helps to explain many observations that you make of the world around you. Everyday you interact with the natural world and with devices where the explanation for what you experience comes from physics.

There are many jobs or areas of interest for which people use physics, and which may interest you now and in the future. Lots of the skills that you learn while studying physics can be applied in careers that may not say 'physics' in the title.

Dentist

Sports scientist

Sound engineer

Pilot

Racing car engineer

Optician

Doctor/surgeon

Architect

Physics and the world

From cars to computers, physics affects our everyday life; a life without electricity would be very different. However, every device or process has an energy cost that can add to the warming of our planet. The effects of climate change on our lives are already clear and it is vitally important that we work to reduce that impact. Reducing inefficient energy transfers will mean that energy resources last longer and add less to climate change. Engineers use physics to design cleaner and more efficient devices.

BIG QUESTIONS

How will we keep the lights on?
There are limited amounts of fossil fuels on Earth, and currently we use them to generate electricity. Scientists and engineers are working to make sure that we will still have a supply of electricity when fossil fuels run out.

What can we do to reduce climate change?
Understanding energy transfers and why some processes or devices are more efficient is very important when we are thinking about how to slow, stop, or reverse the effects of climate change.

Why is electromagnetism so important?
Most homes have over 50 electric motors in them. If a current flows in a wire that is in a magnetic field it can make a motor spin. This effect is used in devices such as vacuum cleaners, microwaves, and electric toothbrushes.

Journey through P2

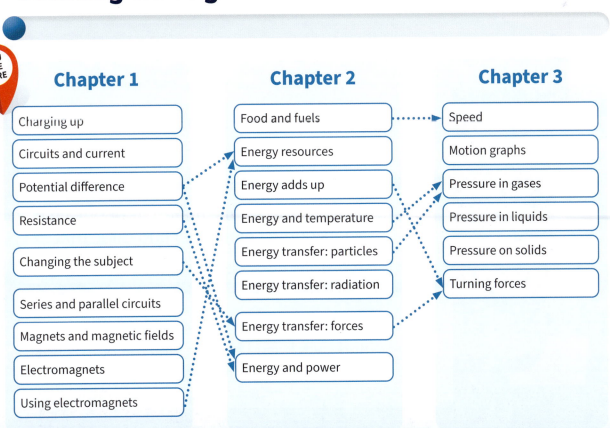

YOU ARE HERE

Chapter 1
- Charging up
- Circuits and current
- Potential difference
- Resistance
- Changing the subject
- Series and parallel circuits
- Magnets and magnetic fields
- Electromagnets
- Using electromagnets

Chapter 2
- Food and fuels
- Energy resources
- Energy adds up
- Energy and temperature
- Energy transfer: particles
- Energy transfer: radiation
- Energy transfer: forces
- Energy and power

Chapter 3
- Speed
- Motion graphs
- Pressure in gases
- Pressure in liquids
- Pressure on solids
- Turning forces

In this chapter you will learn about electric charge and the link between charge and current. You will discover how ideas about current, potential difference, and resistance explain what happens in different types of circuits with different components. These ideas help to explain the circuits that we have in our houses and cars. You will also learn how modelling electric circuits using rope can be very useful.

You will compare permanent magnets and electromagnets, their strength, and the patterns of the magnetic fields they produce. You will learn about the uses of electromagnets and figure out when it is better to use an electromagnet rather than a permanent magnet. These ideas explain how electric motors work, which is important because they are used in a very wide range of electrical devices.

Reactivate your knowledge

1 Draw a diagram showing two magnets that are repelling. Label the poles.

2 Make a list of three materials or objects that conduct electricity and three that do not.

3 Draw a circuit diagram showing a cell, lamp, and switch, and explain why the bulb is not lit when the switch is open (up).

You already know

Magnets have poles that can attract or repel.

Some materials conduct electricity.

Adding cells to circuits increases the brightness of bulbs. Adding bulbs reduces the brightness.

 How to use an equation to calculate weight.

 How to work scientifically to: record observations and data in tables, and use equipment safely.

Journey through P2

YOU ARE HERE

Chapter 1
Charging up

Circuits and current

Potential difference

Resistance

Changing the subject

Series and parallel circuits

Magnets and magnetic fields

Electromagnets

Using electromagnets

Chapter 2
Food and fuels

Energy resources

Energy adds up

Energy and temperature

Energy transfer: particles

Energy transfer: radiation

Energy: forces

Energy and power

Chapter 3
Speed

Motion graphs

Pressure in gases

Pressure in liquids

Pressure on solids

Turning forces

Learning objectives

After this topic, you will be able to:

- describe how charged objects interact
- describe how objects can become charged
- describe what is meant by an electric field.

Reactivate your knowledge

1 Define 'non-contact force'.
2 State when two magnets will attract.
3 State when two magnets repel.

▲ **Figure 1** You can deflect a stream of water with a charged balloon.

Key words

attract, repel, electric charge, positive charge, negative charge, atom, proton, electron, neutron, neutral, electric field

Because of static electricity, you can stick a balloon to a wall or bend a stream of water (Figure 1). Static electricity produces lightning. What is static electricity, and where does it come from?

How do charged objects interact?

Objects can become charged positively or negatively. Charged objects **attract** or **repel** each other, like magnets do (Figure 2). Electrostatics and magnetism are similar but different.

- Positively (+) charged objects *repel* positively (+) charged objects .
- Negatively (−) charged objects *repel* negatively (−) charged objects.
- Positively (+) charged objects *attract* negatively (−) charged objects.

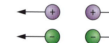
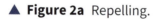

▲ **Figure 2a** Repelling.

▲ **Figure 2b** Attracting.

What is charge and where does it come from?

There are two types of **electric charge**: **positive charge** (+) and **negative charge** (−). Charge is a property of a particle or object, just like mass. Everything is made of particles called **atoms** (Figure 3). Atoms in turn are made of three types of smaller particle:

- **protons**, which have a *positive* charge
- **electrons**, which have a *negative* charge
- **neutrons**, which have no charge.

Atoms contain equal numbers of protons and electrons. Overall, an atom has no charge: it is **neutral**.

▲ **Figure 3** An atom contains three types of particle.

proton
electron
neutron

Link

You can learn more about atoms in C1 2.2 *Atoms*.

A Explain why the atom in Figure 3 is neutral.

Reactivate your knowledge answers
1 A force that can act when objects are not touching 2 When the poles are different 3 When the poles are the same

How do objects become charged?

When you rub a balloon on your jumper, some electrons are transferred from the jumper to the balloon (Figure 4).

- The balloon is now negatively charged. It has a net or overall *negative charge*.
- Your jumper is positively charged. It has a net or overall *positive charge*.
- They will now *attract* each other.

before   after

▲ **Figure 4** Rubbing a balloon transfers electrons from your jumper to the balloon.

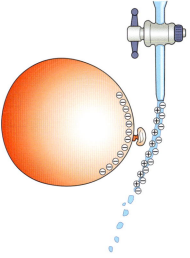

▲ **Figure 5** A charged balloon deflects water.

The balloon is made of rubber. The electrons stay on the balloon. You can use ideas about charge to explain electrostatic phenomena, such as bending a stream of water (Figure 5).

The Greeks noticed that their jewellery produced small shocks due to friction between amber and clothing. The Greek word for amber is 'elektron'.

What is an electric field?

There is an **electric field** around a charge or charged object, just as there is a gravitational field around a mass (Figure 6). If you put a charged object in an electric field, a force will act on it.

> **B** Describe what happens to the electrons in a piece of paper when you bring a balloon near to it.

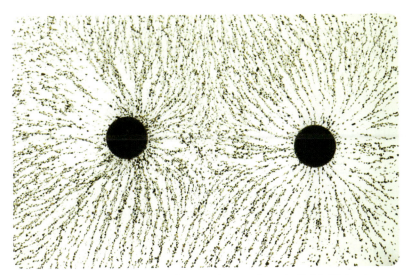

▲ **Figure 6** Pepper grains line up in an electric field. This shows the electric field between two charges that are repelling.

Summary Questions

1 Copy and complete the following sentences.

There are two types of electric charge: _____ charge and _____ charge. When you rub a polythene rod with a cloth you transfer _____ from the cloth to the rod. Two polythene rods would _____ if you brought them close together. A polythene rod would _____ a rod that had a positive charge. A region where there is a force on a charge is called an electric _____.
(6 marks)

2 A student rubs a balloon on their jumper and sticks it to the wall. Explain, in terms of electrons, why the balloon sticks to the wall.
(3 marks)

3 Compare a gravitational field and an electric field.
(4 marks)

Learning objectives

After this topic, you will be able to:

- describe what is meant by current
- describe how to measure current
- draw circuit diagrams.

Reactivate your knowledge

1 Name the charged particle used to explain electrostatic phenomena.
2 Define 'electric field'.
3 Name three circuit components used to make a torch.

▲ **Figure 1** Lightning can strike a plane.

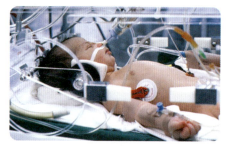

▲ **Figure 2** A baby is kept warm using electric circuits.

free electron   metal atom

▲ **Figure 3** Electrons move randomly.

Confusing words? 🧪

For each of these words, write one sentence using the word with its correct scientific meaning. Write a second sentence where it has a different, everyday meaning.

charge   current   cell

In a thundercloud air moves around, producing regions that have a positive or a negative charge. Electrons jump from one charged area to another and this produces a big current, called lightning (Figure 1).

What is current?

An electric current is used to make lots of devices work. For example, it flows through a heater that keeps the baby warm in an incubator (Figure 2).

- When you complete a circuit, charged particles or charges move in the metal wires.
- The current is the amount of charge flowing per second.

When you press the **switch** on a torch, the light comes on. The switch opens and closes a gap in the circuit. You need to close the gap and make a complete circuit for a current to flow. When people talk about 'electricity' they usually mean 'electric current'.

Where do the charges come from?

The **cell** or **battery** pushes charges around the circuit. You set up an electric field in the wire when you connect the battery. The battery does *not* produce the charges that move. They were already there in the wires. In a metal the charged particles that move are called **electrons** (Figures 3 and 4).

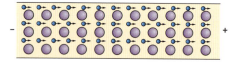

▲ **Figure 4** The electrons move around the circuit when you connect the battery.

A Explain why charges move when you connect a battery.

How do you measure current?

You can measure the current through a component with an **ammeter**. It is connected in the circuit with the component (Figure 5).

Reactivate your knowledge answers
1 Electron 2 A region where a charged particle experiences a force 3 Cell/battery, lamp, switch

- Current is measured in amperes or **amps**.
- The symbol for amps is A. For example, the current in the circuit in Figure 5 is 0.4 A, but the current in a lightning strike is over 1000 A.

> **B** Compare the charge flowing per second in a light bulb and in a lightning strike.

What circuit symbols can I use?

You can build circuits using components such as batteries, bulbs, and **motors**. It would take a long time to draw a picture of each circuit so you can use **circuit symbols** instead (Figures 6b and 7).

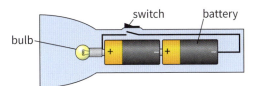

▲ **Figure 6a** This is a picture of a torch…

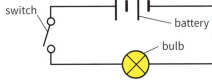

▲ **Figure 6b** …and this is the circuit diagram.

In the torch diagram there are two cells. Cells used together like this are called a battery. People often use the word 'battery' for a single cell, but in physics we call it a cell. You must make sure that you connect cells the right way round or they will not work.

> **C** Suggest what would happen if you turned one of the cells in the torch around.

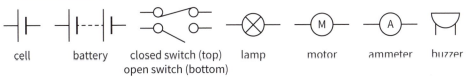

cell   battery   closed switch (top)   lamp   motor   ammeter   buzzer
open switch (bottom)

▲ **Figure 7** Circuit symbols make it simpler to draw circuits.

Modelling electric circuits – part 1

You cannot see what happens in the wires when a current flows. Scientists use models such as the rope model to show what is happening (Figure 8).

▶ **Figure 8** The moving rope is like the current.

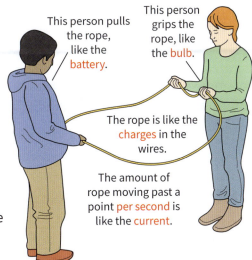

This person pulls the rope, like the battery.

This person grips the rope, like the bulb.

The rope is like the charges in the wires.

The amount of rope moving past a point per second is like the current.

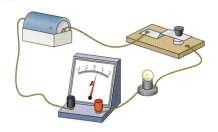

▲ **Figure 5** You connect an ammeter in a circuit to measure current.

Summary Questions

1 Copy and complete the following sentences.

Current is the amount of _____ flowing per _____. In a metal wire, charged particles called _____ move when you connect a battery. You can use a meter called an _____ to measure current. Current is measured in _____, which has the symbol _____. (6 marks)

2 a Draw a circuit diagram to show how you could use a switch to turn a battery-powered motor on and off. (2 marks)

b Describe what happens in the wires when you close the switch. (1 mark)

3 Describe and explain how you would use the rope model to show:

a what happens when you turn one of the cells round in a torch battery (3 marks)
b what happens when you open a switch. (2 marks)

1.3 Potential difference

Learning objectives

After this topic, you will be able to:

- describe what is meant by potential difference
- describe how to measure potential difference
- describe what is meant by the rating of a battery or bulb.

Reactivate your knowledge

1 Name a circuit component you need for a current to flow.
2 Name the circuit component used to measure current.
3 Write down what happens to a bulb when you add more cells.

▲ **Figure 1** You can save someone's life with a big potential difference.

Link

You can learn more about energy transfer in P2 *Energy*.

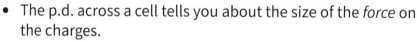

▲ **Figure 2** The long line is the positive terminal, the short line is the negative terminal.

▲ **Figure 4** You can produce a p.d. with fruit and vegetables.

Key words

potential difference, terminal, voltmeter, volt, rating, voltage

A doctor can use a defibrillator to start someone's heart if it stops. Defibrillators produce a large potential difference (sometimes called a voltage), much bigger than a battery can produce (Figure 1).

What is potential difference?

The cell or battery sets up an electric field in wires connected to them. This provides the push to make charges move (Figures 3 and 4). The push is called a **potential difference**, or p.d. for short. The moving charges transfer energy.

- The p.d. across a cell tells you about the size of the *force* on the charges.
- The p.d. also tells you how much *energy* can be transferred to the components in the circuit by the charges.

Chemical reactions between metals and chemicals in a cell produce a p.d. between the two ends, called **terminals** (Figure 2). In an early demonstration of a battery in 1818, Luigi Galvani used a battery to make frogs' legs move. This idea was used by Mary Shelley when she wrote *Frankenstein*.

▲ **Figure 3** Battery size does not relate to p.d.

How do you measure potential difference?

You measure p.d. using a **voltmeter**. You connect it either side of a component, or across it (Figure 5). The circuit symbol is a circle with a 'V' inside it (Figure 6).

- Potential difference is measured in **volts**.
- The symbol for volts is V. For example, the p.d. across the cell in Figure 5 is 6 V. A defibrillator produces a p.d. of about 500 V.

Reactivate your knowledge answers
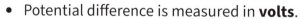
1 Cell or battery 2 Ammeter 3 It gets brighter

You can measure the p.d. of a *cell* by connecting a voltmeter across it. This is also called the **rating**. Voltmeters measure the change in energy transferred to charges by the cell, or from charges to the components.

> **A** Compare the position of an ammeter with the position of a voltmeter when you use them.

Circuit components such as bulbs also have a rating. The bulb in the circuit in Figure 5 has a rating of 6 V. It is designed to work at a p.d. of 6 V, and no higher.

▲ **Figure 5** You connect a voltmeter either side of the component.

> **B** Describe the connection between the rating of a battery and energy.

Do you say 'potential difference' or 'voltage'?

Sometimes people talk about the **'voltage'** of a cell or battery. It is better to talk about p.d. The lifting and falling model in Figure 6 can be helpful when thinking about p.d.

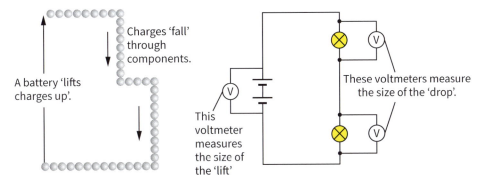

A battery 'lifts charges up'.

Charges 'fall' through components.

This voltmeter measures the size of the 'lift'

These voltmeters measure the size of the 'drop'.

▲ **Figure 6** If the lamps are the same, the voltmeter readings are the same.

It is good practice to draw circuits with the battery on the left with the positive terminal at the top, and the components on the right (Figure 6).

Modelling electric circuits – part 2

You can use the rope model when you are thinking about potential difference. In the rope model:

- a bigger p.d. across the cell would come from the 'battery' person pulling harder
- the direction that the rope moves depends on which way round the battery is connected.

Summary Questions

1 Copy and complete the following sentences.

The potential difference of a cell or battery tells you the size of the _____, and how much _____ can be transferred by the charges. You measure potential difference or p.d. with a _____. The _____ of a battery tells you the p.d. across it, and the _____ on a bulb tells you the p.d. at which it is designed to work. (5 marks)

2 A student connects a circuit with two cells and a buzzer, and listens to the buzzer.

The student adds another cell and listens again. Describe and explain in terms of energy what she hears. (2 marks)

3 Many people get current and potential difference (or voltage) mixed up.

a Use the rope model to explain the difference. (2 marks)

b Explain why it is easier to add an 'ammeter' than a 'voltmeter' to the model. (2 marks)

1.4 Resistance

Learning objectives

After this topic, you will be able to:

- describe what is meant by resistance
- calculate the resistance of a component
- describe the difference between conductors and insulators in terms of resistance.

Reactivate your knowledge

1 State the unit of current.
2 State the unit of potential difference.
3 Which of these objects conduct well: graphite or wood?

▲ **Figure 1** Electrical devices have different currents through them.

The current in the wires connected to a television (Figure 1) is much smaller than the current in the wires to a microwave. The reason for this is to do with resistance.

What is resistance?

Components do different jobs in an electric circuit. Each circuit component has a different **resistance**. This tells you how easy or difficult it is for the charges to pass through the component.

- Resistance is measured in **ohms**.
- The symbol for ohms is Ω. Ω is a letter from the Greek alphabet.

You can use the idea of resistance to explain why the current decreases as you add more bulbs in a circuit. Adding more bulbs increases the resistance, so the current is less.

A Deduce which has a bigger resistance, a television or a microwave?

How do you calculate resistance?

You can use an equation to calculate the resistance of a component, such as those in Figures 2 and 3.

Here is the equation to calculate resistance:

$$\text{resistance } (\Omega) = \frac{\text{potential difference (V)}}{\text{current (A)}}$$

What's the resistance?

A bulb in a circuit has a current of 0.6 A through it and a potential difference of 12 V across it. Calculate the resistance of the bulb.

For example, if you found that the current through a bulb was 0.2 A when the voltage across it was 6 V, you could work out the resistance:

$$\text{resistance} = \frac{\text{potential difference}}{\text{current}}$$

$$= \frac{6\,V}{0.2\,A}$$

$$= 30\,\Omega$$

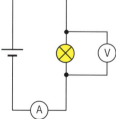

▲ **Figure 2** You can use an ammeter and a voltmeter to find the resistance of a lamp.

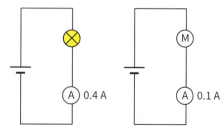

▲ **Figure 3** The currents in these circuits are different, even though the cells are the same.

B In the circuit in Figure 3 suggest which component has the smaller resistance, the motor or the lamp.

What happens inside a wire?

You can use a model with marbles to show what happens inside a wire when a current flows (Figure 5). The charges that move in a wire are electrons.

▲ **Figure 5** You can use marbles and posts to model resistance.

As the marbles fall down the slope they collide with the posts. Inside a wire the moving electrons collide with the atoms of the wire, which is like the resistance. Electrons transfer energy, and the wire gets hot.

C Suggest how to change the model of resistance to show a bigger resistance.

What is the difference between conductors and insulators?

Metals are good **conductors**. Carbon is a non-metal conductor (Figure 4). They have a very low resistance because they contain lots of electrons that can move. Other materials such as plastics do not have many electrons that are free to move. They are good **insulators**.

▲ **Figure 6** A spark happens when the air conducts electricity.

- The resistance of a 10 m piece of copper wire is about 0.2 Ω.
- The resistance of plastic objects is over a thousand million million ohms!

The air is usually an insulator but it can conduct if the potential difference is big enough (Figure 6). Insulators have a high resistance. That does not mean that they do not conduct. It means that it requires a large p.d. to produce a current in them.

▲ **Figure 4** The graphite in a pencil is a non-metal that is a good conductor.

Summary Questions

1 Copy and complete the following sentences.

The resistance of a component tells you how _____ it is for a current to flow. It is calculated using _____ and _____. Inside a metal wire _____ collide with atoms and transfer _____ to them. _____ are materials that contain lots of charges that are free to move. _____ contain fewer charges that can move.
(7 marks)

2 Calculate the resistance of the motor and the lamp in Figure 3, with a potential difference of 12 V across them.
(4 marks)

3 a Explain why glass does not normally conduct.
(1 mark)

b Suggest why glass does conduct when you heat it up until it is nearly melting.
(1 mark)

Learning objectives

After this topic, you will be able to:

- change the subject of an equation
- apply changing the subject of an equation to the equation for resistance.

Reactivate your knowledge

1 State the equation for calculating resistance.
2 State the equation for calculating weight.
3 State **Hooke's Law**.

▲ **Figure 1** The rope model helps to understand the relationship between current, p.d., and resistance.

▲ **Figure 2** You can describe this picture in three ways.

When you think about a circuit, it is the current that depends on the potential difference and the resistance (Figure 1). The three quantities are related, and if we know two of them, we can calculate the third. The relationship between the quantities is shown in an equation.

What does it mean to change the subject?

Here is an example of changing the subject. Look at Figure 2.

We can say:

- The <u>cat</u> is **sitting** on the *mat*.
- The *mat* is the thing that the <u>cat</u> is **sitting** on.
- **Sitting**, is the thing that the <u>cat</u> is doing on the *mat*.

All three statements correctly describe the situation. It is the same with equations.

> **A** Write down the other two versions of 'I am sitting on a chair'.

How do you change the subject?

Just as there are three statements about the cat, there are three ways of writing the equation for resistance. When you write an equation you can use words or symbols. When scientists first investigated current, they called it electrical 'intensity'. This is why we use I.

- The symbol for resistance is R.
- The symbol for p.d. is V.
- The symbol for current is I.

In the table on the next page, the word equations are on the left, and the symbol equations are on the right.

Key words

Hooke's Law, relationship

Reactivate your knowledge answers

1 resistance = $\frac{\text{potential difference}}{\text{current}}$ 2 weight = mass × gravitational field strength 3 The extension of a spring is proportional to the force up to the elastic limit

resistance (Ω) = $\dfrac{\text{potential difference (V)}}{\text{current (A)}}$	$R = \dfrac{V}{I}$
current (A) = $\dfrac{\text{potential difference (V)}}{\text{resistance }(\Omega)}$	$I = \dfrac{V}{R}$
potential difference (V) = current (A) × resistance (Ω)	$V = IR$

How can we work out these other two versions? Here we want to find the value of V. We need to remove I from the right hand side of the equation.

$R = \dfrac{V}{I}$ multiply both sides by I

$R \times I = \dfrac{V \times I}{I}$ cancel the I

$R \times I = V$ or $V = IR$

B Work out the current equation using $V = IR$ and dividing by R.

How can I check that I have done it correctly?

Sometimes it's easier to use numbers, not words or symbols.

Think about this equation.

$$6 = 2 \times 3$$

It is quite easy to see that

$$2 = \dfrac{6}{3} \quad \text{and} \quad 3 = \dfrac{6}{2}$$

You can use this technique to check that you have rearranged an equation correctly.

C Work out the other two versions of $2 = 0.1 \times 20$.

In terms of circuits, it makes more physical sense to start with the equation $I = \dfrac{V}{R}$ than either of the other two equations. This equation says:

- you choose the p.d. and the resistance and get a current as a result of those choices
- the bigger the p.d., the *bigger* the current. The p.d. is on the top.
- the bigger the resistance, the *smaller* the current. The resistance is on the bottom.

▲ **Figure 3** Springs extend when you hang weights from them.

Summary Questions

1 Copy and complete the following sentences.

Equations show the _____ between quantities. You can change the _____ of an equation by multiplying or _____. (3 marks)

2 Start with the equation for weight and derive the equations for:

a mass (2 marks)

b gravitational field strength (2 marks)

3 Springs (Figure 3) have a spring constant that relates to their stiffness. Stiff springs have a big spring constant. Use this information to deduce an equation relating force (F), extension (x), and spring constant (k). Find the version that makes the most physical sense. (4 marks)

Learning objectives

After this topic, you will be able to:

- describe the difference between series and parallel circuits
- describe how current varies in series and parallel circuits
- describe how potential difference varies in series and parallel circuits.

Reactivate your knowledge

1 Define 'current'.
2 Give the equation for resistance.
3 State what pulling the rope in the rope model is like in a circuit.

▲ **Figure 1** Modern Christmas lights stay on if one bulb blows.

Christmas lights make a great display (Figure 1). In old sets of lights, if one of the bulbs broke, they would all go out.

What are the two types of circuit?

In the old Christmas lights, the bulbs were connected in **series** (Figure 2). All the bulbs were on one loop – the same loop as the battery and the switch. There is another type of circuit called a **parallel** circuit (Figure 3). In a parallel circuit there is more than one loop or branch. Parallel circuits are sometimes called 'branching circuits'.

Parallel circuits are very useful because:

- if one bulb breaks, the other lights stay on
- you can control each lamp separately in a parallel circuit by adding a switch to each branch.

Each bulb is independent of the others.

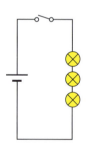

▲ **Figure 2** A series circuit has one loop.

> **A** State two differences between series and parallel circuits.

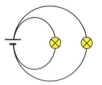 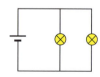

▲ **Figure 3** These are both parallel circuits.

What happens to the current?

Series circuits

In a series circuit the current is the same everywhere (Figure 4).

If you add components to a series circuit:

- the current *decreases*
- the resistance of the circuit *increases*.

Parallel circuits

A parallel circuit has more than one loop. In Figure 5, the current in each branch of the circuit is the same. The ammeters A_2 and A_3 show the same reading.

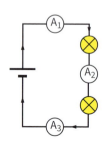

▲ **Figure 4** The current in a series circuit.

▲ **Figure 5** The current in a parallel circuit.

Reactivate your knowledge answers
1 Current is the charge flowing per second 2 Resistance = p.d./current 3 The p.d./battery

The ammeters A$_1$ and A$_4$ measure the total current. The currents in all the branches of a parallel circuit add together to make the total current. Here the total current is double the current in each branch.

If you add another branch to a parallel circuit:

- the current in the other branches stays the same
- the total current *increases*
- the resistance of the circuit *decreases*.

> **B** If the current in A$_2$ in Figure 5 is 2A, calculate the current in A$_1$. Assume the lamps are identical.

Modelling circuits – part 3

You can use the rope model when you are thinking about different types of circuit:

Series circuits

- The rope moves at the same speed everywhere.
- As more people hold the rope, the rope moves more slowly.

Parallel circuits

- There are more loops of rope.
- All the loops are driven by the same 'battery' person.

> **C** Describe how the rope model shows that the current in a series circuit is the same everywhere.

What happens to the potential difference?

Series circuits

The potential difference across each component *adds up to* the potential difference across the battery (Figure 6).

Parallel circuits

The potential difference across each component *is the same as* the potential difference across the battery (Figure 7).

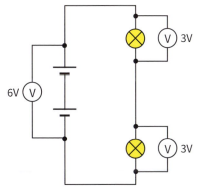

▲ **Figure 6** The p.d. in a series circuit.

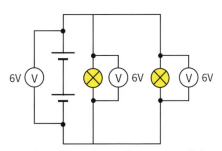

▲ **Figure 7** The p.d. in a parallel circuit.

Current issues

In a circuit with a single cell and a single buzzer, the current is 0.2 A. Calculate the current if you add another buzzer in series with the first bulb. Explain your answer.

Key words

series, parallel

Summary Questions

1 Copy and complete the following sentences.

A series circuit has **more than one/one** loop. A parallel circuit has **more than one/one** loop. If a bulb in a **parallel/series** circuit breaks, the rest of the bulbs stay on. If a bulb in a **parallel/series** circuit breaks, the rest of the bulbs go out.
(4 marks)

2 Use the equation for resistance to explain why the resistance of a series circuit increases as you add more bulbs. (2 marks)

3 A student has a 10 Ω lamp, and a 6 V battery. They connect an ammeter in the circuit, and a voltmeter across the lamp.

a Calculate the current in the circuit. (2 marks)
b Write down the reading on the voltmeter. (1 mark)

The student adds another lamp in series.

c Describe what happens to the reading on the ammeter, and on the voltmeter. (1 mark)

Learning objectives

After this topic, you will be able to:

- define magnetic field
- describe how to investigate and represent the shape of a magnetic field
- describe the Earth's magnetic field.

▲ **Figure 1** Ferrofluid is a special liquid that is magnetic.

With a magnet you can make something move without even touching it such as magnetic liquid (Figure 1).

A **magnet** has a **north pole** and a **south pole** that attract or repel (Figure 3).

- North poles *repel* north poles.
- South poles *repel* south poles.
- North poles *attract* south poles.

Only certain materials are attracted to a magnet. They are called **magnetic materials**. Iron is a magnetic material, and so is steel because steel contains iron. Cobalt and nickel are also magnetic.

▲ **Figure 2** Information on a credit card is stored in a magnetic strip.

A Explain how you can tell that a material is magnetic, but not a magnet.

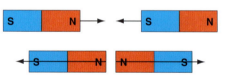

▲ **Figure 3** Magnets can attract or repel other magnets.

What is a magnetic field?

In an electric field there is a force on a charge. In a **magnetic field** there is a force on a magnet or a magnetic material (Figure 4).

B Give one difference between a magnetic field and a gravitational field.

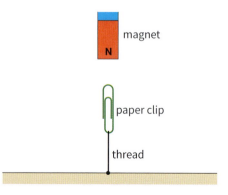

magnet

N

paper clip

thread

▲ **Figure 4** There is a force on a steel paper clip in a magnetic field.

How do you investigate the shape of a magnetic field?

You can find out the shape of a magnetic field in two ways:

- using plotting compasses
- using iron filings

The needle of a compass lines up with the magnetic field. So do the iron filings. You can draw lines called **magnetic field lines** to represent the field (Figures 5 and 6).

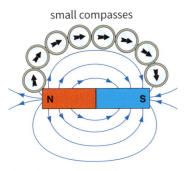

▲ **Figure 5** Plotting compasses showing the shape and direction of a magnetic field.

small compasses

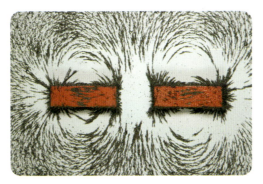

▲ **Figure 6** Iron filings used to show magnetic field lines.

The field lines are *not* the field, just a way to represent it. The lines go from the north pole to the south pole of the magnet, with arrows pointing from the north to the south pole.

- If the magnetic field lines are *closer together* this shows that the magnetic field is *stronger*.
- A permanent magnet is a magnet that has its own magnetic field.

C Explain why the filings used to investigate magnetic fields are not made of aluminum.

What shape is the Earth's magnetic field?

If you suspend a magnet by a thread it will line up in a direction pointing north to south. This is because it is in the magnetic field of the Earth (Figures 7 and 8). The Earth behaves as if there is a huge bar magnet inside it. The Earth's magnetic field keeps flipping. About 500 000 years ago the magnetic north pole was actually the south pole.

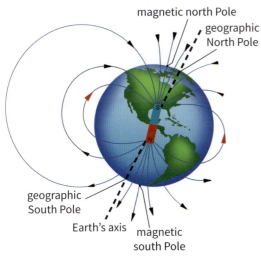

magnetic north Pole
geographic North Pole
geographic South Pole
Earth's axis
magnetic south Pole

▲ **Figure 7** The Earth's magnetic field is the same as that of a big bar magnet with the south pole at the top of the planet.

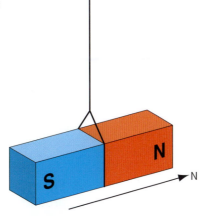

▲ **Figure 8** A suspended magnet lines up with the Earth's magnetic field.

How strong?

A student wants to measure the strength of different types of magnet by holding up a paperclip as shown in Figure 4. Draw a table for their results.

Key words

magnet, north pole, south pole, magnetic material, magnetic field, magnetic field line

Summary Questions

1 Copy and complete the following sentences.

Magnets have a _____ pole and a _____ pole. Two poles that are the same will _____ and two poles that are different will _____. A magnetic field is a region where there is a _____ on a magnetic material. You can investigate a magnetic field using iron _____. (6 marks)

2 Explain why the needle of a compass always points in the same direction wherever you point it in a room. (2 marks)

3 In Figure 6, there is a point between the two magnets where you can place a steel ball and it will not move.

a Explain why, in terms of fields and forces. (2 marks)
b Suggest and explain what would happen to this point if the magnet on the left was stronger than the magnet on the right. (2 marks)

Learning objectives

After this topic, you will be able to:

- describe the magnetic field around a current carrying wire
- describe how to make an electromagnet
- describe how to change the strength of an electromagnet.

Reactivate your knowledge

1 Define 'magnetic field'.
2 Name one way to investigate the shape of a magnetic field.
3 State how you know a magnetic field is strong.

▲ **Figure 1** You cannot turn a fridge magnet off.

Permanent magnets like fridge magnets (Figure 1) are fun, but you can't turn them off.

What shape is the magnetic field around a wire?

A wire with an electric current flowing through it has a magnetic field around it. You can investigate the field with a plotting compass. The field lines are circles (Figure 2).

> **A** Describe how you know the field gets weaker further from the wire.

How do you make an electromagnet?

You can make a circular loop of wire and pass a current through it. The magnetic field lines at the centre of the loop are straight (Figure 3).

The magnetic field around a single loop isn't very strong. If you put lots of loops together to make a coil the field is much stronger (Figure 4). The magnetic fields add together. This is an **electromagnet**. The magnetic field is only produced when the current is flowing in the wire. The shape of the magnetic field is just like the shape of the magnetic field around a bar magnet.

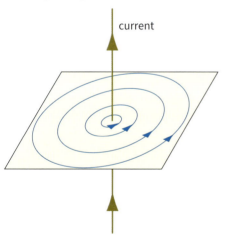

▲ **Figure 2** The magnetic field around a straight wire.

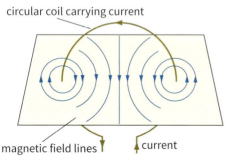

▲ **Figure 3** The magnetic field around a loop of wire.

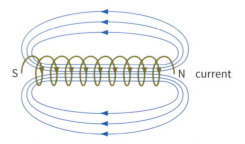

▲ **Figure 4** The magnetic field around a coil of wire.

Reactivate your knowledge answers

1 A region where a magnetic material experiences a force 2 Using iron filings or a plotting compass 3 The field lines are close together

You can turn an electromagnet on and off by turning the current on and off. Electromagnets usually have a magnetic material in the centre of the coil, called a **core.** This makes the electromagnet much stronger. Most cores are made of iron. Iron is easy to **magnetise** but loses its magnetism easily. Steel is hard to magnetise but keeps its magnetism when the field is removed (Figure 5).

iron nails   steel pins

magnet removed   magnet removed

▲ **Figure 5** Steel stays magnetic when you remove the magnet.

▲ **Figure 6** The strength of an electromagnet depends on the number of turns on the coil, the current, and the core.

B Describe one problem with using steel as the core of an electromagnet.

How do I make an electromagnet stronger?

You can increase the strength of an electromagnet (Figure 6) by:

- using more turns, or loops of wire
- increasing the current flowing in the wire using a magnetic material in the core.

How is the Earth's magnetic field produced?

Scientists think that the magnetic field of the Earth is produced by the movement of charged particles at the Earth's centre. This is like a current producing a magnetic field. They are not sure why the magnetic north pole moves.

Summary Questions

1 Copy and complete the following sentences.

When a _____ flows in a wire it produces a _____ around it. You can make an electromagnet stronger by having _____ coils or a _____ current. The shape of the _____ around an electromagnet is the same as that around a bar magnet.
(5 marks)

2 Describe how to use a nail, a piece of wire, crocodile clips, leads, and a battery to make an electromagnet. (2 marks)

3 Explain in detail why the number of coils, and the type of core affect the strength of an electromagnet. (4 marks)

1.9 Using electromagnets

Learning objectives

After this topic, you will be able to:

- describe some uses of electromagnets
- compare permanent and electromagnets
- describe how a simple motor works.

Reactivate your knowledge

1 Name three things you need to make an electromagnet.
2 Name two ways to make an electromagnet stronger.
3 Name three magnetic materials.

▲ **Figure 1** You can travel at over 200 mph on a maglev train.

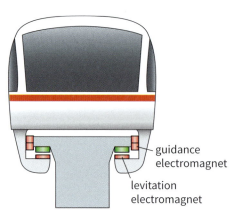

▲ **Figure 2** Electromagnets lift a maglev train and push it forward.

guidance electromagnet
levitation electromagnet

Have you ever travelled on a high-speed train? Trains that use electromagnets can go faster than a Formula 1 car. They don't have an engine. How do they work?

How do you lift a train?

You have learned that magnets can repel each other. Engineers have used this fact to build trains that use magnetic levitation (Figures 1 and 2). This means the train is lifted up using magnets. By removing friction, the train can travel much faster than normal trains. Electromagnets move the train forward so it doesn't need a motor.

How do you switch on dangerous equipment?

An X-ray machine can be very dangerous. It uses a very high potential difference. The radiographer using the machine uses a **relay** to turn the machine on, instead of a normal on/off switch. A relay uses a small current in one circuit to operate a switch in another circuit (Figure 3).

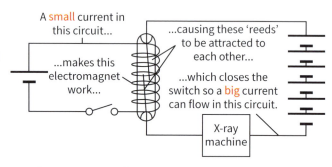

A small current in this circuit...
...makes this electromagnet work...
...causing these 'reeds' to be attracted to each other...
...which closes the switch so a big current can flow in this circuit.
X-ray machine

▲ **Figure 3** A small current can turn on a much bigger current in a separate circuit.

A Suggest the poles on the reeds when the relay is switched on.

How do you start a car?

A car battery produces a large current that can be very dangerous. The driver switches on the circuit in the battery to start the car. They can do this safely using an electromagnet switch (Figure 4).

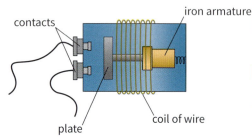

iron armature
contacts
plate
coil of wire

▲ **Figure 4** A starter motor uses an electromagnetic switch.

Reactivate your knowledge answers
1 Wire, battery, nail 2 Add more coils/use a bigger current/use a core 3 Iron/steel, nickel, cobalt

How do you lift a car?

You can use an electromagnet to move large pieces of iron or steel in a factory, or to move cars in a scrap yard (Figure 5).

How do you sort metal?

You can use an electromagnet to sort out scrap metal. Iron and steel will be attracted to the electromagnet. Other metals, such as aluminium, will not.

B Explain why you could not sort copper from aluminium using an electromagnet.

current on   current off

▲ **Figure 5** Electromagnets can lift cars.

Permanent magnet or electromagnet?

Permanent magnets and electromagnets both have their uses. There are two main differences between permanent magnets and electromagnets.

- You can turn an electromagnet on and off.
- You can make electromagnets that are much stronger than permanent magnets.

C Explain why you need electromagnets to levitate a train.

How do you make a motor?

The turntable in a microwave needs to turn so that your food cooks evenly. The motor that makes it move is just one of over 50 electric motors in your home. You can make a simple **motor** using two magnets, a coil of wire, and a battery (Figure 6).

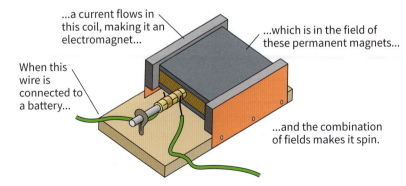

...a current flows in this coil, making it an electromagnet...

...which is in the field of these permanent magnets...

When this wire is connected to a battery...

...and the combination of fields makes it spin.

▲ **Figure 6** A simple motor.

Summary Questions

1 Copy and complete the following sentences.

Electromagnets can be used to levitate _____ and push them forward. A _____ acts like a switch to turn on circuits that can be dangerous. An electric motor _____ when a current flows in it. A permanent magnet _____ be turned off.

(4 marks)

2 a State the parts of an electric motor. (2 marks)

b Describe how a motor works. (2 marks)

3 Design a system that uses electromagnets to hold open fire doors. The fire doors should close automatically when the fire alarm button is pressed. Explain how your system works. (4 marks)

In this chapter you have learnt about charge, current, potential difference, and resistance and how they explain the behaviour of charged objects and circuits. You have seen how potential difference is related to energy per charge, and current is related to charge flowing per second. You learned that resistance determines the current for a given potential difference. You have seen how series circuits have one loop, and parallel circuits have more than one loop, and how they are used.

You have learnt how the magnetic fields around permanent magnets, and the Earth, have a similar pattern that can be investigated with compasses or iron filings. You have seen that electromagnets can be constructed with wire, batteries, and iron cores to be much stronger than permanent magnets and can be turned on and off. You have also learnt some of the many uses of electromagnets, and how simple electric motors work.

Metacognition and self-reflection task

To check your understanding of the differences between current, potential difference, and resistance, for *each* one draw a grid of four squares and write these titles in the boxes: definition, equation with units, example, non-example.

Complete the grid for each of current, potential difference, and resistance.

Did you find it difficult to complete the grid for any of the three?

Journey through P2

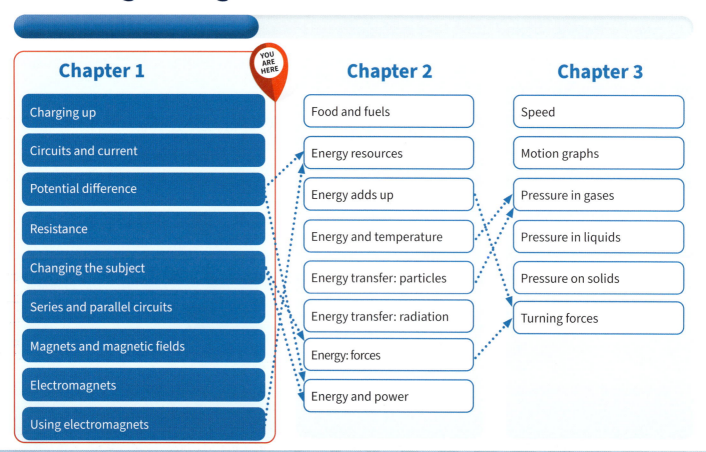

Chapter 1	Chapter 2	Chapter 3
Charging up	Food and fuels	Speed
Circuits and current	Energy resources	Motion graphs
Potential difference	Energy adds up	Pressure in gases
Resistance	Energy and temperature	Pressure in liquids
Changing the subject	Energy transfer: particles	Pressure on solids
Series and parallel circuits	Energy transfer: radiation	Turning forces
Magnets and magnetic fields	Energy: forces	
Electromagnets	Energy and power	
Using electromagnets		

YOU ARE HERE

Chapter 1 Summary Questions

1 Choose the correct word or phrases in bold in these sentences.

a When you rub a cloth on a rod, **atoms/electrons** are transferred.

b A positively charged rod will **attract/repel** a negatively charged rod.

c There is a current when **atoms/charges** flow.

(3 marks)

2

a Copy and complete Figure 1 to show the magnetic field around a bar magnet by adding the labels 'N' and 'S'. (1 mark)

▲ **Figure 1**

b Describe what would happen to the magnets in the diagrams A and B below.

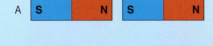

(2 marks)

c Complete this sentence:
One advantage of using an electromagnet instead of a permanent magnet is... (1 mark)

(4 marks)

3 A student makes an electromagnet.

a List the equipment that they need. (3 marks)

b Copy and complete the table to say what would happen to the strength of the electromagnet when the student makes these changes. (3 marks)

Change	Strength will...
Increase the number of coils	
Decrease the current	
Use an aluminium core	

(6 marks)

4

a Draw a circuit diagram for the circuit in Figure 2 below.

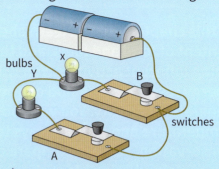

▲ **Figure 2**

(2 marks)

b State whether this is a series or a parallel circuit. (1 mark)

c Copy and complete the table to show what would happen to bulbs X and Y when you press the switches.

Switches closed	Bulbs lit
A	
B	
A and B	

(3 marks)

d Describe how you could measure the current flowing in each bulb. (2 marks)

(8 marks)

5 A student connects one bulb, an ammeter, and a cell in series. They connect a voltmeter across the bulb.

a Draw a circuit diagram for this circuit. (2 marks)

The current through the bulb is 0.4 A. The potential difference across the bulb is 6 V.

b Explain what is meant by potential difference. (1 mark)

The bulb has a rating of 12 V.

c State what is meant by the rating of a lamp. (1 mark)

d Calculate the resistance of the lamp. (2 marks)

A different component has a resistance of 10 Ω.

e Calculate the current through the component when there is a potential difference of 6V across it. (2 marks)

(8 marks)

6 A student rubs a rod with a cloth and uses the rod to pick up small pieces of paper. Explain in detail how this happens.

(6 marks)

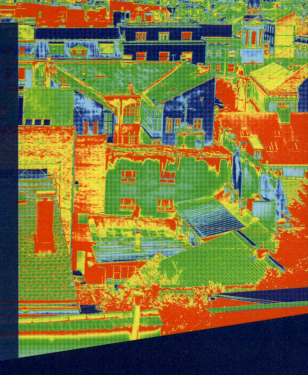

2 Energy

In this chapter you will learn about the energy content of food and fuels, and the energy you use doing different activities. You will compare different energy resources and find out how they are used to generate electricity. You will compare energy and temperature and explore ways to model energy and its conservation. You will compare energy transfers that are explained using ideas about particles and those that are explained using radiation. You will also learn how to do calculations of work and power.

The ideas in this chapter will explain your experiences with devices and processes that involve energy transfers, such as cooking, generating electricity, electrical devices, and transportation. You will consider how ideas about energy are necessary to understand climate change.

Reactivate your knowledge

1 Draw particle diagrams of ice (solid water), liquid water, and steam (water in the gas state). Describe the motion of the particles in each state.

2 Name the unit of temperature we use in science, and the device we use to measure it.

3 Calculate the weight of a person with a mass of 50 kg on Earth where g = 10 N/kg.

You already know

Temperature describes how hot or cold something is.

The different particle arrangements of a substance make it a solid, liquid, or a gas.

An electric current transfers energy, and forces change motion.

 How to calculate quantities using an equation.

 How to work scientifically to: record observations and data in tables.

Journey through P2

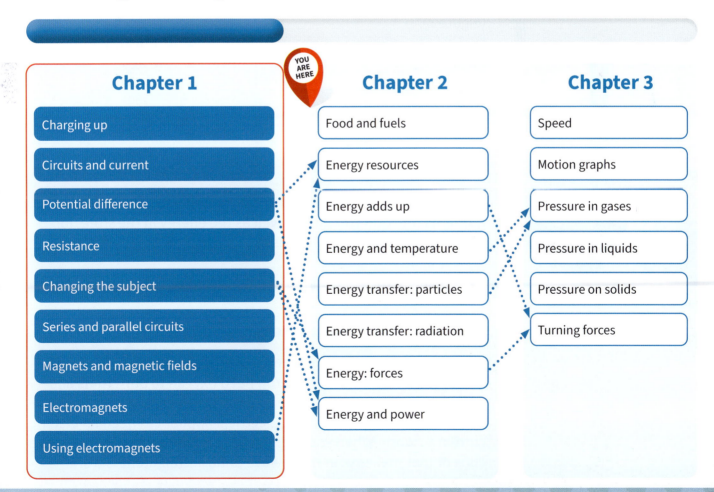

Chapter 1	Chapter 2	Chapter 3
Charging up	Food and fuels	Speed
Circuits and current	Energy resources	Motion graphs
Potential difference	Energy adds up	Pressure in gases
Resistance	Energy and temperature	Pressure in liquids
Changing the subject	Energy transfer: particles	Pressure on solids
Series and parallel circuits	Energy transfer: radiation	Turning forces
Magnets and magnetic fields	Energy: forces	
Electromagnets	Energy and power	
Using electromagnets		

YOU ARE HERE

2.1 Food and fuels

Learning objectives

After this topic, you will be able to:

- compare the energy values of foods and fuels
- compare the energy in foods and fuels with the energy needed for different activities.

Reactivate your knowledge

1 Name a fuel that you burn.
2 Name a fuel that you put in a car.
3 State which of these activities is more tiring – sitting or walking.

▲ **Figure 1** You need the energy stored in food.

▲ **Figure 2** A food label.

What did you have for breakfast? You need energy from food (Figure 1) to do many things, including walking, breathing, and even reading this! Your brain needs energy to work.

How much energy in food?

Different foods are stores of different amounts of **energy**. Energy is measured in **joules** (J). One joule is a very small amount of energy, so we often use **kilojoules** (kJ). 1 kJ = 1000 J. 10 kJ = 10 000 J.

> **A** Calculate the number of joules in 200 kJ.

A food label tells you how much energy is stored in the food (Figure 2).

Food	Energy (kJ) per 100 g
apple	200
banana	340
peas	250
chips	1000
cooked beef	1000
chocolate	1500

▲ **Table 1** Energy stored in food.

When you choose which foods to eat you need to consider which nutrients the food contains as well as the energy in the store, for example, vitamins and minerals.

> **B** Calculate the energy in kJ in 200 g of apple.

How much energy in fuels?

Coal and chocolate are both stores of energy (Figure 3). Oil, wood, and other fuels are stores too. You need oxygen to burn **fuels** and to utilise the energy in food. People use the energy in fuels to heat their house or cook their food. Electrical appliances need an electric current to work. When you burn fuel in a power station it produces a current that makes your microwave or hair straighteners work.

![coal and chocolate]
▲ **Figure 3** In terms of energy stored, coal and chocolate are about the same.

Reactivate your knowledge answers
1 E.g., coal, wood 2 Petrol/diesel 3 Walking

How much energy do you need each day?

You need different amounts of energy depending on what you do each day.

Sleeping: 300 kJ per hour

Working: 600 kJ per hour

Playing: 3600 kJ per hour

Relaxing: 360 kJ per hour

▲ **Figure 4** Energy used in activities.

There is an energy cost to everything that you do. You need energy to keep your body warm, to breathe, move, and talk. While you are growing you need energy for your bones, muscles, and brain to grow.

Activity	Energy (kJ) for each minute of activity
sitting	6
standing	7
washing, dressing	15
walking slowly	13
cycling	26
running	60
swimming	73

▲ **Table 2** Energy needed for different activities.

Athletes need a lot more energy than the average person. People who walk to the North or South Pole need even more energy because they need extra energy to keep warm.

> **C** Calculate the energy needed to sit still for 10 minutes.

What is an 'energy balance'?

An adult should just take in the energy they need for the activities that they do. If you take in more energy than you need your body produces fat to store the extra energy.

Link

You can learn more about nutrition in B2 1.3 *Unhealthy diet*.

How far?

On average, people can walk about 90 m per minute, and run about 150 m per minute. Calculate how far you would need to run to use the energy in 50 g of chocolate.

Key words

energy, joule, kilojoule, fuel

Summary Questions

1 Copy and complete the following sentences.

Energy is stored in _____ and _____. The amount of energy stored is measured in _____. When you are asleep your body needs energy for keeping warm and _____. Children need more energy than adults because they are _____.
(5 marks)

2 Calculate the number of minutes you would need to cycle for to use the energy in 200 g of chips. Show your working. (2 marks)

3 Use the information in Table 2 to calculate the approximate energy cost of the activities that you do in one day. Compare the number of apples with the amount of chips that you would need to eat to give you this energy. (4 marks)

Learning objectives

After this topic, you will be able to:

- describe how fossil fuels are formed
- describe the difference between a renewable and a non-renewable energy resource
- describe how electricity is generated by renewable and non-renewable resources.

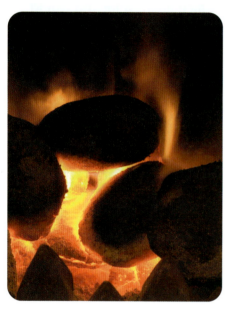

▲ **Figure 1** Coal is one of many energy resources.

Have you ever thought about where the gas and electricity that you use in your house come from? All the energy you use in your home comes from the energy resources on our planet.

How are fossil fuels formed?

Coal (Figure 1), oil, and natural gas are energy resources that were formed millions of years ago. That is why they are called **fossil fuels**. Oil and natural gas are made from the fossilised remains of sea creatures. Coal is the fossilised remains of trees. The trees and sea creatures were compressed and heated over millions of years, and that produced coal, oil, and natural gas.

Coal, oil, and natural gas are **non-renewable**. That doesn't mean that you can't use them again. It means that you cannot easily get more of them when they run out.

A Compare coal and oil in terms of how they are formed.

What's in a power station?

Thermal power stations burn coal and natural gas (Figure 2). Oil is mainly used to produce petrol, plastics, and other useful materials.

The generator produces the potential difference that means a current flows in a kettle in your home. Thermal power stations are very reliable.

B Suggest why most power stations are built next to a river or reservoir.

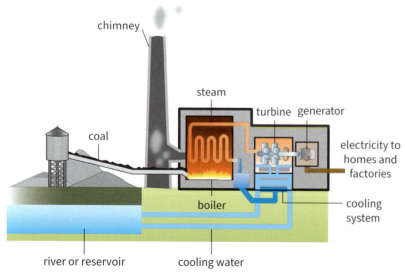

▲ **Figure 2** A power station burns fossil fuels to drive a generator.

One problem with burning fossil fuels is that they produce a lot of carbon dioxide. Carbon dioxide is a greenhouse gas, so it can contribute to climate change.

Burning fossil fuels also produce pollutants that can affect peoples' health.

Nuclear power stations are similar to coal power stations, but they use **uranium** as a fuel. They do not produce carbon dioxide while they are working, but the waste they produce is very dangerous.

What are renewable resources?

Scientists agree that it would be better if we did not burn so many fossil fuels. They have found some alternative ways to produce a current. These resources are **renewable** because they will not run out, for example, sunlight. Most renewable resources except solar cells need a generator to produce a current, just like a power station.

C Compare wind turbines and biomass in terms of how electricity is generated.

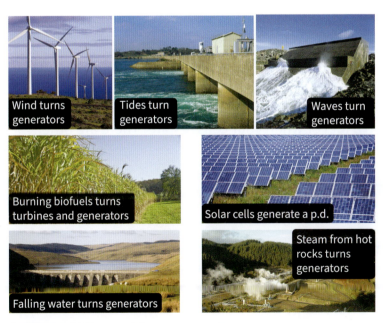

Wind turns generators

Tides turn generators

Waves turn generators

Burning biofuels turns turbines and generators

Solar cells generate a p.d.

Steam from hot rocks turns generators

Falling water turns generators

▲ **Figure 3** Renewable energy sources.

Renewable resources do not produce much carbon dioxide when they produce a current. They do produce carbon dioxide when they are being built. Renewable resources can be unreliable. They can affect their local environment because they need a lot of land, and change animal and human habitats.

Link

You can learn more about greenhouse gases in C2 4.6 *Climate change*.

Chris the carbon atom

Write a children's story that follows the journey of Chris the carbon atom. Chris starts out in the trunk of a tree that is turned into coal and then is used to generate electricity. At the end of the journey, he is in a molecule of carbon dioxide.

Key words

energy resource, fossil fuel, non-renewable, thermal power station, nuclear power station, uranium, renewable.

Summary Questions

1 Copy and complete the following sentences.

Coal is a _____ resource because it will run out. It is called a _____ _____ because it took millions of years to form. Wind is a _____ resource because it won't run out.

(3 marks)

2 Describe how electricity is generated from a fossil fuel like natural gas. (4 marks)

3 Compare how water is used to generate electricity in thermal power stations and by renewable resources. (4 marks)

Learning objectives

After this topic, you will be able to:

- describe energy before and after a change
- describe what brings about changes in energy
- use the law of conservation of energy.

Reactivate your knowledge

1 Name two non-renewable energy resources.
2 State how long coal takes to form.
3 State the main advantage of using fossil fuels to generate electricity.

▲ **Figure 1** Energy is a bit like money.

Key words

law of conservation of energy, chemical store, energy store, thermal, kinetic, gravitational potential, elastic, electromagnetic, nuclear, dissipated

Do you have some money in your pocket? If you know how much you left home with, and you didn't spend any on the way, then you know how much you have now (Figure 1).

What is conservation of energy?

Energy cannot just disappear, and you cannot end up with more than you had at the start. Energy cannot be created or destroyed, only transferred. This is the **law of conservation of energy**. It is important to keep track of energy because some energy resources are limited.

A Suggest why energy is like money.

What are energy stores?

There is an amount of energy you can calculate associated with food and fuels (and oxygen). You can think of that energy as being in a **chemical store**. Energy is transferred from the chemical store when you burn a fuel or when your cells respire. There are other types of **energy store** (Table 1):

What is an energy analysis?

A camping stove burns gas, which is a fuel (Figure 2).

If you could measure the energy in the chemical and thermal stores before and after you heat up a saucepan of soup, you would see that:

total energy before = total energy after

Energy to do with...	Type of store
food, fuels, batteries	chemical
hot objects	**thermal**
moving objects	**kinetic**
position in a gravitational field	**gravitational potential**
changing shape, e.g., stretching	**elastic**
electric or magnetic fields	**electromagnetic**
nuclear fuels or processes in the Sun	**nuclear**

▲ **Table 1** Types of energy store.

	Type of store	Energy to do with...
What we have	unburnt fuel, more oxygen, cold soup	less fuel, more carbon dioxide, more water, hot soup (and slightly hotter air)
Thinking about energy	more energy in the chemical store, less energy in the thermal store	less energy in the chemical store, more energy in the thermal store

▲ **Table 2** Energy analysis table.

Reactivate your knowledge answers
1 Two from coal, oil, gas 2 It takes millions of years to form 3 It's very reliable

How do you transfer energy between stores?

Electric current, light, sound, and forces are ways of transferring energy between stores. After you use your phone, there is less energy in the chemical store of the battery, and more energy in the thermal store of the surroundings.

> **B** Suggest a situation where energy is transferred by an electric current.

If energy is conserved, why do we need to save it?

There is no 'law of conservation of fuels'. When we have used up non-renewable energy resources, we cannot get any more.

In a car, you want the burning fuel to transfer energy to the store that you want (the kinetic store of the car), not to other stores that you don't want (such as a thermal store). You want the car to move, not heat up (Figure 3).

▲ **Figure 3** Fuel used to heat the outside of the car is wasted.

In many situations wasted energy is transferred to the thermal store of the surroundings. Scientists say that the energy is **dissipated**.

When we talk about 'saving energy', what we really mean is saving energy resources like fossil fuels.

> **C** Describe how energy is dissipated when you use a kettle to boil water.

Why do things happen?

It is tempting to say that things happen because they have energy. Energy tells you what changes are possible, but it does not explain why things happen. Forces, not energy, explain why things move.

▲ **Figure 2** Camping gas and oxygen together make a chemical store.

Summary Questions

1 Copy and complete the following sentences.

The law of conservation of energy says that energy cannot be **created/dissipated** or **destroyed/transferred**. When you burn coal, you transfer energy from a **chemical/thermal** store to a **chemical/thermal** store. You **can/cannot** explain why things happen using energy. (5 marks)

2 a Describe where and how energy is stored in a torch. (2 marks)

b Explain what happens to the energy stored in a torch when it is switched on. (2 marks)

3 Complete an energy analysis table like Table 2 to show what happens when you cook sausages on a camp fire by burning wood. (4 marks)

2.4 Energy and temperature

Learning objectives

After this topic, you will be able to:

- state the difference between energy and temperature
- describe what affects temperature rise
- explain what is meant by equilibrium.

Reactivate your knowledge

1 Name the unit of energy.
2 Name a unit of temperature we usually use.
3 Describe what is meant by an 'energy store'.

▲ **Figure 1** Rock melts at 1200 °C to form lava.

▲ **Figure 2** Some thermometers use sensors to measure temperature.

Key words

temperature, thermometer, equilibrium

People visit places where there is molten rock. It takes a lot of energy to melt rock (Figure 1).

What is temperature?

Something that is hotter than your skin will feel hot, and something that is colder than your skin will feel cold. You cannot measure **temperature** with your skin. You use a **thermometer** to measure temperature. Some thermometers have a liquid inside a very thin glass tube that expands when it is heated. Other thermometers are digital (Figure 2). We measure temperature in degrees Celsius (°C).

A Suggest when a bowl of warm water might feel cold.

What's the difference?

There is a difference between energy in a thermal store and temperature.

- The energy in a thermal store is a measure of the motion of all the particles.
- The temperature is a measure of the *average* speed of motion of the particles, which does not depend on how many there are.

There is much more energy in the thermal store of this swimming pool than in a beaker of water....

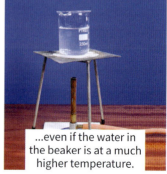

...even if the water in the beaker is at a much higher temperature.

▲ **Figure 3** Energy in a thermal store is not the same as temperature.

Reactivate your knowledge answers
1 Joules 2 Degrees Celsius, °C 3 Ways in which energy can be calculated

B Explain why there is more energy in the thermal store of a bath than a cup of tea.

What happens when you heat things up?

Heating changes the movement or arrangement of particles.

- If you heat a solid the particles vibrate more.
- If you heat a liquid or a gas the particles move faster.
- You can change the arrangement of particles by heating a substance to its melting or boiling point.

Individual particles in a solid, liquid, or gas don't get hotter. They move or vibrate faster.

solid   liquid   gas

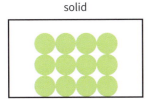 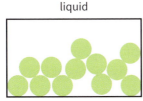 

▲ **Figure 4** Particles in solids, liquids, and gases.

The temperature rise of a material depends on:

- the mass of material
- what the material is made of
- the energy transferred to it.

C State what happens to the movement of particles in lava as it cools.

Which way?

Hot objects cool down. Energy is never transferred from a cold object to a hot object, only from a hot object to a cooler object. The temperature difference is reduced and eventually both objects will end up at the same temperature. They will be in **equilibrium**. No more energy is transferred between their thermal stores.

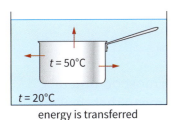

energy is transferred

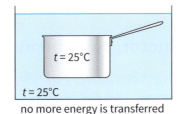

no more energy is transferred

▲ **Figure 5** A pan reaching thermal equilibrium.

You might hear someone say "Shut the door, you'll let the cold in!"
Rewrite the statement so that it is scientifically correct and explain why it is now correct.

Link

You learnt about particles in C1 1.1 *The particle model*.

Summary Questions

1 Copy and complete the following sentences.

You measure _____ in degrees Celsius using a _____. _____ does not depend on the amount of material that you have, but the _____ stored does. The particles in a _____ vibrate more when you heat the solid. Energy moves from hotter objects to colder objects until they are in _____. (6 marks)

2 Sort these things in order from least energy stored to most energy stored: a saucepan full of water at 50 °C, a cup of water at 30 °C, a saucepan full of water at 30 °C. (1 mark)

3 You are cooking a pizza. When the pizza is cooked you remove the tray from the oven. Eventually it reaches room temperature again. Describe and explain what happens to the movement of the particles in the metal tray during this time. (4 marks)

Learning objectives

After this topic, you will be able to:

- describe how energy is transferred by particles in conduction
- describe how energy is transferred by particles in convection
- explain how an insulator can reduce energy transfer.

Reactivate your knowledge

1 State whether particles in a liquid move faster or more slowly as you heat it.
2 Define 'insulator' in terms of circuits.
3 Name a non-metal that conducts electricity.

Have you ever lit a wooden splint in a Bunsen burner flame? The end of the splint is at a temperature of about 1000 °C but you can still hold the other end (Figure 1).

How is energy transferred?

When you put a saucepan of soup on the stove, the soup heats up. The bottom of the saucepan is made of metal. A metal is a good **conductor** of energy. Energy is transferred through it very quickly. This is **conduction**. Energy can be transferred by conduction, **convection**, or **radiation**.

> **A** State which is the better conductor: aluminium or glass.

What is conduction?

In conduction in solids, particles transfer energy by colliding with other particles when they vibrate. This is a slow process.

In metal solids there are electrons that can move (Figure 2). They also transfer the energy by colliding with the atoms. This happens much more quickly. We use the same idea to explain conduction in circuits.

Energy transfer happens until the two surfaces are at the same temperature. If you keep one surface warm by heating it, then you will maintain the temperature difference. The solid will continue to conduct.

Solid conductor, solid insulator?

Energy is not transferred very quickly through most non-metals, like wood. They are **insulators**. This does not mean that they do not conduct at all but that energy is transferred very slowly through them. They are poor conductors.

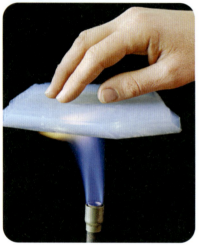

▲ **Figure 1** This special material is called aerogel. Like wood, energy is transferred very slowly through it.

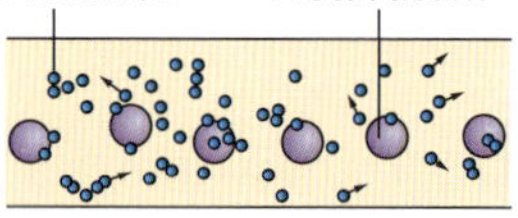

Free electron · Metal atom

thermal store at a high temperature — thermal store at a low temperature

▲ **Figure 2** Energy transfer in a solid metal.

▲ **Figure 3** The capsule that brought these astronauts back is insulated so that they do not burn up in the atmosphere.

Reactivate your knowledge answers
1 Faster 2 A material that does not allow a current to pass through easily 3 Graphite

B Suggest whether graphite is a good or bad conductor of energy.

Insulating liquids and gases

Liquids are also poor conductors. Divers wear wetsuits, which use a thin layer of water against the skin as an insulator to keep them warm (Figure 4).

Gases do not conduct well at all because their particles are much further apart than the particles in a solid. Duvets and warm clothing are designed to trap small pockets of air, which is a good insulator.

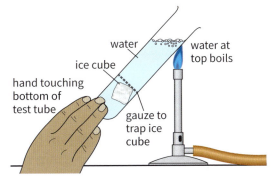

▲ **Figure 4** Poor heat conduction of water.

What is convection?

When you heat water in a pan it all heats up, not just the layer in contact with the bottom of the saucepan. A **convection current** in a saucepan of water heats all of the water up (Figure 5).

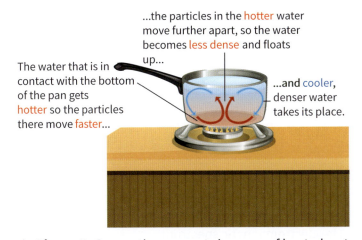

…the particles in the hotter water move further apart, so the water becomes less dense and floats up…

The water that is in contact with the bottom of the pan gets hotter so the particles there move faster…

…and cooler, denser water takes its place.

▲ **Figure 5** Convection currents in a pan of heated water.

C Give the place in the pan in Figure 5 where the water is most dense.

How does sound transfer energy?

When you play music, energy is transferred to the surroundings. The air and walls get a bit warmer. The particles in the air move a bit faster, and the particles in the walls vibrate more.

Key words

conductor, conduction, convection, radiation, insulator, convection current

How fast?

A student wants to investigate how the temperature of a liquid affects how long it takes to cool down. Write a plan for the investigation, including a risk assessment.

Summary Questions

1 Copy and complete the following sentences.

Energy is transferred through a solid by _____ if one end is a different _____ to the other. Liquids and solids transfer energy by _____ because the particles can _____. Energy is transferred much more _____ through an insulator than it is through a conductor. (5 marks)

2 a Explain in terms of particles why conduction happens in solids but not in liquids and gases. (2 marks)

b Explain in terms of particles why convection happens in liquids and gases but not in solids. (2 marks)

3 An electric kettle contains an element at the bottom that gets hot when you switch it on. Explain how all the water in a kettle boils. (4 marks)

Learning objectives

After this topic, you will be able to:

- describe what is meant by radiation
- give the waves of the electromagnetic spectrum
- compare energy transfer by conduction, convection, and radiation.

Reactivate your knowledge

1 Name the radiation that the eye detects.
2 State what happens when light hits a mirror.
3 Name the states of matter that convection happens in.

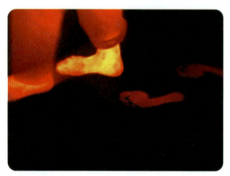

▲ **Figure 1** A special camera shows your thermal footprint.

▲ **Figure 2** A thermal imaging camera produces a coloured image of the fire.

Link ↗

You learnt about the properties of light in P1 3.1 *Light*.

Key words +🔑+

radiation, infrared radiation, electromagnetic spectrum, thermal imaging camera.

You leave thermal footprints on the floor when you walk across it in bare feet. You can't see them because your eyes only detect visible light (Figure 1).

What is radiation?

Waves or particles emitted by a substance are called **radiation**. Very hot things such as burning coal give out light as well as **infrared radiation**. Some people call infrared 'thermal radiation' or 'heat'. The Sun emits lots of different types of radiation, including light and infrared. Both light and infrared radiation are part of the **electromagnetic spectrum**, and travel as waves (Figure 3).

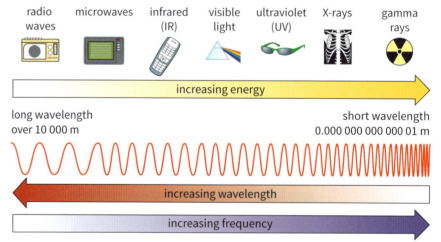

radio waves | microwaves | infrared (IR) | visible light | ultraviolet (UV) | X-rays | gamma rays

increasing energy →

long wavelength over 10 000 m .... short wavelength 0.000 000 000 000 01 m

← increasing wavelength

increasing frequency →

▲ **Figure 3** The electromagnetic spectrum.

A Name two objects apart from burning coal that emit both light and infrared.

How is energy transferred by radiation?

Light and infrared reach the Earth from the Sun by travelling through space. Space is a vacuum. There are no particles in a vacuum.

Reactivate your knowledge answers
1 Light 2 Reflects 3 Gases and liquids

What emits infrared?

All objects (including you, and very cold objects) give out, or emit, radiation.

- The type of radiation that they emit depends on their temperature.
- How much radiation they emit per second depends on the type of surface.
- Infrared can be transmitted, absorbed, or reflected, just like light.

B Suggest an object that would emit more infrared than a mouse.

▲ **Figure 4** The mouse is at a higher temperature than the snake.

What absorbs or reflects infrared?

On a sunny day your skin absorbs infrared from the Sun. A **thermal imaging camera** absorbs infrared and produces an image (Figures 2 and 4). The colours in the image are 'false'. The camera works out which areas are hotter and shows them redder in the image.

You might feel hotter when you wear dark clothing because:

- dark colours absorb infrared
- light-coloured and shiny surfaces reflect infrared (Figure 5).

▲ **Figure 5** Infrared is reflected by the foil, keeping the runner warm.

C Suggest which colours of clothing will dry fastest on a washing line.

How do conduction, convection, and radiation compare?

Energy is transferred by heating in conduction and convection, and by radiation.

- You need particles to transfer energy by conduction or convection.
- Radiation can travel through a vacuum and gases.
- Different types of radiation travel through different solids. Infrared can travel through black plastic, but light cannot.

Summary Questions

1 Copy and complete the following sentences.

The Sun and fire are examples of _____ of infrared. All objects emit _____ but the type of radiation depends on the _____. The waves of the electromagnetic spectrum are: radio, _____, infrared, _____, ultraviolet, _____, gamma. Just like light, infrared does not need _____ to travel through. It can travel through empty space, or a _____. (8 marks)

2 Explain why:

a houses are painted white in hot countries (1 mark)
b the inside of a flask designed to keep water hot is silver. (1 mark)

3 Draw a Venn diagram about conduction, convection and radiation. (4 marks)

Learning objectives

After this topic, you will be able to:
- describe what is meant by 'work' in physics
- calculate work done
- apply the conservation of energy to simple machines.

Reactivate your knowledge

1 Name the unit of force.
2 Define 'weight'.
3 State the law of conservation of energy.

If you drive in the mountains, you will always take roads that wind backwards and forwards (Figure 1). The reason is to do with forces and energy.

What is work?

Not all energy transfers are to do with heating, current, or radiation. You can transfer energy by using a force, which is doing **work**. In physics the word 'work' has a special meaning.

- When you lift a book you do work against gravity.
- When you slide the book you do work against friction.
- Forces which do not cause movement do no work.

work done = force × distance in the direction of the force
(J)   (N)   (m)

▲ **Figure 1** You cannot drive straight up a tall mountain.

▲ **Figure 2a** Lifting a book.

work done = force × distance

= 2 N × 1 m

= 2 J

▲ **Figure 2b** Sliding a book.

work done = force × distance

= 1 N × 0.2 m

= 0.2 J

The unit of work is the joule because work is a way of transferring energy (Figure 2). Work can also be measured in newton-metres, or Nm.

A Explain why holding a book is not doing work.

Key words

work, simple machine, lever, ramp, newton-metre

Reactivate your knowledge answers
1 Newtons 2 Force of the Earth on an object 3 Energy cannot be created or destroyed only transferred between stores

How do machines make life easier?

A **simple machine** makes it easier to lift things, move things, or turn things. It reduces the force that you need to do a job, or increases the distance that something moves when you apply a force.

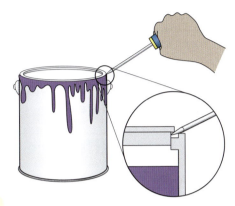

▲ **Figure 3** A screwdriver used this way is a lever.

How do levers work?

Most people use a **lever** to open a tin of paint (Figure 4). If you put a screwdriver between the lid and the rim of the tin, you can open the tin with a much smaller force (Figure 3). A lever is a force multiplier.

B Use the paint tin example to explain why a lever is a force multiplier.

▲ **Figure 4** Using leverage to open a can of paint.

Why are mountain roads winding?

A winding mountain road is a **ramp**. A ramp (Figure 5) is a simple machine. You may have seen ramps at the side of stairs. The longer the ramp for a particular height, the smaller the force that you need to travel that height.

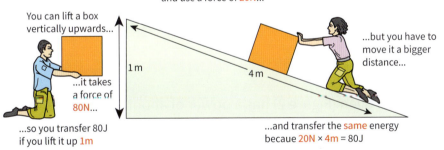

You can lift a box vertically upwards...
1 m
...it takes a force of **80N**...
...so you transfer 80J if you lift it up **1m**

Alternatively, you can push it up a ramp, and use a force of **20N**...
4 m
...but you have to move it a bigger distance...
...and transfer the **same** energy becaue **20N × 4m = 80J**

▲ **Figure 5** Moving a box with and without a ramp.

C Show that you do 80 J of work lifting the box in Figure 5 vertically.

Do you get something for nothing?

A small force acting over a big distance can transfer the same energy as a big force acting over a small distance. The reason is the law of conservation of energy. If you increased the distance as well as the force then you would need to put more energy in because you cannot get out more energy than you put in. You cannot get something for nothing.

Summary Questions

1 Copy and complete the following sentences.

You need to know the _____ and the _____ to calculate work done. A simple _____ like a _____ can be used to open a paint tin because it is a _____ multiplier. A _____ on a hill can make it easier to move uphill. All simple machines obey the law of _____ of energy. You cannot get more _____ out than you put in. (8 marks)

2 You can use a stone under a plank of wood to lift a heavy rock.

a State the type of machine that you can make with this equipment. (1 mark)

b Calculate the work done by lifting a rock of weight 200 N a distance of 0.25 m. (2 marks)

3 A person with a weight of 600 N climbs Mount Everest, a vertical height of 10 km. Compare the work done climbing Mount Everest and climbing 2.5 m upstairs to bed. (4 marks)

Learning objectives

After this topic, you will be able to:

- describe the difference between energy and power
- calculate power and energy
- calculate the cost of using domestic appliances.

Reactivate your knowledge

1 Give the equation for calculating work.
2 Name the unit of work.
3 Give the number of joules in a kilojoule.

▲ **Figure 1** The power rating of this heater is 2000 W.

Key words

power rating, watt, kilowatt, kilowatt hour

▲ **Figure 2** The power rating of this oven is 12 000 W.

Some microwaves cook popcorn faster than others. Why is there a difference?

What is the difference between energy and power?

Microwave ovens transfer energy by an electric current and by radiation. Microwaves have a **power rating** in **watts** (W). The power rating tells you how much energy is transferred *per second*, or the rate of transfer of energy. The power of a microwave oven is about 800 W. If you want to transfer a lot of energy you turn it on for a long time.

Energy transferred (J) = power (W or J/s) × time (s)

> **A** Calculate the energy transferred by a 800 W microwave in 10 seconds.

How do you calculate power?

You can change the subject of this equation to calculate power:

$$\text{power (W)} = \frac{\text{energy (J)}}{\text{time (s)}}$$

A traditional oven (Figure 2) has a power of about 12 000 W, or 12 **kilowatts**. 12 000 W is the same as 12 kilowatts, or 12 kW.

- There are 1000 W in 1 kW. You divide by 1000 to convert watts to kilowatts.
- An oven with a rating of 12 kW transfers energy at a rate of 12 000 J per second.
- This is the same as 12 kilojoules per second because there are 1000 J in 1 kJ.

What are you paying for?

When you pay an electricity bill you are paying for a fuel such as coal to be burnt in a power station. The power station generates the potential difference that we call 'mains electricity'. You are charged

Reactivate your knowledge answers
1 work = force × distance 2 Joules 3 1000

for the number of hours that you use each appliance, and for the power of the appliance.

You can calculate energy use in **kilowatt hours** (kWh), or joules. This is the unit that electricity companies use to calculate your bill.

A kilowatt hour is calculated like this:

Suppose you use a 12 kW (12 000 W) oven for 1 hour (3600 seconds):

energy used in kWh = 12 kW × 1 hour

= 12 kWh

energy used in J = 12 000 J/s × 3600 s

= 43 200 000 J

The number of joules is very big, so it is more convenient to use kWh.

To reduce your energy bills you could use:

- fewer appliances
- appliances that require less power to produce the same output
- appliances for fewer hours.

Insulation in a house reduces the rate at which energy is transferred to the surroundings, so it reduces the rate at which you need to supply energy to heat the house.

▲ **Figure 4** The bulbs are the same brightness but the one on the right has a much lower power.

> **B** Compare the unit of energy with the unit used on electricity bills.

How powerful are you?

You can transfer energy by using a force. When you run uphill you do work against gravity. You use a force over the height that you travel. If you know your weight and the height you have moved, you can calculate the work done. If you know how long it took, you can work out your power.

▲ **Figure 3** Some houses transfer more energy to the surroundings than others.

Summary Questions

1 Copy and complete the following sentences.

Energy is measured in _____ and power is measured in _____. Power is the energy transferred per _____. You pay for the number of _____ that are transferred to your house by electricity. You could save money by using appliances with a _____ power rating, or by using them for _____ time.
(6 marks)

2 A 10 kW cooker takes 1 ½ hours to cook a chicken.

a Calculate the energy transferred in kWh. (2 marks)
b Calculate the cost of cooking the chicken if the electricity company charges 15p per kWh. (2 marks)

3 Explain why the cost of using a kettle with a power rating of 2 kW and a kettle rated 1.2 kW might be approximately the same even though the power ratings are different.
(4 marks)

In this chapter you have learnt about energy, how it is stored, transferred, and how to do calculations of energy transfer involving forces, which we call *work*, and rate of energy transfer, which we call *power*.

You have seen how an energy analysis can help to identify useful energy transfers, and how energy is dissipated, because energy is always conserved. You have compared different energy resources, and different methods of energy transfer, which explains energy dissipation, and how different insulation methods work. You have seen the link between electric current, power, and how energy is calculated on an electricity bill.

Metacognition and self-reflection task

Mind maps help you to see the connections between different concepts. Write all the key words on post-it notes and make a mind map on a big piece of paper. Draw lines between them and write the reason why they are related next to the line. Take off the post-it notes and try to put them back in the correct place a week later. Did you struggle with some words more than others?

Journey through P2

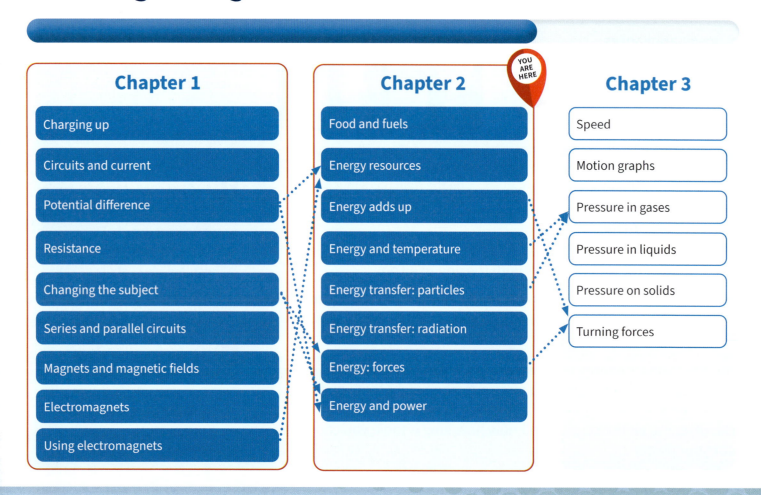

Chapter 1	Chapter 2	Chapter 3
Charging up	Food and fuels	Speed
Circuits and current	Energy resources	Motion graphs
Potential difference	Energy adds up	Pressure in gases
Resistance	Energy and temperature	Pressure in liquids
Changing the subject	Energy transfer: particles	Pressure on solids
Series and parallel circuits	Energy transfer: radiation	Turning forces
Magnets and magnetic fields	Energy: forces	
Electromagnets	Energy and power	
Using electromagnets		

YOU ARE HERE

Chapter 2 Summary Questions

1 Here are some energy resources. List the renewable energy resources.

    wind solar oil coal geothermal gas
                            (1 mark)

2 Almost all electrical appliances have a power rating.

a State which definition of power below is correct.
                                   (1 mark)

    A the energy transferred per hour.
    B the energy transferred.
    C the energy transferred per second.
    D the force multiplied by a distance.

b Select all the units of power from this list:
    kW J watts kilojoules kilowatts W joules kJ
                                (1 mark)
                                (2 marks)

3 Figure 1 shows an experiment to demonstrate convection.

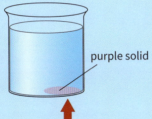

purple solid

Bunsen burner heats here

▲ **Figure 1**

a Describe what will happen to the purple colour during heating.
                            (3 marks)

b Explain how this shows energy transfer by particles.
                            (4 marks)

c Name the type of radiation that the beaker emits.
                            (1 mark)
                            (8 marks)

4 A student reads that you use 15 kJ per minute by walking, and that there are 1500 kJ in 100 g of chocolate.

a They calculate the number of minutes of walking that would use the energy in 100 g of chocolate. Select the correct answer from the list below:
    0.01 min   10 min   100 min   1000 min   **(1 mark)**

b Suggest whether the answer to part a would be bigger or smaller if you were walking quickly. Explain your answer.
                            (2 marks)
                            (3 marks)

5 A tennis ball has 10 J of energy when it is 1 m above the floor.

a Name the store associated with this energy.   **(1 mark)**

b A student states that there will be 10 J of energy in the kinetic store just before it hits the ground.

    i Explain why the student has made that statement.
                            (1 mark)

    ii Explain why the student might not be correct.
                            (1 mark)

c Explain why the ball moves.   **(2 marks)**
                            (5 marks)

6 Someone lifts a suitcase into the back of a car as shown in Figure 2.

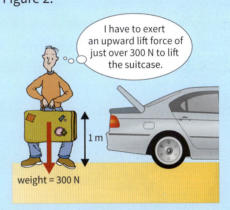

I have to exert an upward lift force of just over 300 N to lift the suitcase.

1 m

weight = 300 N

▲ **Figure 2**

a Name the force against which the person is doing work.
                            (1 mark)

b Calculate the work done.   **(3 marks)**

c Write down another measurement that you would need to make to be able to work out the power to lift the suitcase into the car.   **(1 mark)**.

d Describe how you would use that measurement and your answer to part **b** to calculate the power.   **(1 mark)**
                            (6 marks)

7 A student reads that a human being would glow like a 60 W lightbulb if they converted all of the energy from their food into light. An average human consumes 2000 calories every day which is about 8000 kJ.
Do you agree? Justify your answer with calculations. Show your working.   **(5 marks)**

8 Explain in detail why insulating your house will reduce your energy bills.   **(6 marks)**

Motion and pressure

In this chapter you will learn how to interpret a motion graph, which is a graph of distance against time. You will learn how to calculate speed from data, or from the graph.

You will learn how the pressure of a gas depends on temperature or volume, and why the atmosphere exerts a pressure that changes with height. You will compare pressure in gases to pressure in liquids and learn how to calculate the pressure exerted on the surface of a solid. You will learn how forces can make objects turn around a pivot and why some objects are more stable than others.

Reactivate your knowledge

1 Describe a situation where the forces on a moving object are balanced and another where they are unbalanced.

2 Compare the arrangement of particles and their motion in a liquid state and a gas state.

3 Calculate the area of a square with a side of 10 cm, and the area of a rectangle of sides 10 cm and 20 cm.

You already know

Objects are stationary or move at a steady speed unless a resultant force acts; a resultant force can make an object speed up, slow down, or change direction.

The particles in a substance are arranged differently in the solid, liquid, and gas states and particles in a gas move faster if the temperature of the gas increases.

How to calculate the area of regular objects like squares and rectangles.

 How to use an equation to calculate weight, resistance, work, power.

 How to work scientifically to: make measurements, record data in tables, draw graphs, and make conclusions from a graph.

Journey through P2

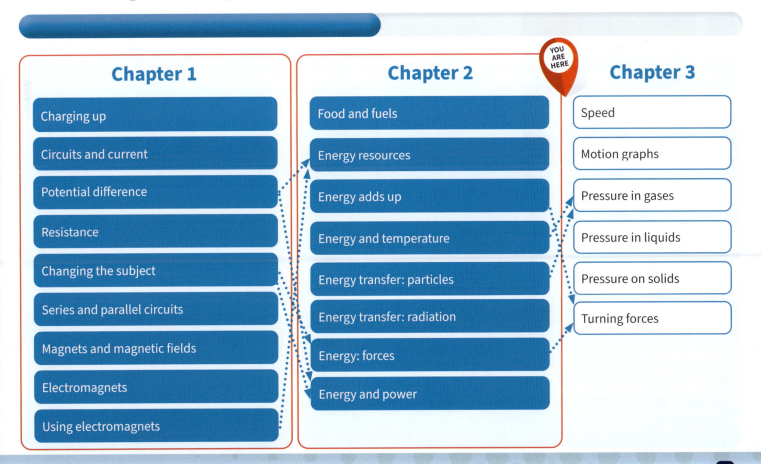

Chapter 1	Chapter 2	Chapter 3
Charging up	Food and fuels	Speed
Circuits and current	Energy resources	Motion graphs
Potential difference	Energy adds up	Pressure in gases
Resistance	Energy and temperature	Pressure in liquids
Changing the subject	Energy transfer: particles	Pressure on solids
Series and parallel circuits	Energy transfer: radiation	Turning forces
Magnets and magnetic fields	Energy: forces	
Electromagnets	Energy and power	
Using electromagnets		

YOU ARE HERE

Learning objectives

After this topic, you will be able to:

- calculate speed
- describe the difference between average and instantaneous speed
- describe relative motion.

▲ **Figure 1** A cheetah can travel faster than a car.

▲ **Figure 2** A speed camera measures how long it takes a car to travel a certain distance by taking a photo at the start of the distance and another at the end. It can then calculate the car's speed.

It feels fast going downhill on a bike. Even going downhill on a bike you could not travel as fast as a cheetah (Figure 1).

How fast?

Speed is a measure of how far something travels in a particular time. In science you measure speed in **metres per second** (m/s). Car speed and speed limits are measured in miles per hour (mph) or kilometres per hour (km/h). A traffic speed camera, Figure 2, makes these measurements. A very fast car can move at over 300 km/h, but when you walk to school you are probably walking at 5 km/h or about 1 m/s. Table 1 shows some speeds in different units.

	Speed in m/s	Speed in km/h	Speed in mph
Walking quickly	1.7	6.1	3.8
Sprinting	10	36	22
Typical speed limit	14	50	31
Cheetah	33	119	74
Aeroplane cruising speed	255	918	570
Sound in air	330	1190	738
Light in air	300 000 000	10 000 000 000	670 000 000

▲ **Table 1**

A State the unit of speed that you use in science.

How do you calculate speed?

To find the speed of an object moving at a steady speed you need to measure the time it takes to travel between two points. You work out the speed from the distance travelled divided by the time taken:

$$\text{speed (m/s)} = \frac{\text{distance travelled (m)}}{\text{time taken (s)}}$$

Marathon times

A marathon runner runs the 42 km in 2 hours 30 minutes, or 2.5 hours. Calculate the average speed of the runner in km/h.

A long-distance runner runs part of their race at a steady speed. It takes them 20 seconds to run 100 m.

$$speed = \frac{100\,m}{20\,s}$$
$$= 5\,m/s$$

When you are using an equation, it is helpful to write it out like this. If you write the units of distance and time in the equation then you will have the correct units for the speed.

Instantaneous or average speed?

A runner will take many seconds, minutes, or hours to run a race. They do not run at exactly the same speed throughout the race.

The speed that the runner is travelling at any time during the race is the **instantaneous speed**. This is the speed that you see on the speedometer in a car. You can work out the **average speed** by dividing the *total* distance by the *total* time that it took to run the race. This average speed makes it easier to compare how fast different people, boats, or cars, travel.

▲ **Figure 3** A sprinter's speed changes during a race.

> **B** A ball falls and hits the ground. State where its instantaneous speed is fastest.

What is relative motion?

Figure 4 shows an example of **relative motion**. Relative motion means how fast one thing is travelling compared to another. For example, being on a moving train looking at a stationary one feels the same as being on a stationary train looking at a moving one. Speed is relative. If two cars are moving at the same speed in the same direction their relative speed is zero. We usually measure speed relative to the ground.

The green car is moving at 10 km/h relative to the red car...

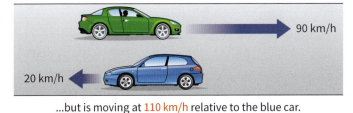
...but is moving at 110 km/h relative to the blue car.

▲ **Figure 4** Relative speeds.

> **C** State the speed of the red car relative to the ground.

Summary Questions

1 Copy and complete the following sentences.

To calculate speed, you need to know the _____ and the _____. To calculate average speed, you divide the _____ _____ by the _____ _____. The instantaneous speed is the speed at any _____. You measure speed _____ to a stationary object. (7 marks)

2 A runner runs 100 m in 12.5 seconds. Calculate their average speed. (2 marks)

3 A car is travelling east at 50 km/h. On the same road another car is travelling west at 20 km/h. The cars are moving away from each other. Describe their relative motion. (2 marks)

4 a Change the subject of the speed equation to find time. (2 marks)

b Calculate the time in seconds it would take sound and light to reach you from a lightning strike that is 6 km away. (2 marks)

Learning objectives

After this topic, you will be able to:

- interpret distance–time graphs
- calculate speed using a distance–time graph.

Reactivate your knowledge

1 Give the equation for speed.
2 State the difference between instantaneous and average speed.
3 Estimate walking speed in m/s.

Key words

distance–time graph, acceleration

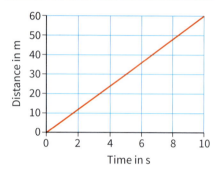

▲ **Figure 2** A distance–time graph for a constant speed.

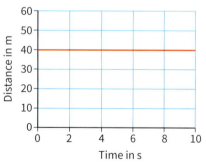

▲ **Figure 3** A distance–time graph for a stationary object.

▲ **Figure 4** The car and motorbike are travelling at different speeds.

How long does it take you to get to school? You can tell the story of a journey with a graph.

What is a distance–time graph?

A **distance–time graph** is a useful way of showing how something moves. It shows the distance that something travels over a certain time.

Figure 1 shows Lucy's journey to school. The line shows how far she travelled each minute of the journey.

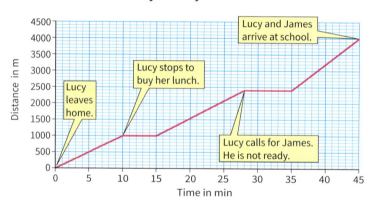

▲ **Figure 1** A distance–time graph for Lucy's journey to school.

What does the graph tell us?

Figure 2 is a very simple distance–time graph. The object moves the same distance each second.

What happens if you stay still? The line on the distance–time graph is horizontal (Figure 3).

> **A** State how you know that the speed of the objects in the graphs in Figures 1 and 3 is not changing.

The slope of a distance–time graph tells you the speed. If the line is steep the object is moving fast. If it is not very steep then the object is moving more slowly.

Reactivate your knowledge answers
1 Speed = distance ÷ time 2 Instantaneous speed = speed at a certain time, average speed = total distance ÷ total time 3 1 – 2 m/s

In Figure 4, a car and motorbike are driving down the same road at different but steady speeds. Figure 5 shows the distance–time graph for both vehicles. The line for the motorbike shows a faster speed and the line for the car shows a slower speed.

> **B** Suggest where the line for you walking at a steady speed might be drawn on the graph for the car and motorcycle.

▲ **Figure 5** A distance–time graph for two different speeds.

What is acceleration?

When you are travelling the speed changes during the journey.

If your speed is changing you are **accelerating**. Acceleration tells you how quickly your speed is changing (speeding up or slowing down). The slope (gradient) of the graph changes.

When you drop a ball, it gets faster and faster. It accelerates towards Earth. The distance–time graph is curved. The distance–time graph is also curved if an object is slowing down.

▲ **Figure 6** The ball accelerates.

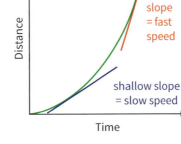

▲ **Figure 7** A distance–time graph for an accelerating object.

> **C** Write down whether the blue and red lines are showing average or instantaneous speeds.

How do you work out speed from a distance–time graph?

You can calculate speed from a distance–time graph. For example, in the first section of Lucy's graph, she walks 1000 m in 10 minutes or 600 seconds.

$$\text{average speed} = \frac{\text{total distance}}{\text{total time}}$$

$$= \frac{1000\,\text{m}}{600\,\text{s}}$$

$$= 1.7\,\text{m/s}$$

Summary Questions

1 Copy and complete the following sentences.

A distance–time graph shows the _____ that an object travels in a certain _____. The _____ of the line tells you the speed. If the line is horizontal the object is _____. If the line is a curve getting steeper the speed of the object is _____. (5 marks)

2 Look at the graph for Lucy's journey to school.

a Calculate Lucy's speed for the final 10 minutes of the graph. (4 marks)
b State the value of the speed in the horizontal sections of the graph. (1 mark)

3 Imagine two students travelling 3 km to school. One walks and the other travels by car.

a Describe and explain one similarity that there might be between the two graphs. (2 marks)
b Describe and explain one difference that there might be between the two graphs. (2 marks)

Learning objectives

After this topic, you will be able to:

- describe the factors that affect gas pressure
- describe what is meant by atmospheric pressure
- describe how atmospheric pressure changes with height.

Reactivate your knowledge

1 Name the force that slows down objects moving through the air.
2 Define 'unbalanced force'.
3 Write down what happens to the speed of gas molecules as you heat the gas.

▲ **Figure 1** The moment when a balloon bursts.

Hot gas
Faster molecules
More collisions
Higher pressure

Cold gas
Slower molecules
Fewer collisions
Lower pressure

▲ **Figure 2** Hot gas and cool gas.

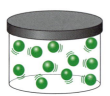

Large volume
Fewer collisions
Smaller pressure

Smaller volume
More collisions
Bigger pressure

▲ **Figure 3** The effect of volume on gas pressure.

Have you ever blown a balloon up until it bursts (Figure 1)?

What is gas pressure?

When you blow up a balloon there are millions of air molecules hitting the inside of the balloon. The collisions between the air molecules and the balloon produce **gas pressure** (air pressure). Lots of collisions per second make a high gas pressure because there is a big force over a small area. Gas pressure is exerted in all directions.

How do temperature and volume affect pressure?

When a gas cools down its molecules move more slowly. If the container doesn't change shape, then the pressure goes down. There are fewer collisions with the sides of the container.

A Suggest what happens to a balloon if you warm it up.

If you squash a gas into a smaller volume there will be more collisions between the gas molecules and the walls of the container. The pressure increases.

What is a compressed gas?

When you pump up a bicycle tyre you increase the gas pressure. As you pump more gas into a container the gas becomes **compressed**. There are more molecules in the same space, so there are more collisions. The pressure is bigger. You need a strong container to hold a compressed gas.

B Write down what happens to the force on the inside of the tyre as you pump in more gas.

Reactivate your knowledge answers
1 Air resistance/drag 2 The forces do not cancel out 3 They speed up

What is atmospheric pressure, and how does it change with height?

There is air all around you. The air exerts a pressure on your body all the time called **atmospheric pressure**. You do not feel the pressure. It is cancelled out by the pressure of the gases and liquids in your body pushing out. You can see the effects of atmospheric pressure in Figure 4.

▲ **Figure 4** Marshmallows contain pockets of air that expand when you pump out the air around them.

The atmospheric pressure at sea level is bigger than the atmospheric pressure high up a mountain. Gravity pulls the air particles towards the Earth. Where the particles are closer there are more collisions. The pressure is higher. **Density** is how close the particles are in a substance. Gas has a higher density at sea level (Figure 5).

Mountain climbers may find it hard to get enough oxygen. They may take oxygen tanks when they climb. The tanks contain oxygen gas that has been compressed into a small volume.

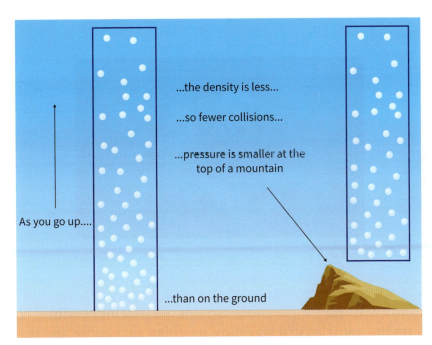

...the density is less...

...so fewer collisions...

...pressure is smaller at the top of a mountain

As you go up....

...than on the ground

▲ **Figure 5** Atmospheric pressure.

c Compare the mass of gas in 1 m³ at the top and bottom of a mountain.

Link

You can learn more about gas pressure in C1 1.7 *Gas pressure*.

Summary Questions

1 Copy and complete the following sentences.

A gas exerts a pressure on the walls of its container because the particles **collide with/stick to** the walls. If the gas gets hotter the pressure will be **bigger/smaller**. If the volume gets bigger the pressure will be **bigger/smaller.** As you go up a mountain the air pressure is **bigger/smaller** because there are **fewer/more** gas particles.

(5 marks)

2 A climber climbs a mountain.

a Explain why they might take a cylinder of oxygen with them.   (2 marks)

b Explain why the oxygen needs to be compressed.   (2 marks)

3 A teacher heats some water in a drinks can until it is boiling and steam comes out of the can. She quickly turns the can over and puts it into some cold water.

a Describe and explain what happens to the pressure inside the can when she puts it in the cold water. (2 marks)

b Explain why the can collapses.   (2 marks)

213

3.4 Pressure in liquids

Learning objectives

After this topic, you will be able to:

- describe how liquids exert a pressure in all directions
- describe how liquid pressure changes with depth
- explain floating and sinking in terms of pressure.

Reactivate your knowledge

1 State what produces gas pressure.
2 State what happens to atmospheric pressure as you go down a mountain.
3 Define 'upthrust'.

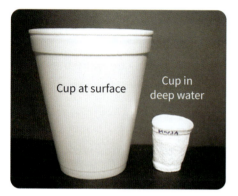

▲ **Figure 1** At 3000 m water exerts a big pressure.

How do you squash a polystyrene cup without touching it? Take it deep beneath the sea and the pressure in the water will do it for you as shown in Figure 1.

What is liquid pressure?

When you swim underwater the water exerts a pressure on you. The water molecules are pushing on each other and on surfaces, and this **liquid pressure** acts in all directions.

When you squeeze a bag with holes in it the water is pushed out of all the holes because of liquid pressure (Figure 2). The water comes straight out of each hole and then falls because of gravity.

> **A** State the angle between the jet of water leaving the bag, and the surface.

▲ **Figure 2** The water comes out in all directions.

Key words

liquid pressure, incompressible

Link

You learnt about upthrust in P1 1.1 *Introduction to forces*.

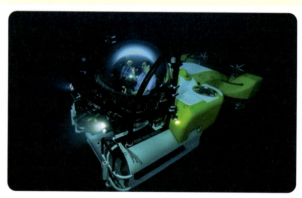

▲ **Figure 3** You need strong vessels to go deep underwater.

If you put water in a syringe, cover the end, and try to compress the liquid you will find it impossible. Liquids are **incompressible**. This is because the particles in a liquid are touching each other and there is very little space between them. Liquids pass on any pressure applied to them.

> **B** Explain why a gas in a syringe is compressible but a liquid is not.

 214

Reactivate your knowledge answers
1 Collisions between gas molecules and a surface 2 It increases/gets bigger 3 The upwards force of water or air on an object

How does pressure change with depth?

The wall of a dam is not straight (Figure 4). It curves outwards at the bottom. The pressure at the bottom of the lake is bigger than the pressure at the top. The pressure at a particular depth in a liquid depends on the weight of water above it. The water pressure at the bottom of the Atlantic Ocean is equivalent to the weight of eight cars pushing on an area the size of your thumb. Submarines are made of strong materials (Figure 3)

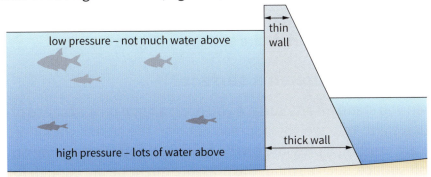

▲ **Figure 4** A dam is thicker at the bottom.

Why do some things float and others sink?

Upthrust acts on any object that is floating, or is submerged in a fluid like a liquid or gas (Figure 5).

A rubber duck floats because there are lots more water molecules hitting the bottom of the rubber duck than there are

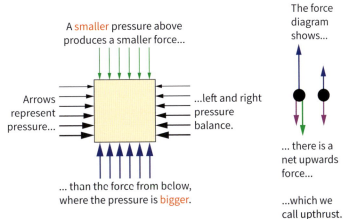

▲ **Figure 5** This object is submerged. The arrows show the forces acting on the object because of the pressure in the water.

air molecules hitting the top. This produces the upthrust. The duck sinks until there is enough upthrust to balance the weight.

If the area in contact with the water is too small, there is not enough upthrust to make the object float.

C Explain why a very heavy supertanker can float.

When a submarine is underwater, there is a difference in pressure between the top and bottom of the submarine. That produces the upthrust.

A primary-school student says that 'heavy things sink and light things float'. Use the example of a ferry to explain to them why that is not the case.

Summary Questions

1 Copy and complete the following sentences.

The pressure in a liquid acts in _____ directions. The pressure _____ as you go deeper because the _____ of the water above you gets _____. The difference in pressure explains why there is a force called _____ on a floating object.
(5 marks)

2 Explain, in terms of pressure, why:

a a boat made of modelling clay floats. (2 marks)
b the same mass of modelling clay shaped into a ball sinks. (2 marks)

3 You fill a bucket with water.

a Describe how the water pressure changes as you go from the top to the bottom of the bucket. (1 mark)

You push a ping pong ball to the bottom of the bucket of water.

b Explain why the ball moves up when you let it go. (2 marks)

3.5 Pressure on solids

Learning objectives

After this topic, you will be able to:

- describe what is meant by pressure on a surface
- calculate pressure
- apply ideas of pressure to different situations.

Reactivate your knowledge

1 State the direction of gas and liquid pressure on a surface.
2 State the unit of force.
3 State two units of area.

▲ **Figure 1** There is no wind on the Moon to blow Neil Armstrong's footprints away.

▲ **Figure 2** The tracks on the earthmover stop it sinking into the mud.

Key words

pressure, newtons per metre squared, pascal

Link

You can learn more about upthrust in P1 1.1 *Introduction to forces*.

When Neil Armstrong walked on the Moon in 1969, he left footprints. The footprints are still there (Figure 1).

What is pressure on a surface?

When you stand on any surface you exert a force on it because of your weight. Your weight is spread out over the area of your foot. You are exerting a pressure on the ground. If you are standing on a soft surface, such as mud, the pressure might be big enough for you to sink.

An earthmover is very heavy. It has a weight of about a million newtons, the same as about 15 000 people! A single person standing on the same muddy ground might sink. The earthmover does not sink because its weight is spread out over a bigger area (Figure 2).

Pressure is a measure of how much force is applied over a certain area. The pressure acts in a direction that is at 90°, or normal, to the surface.

> **A** Compare the direction of gas and liquid pressure with pressure on a surface.

How do you calculate pressure?

You calculate pressure using this equation:

$$\text{pressure (N/m}^2) = \frac{\text{force (N)}}{\text{area (m}^2)}$$

You measure force in newtons (N) and area in metres squared (m²).

Pressure is measured in **newtons per metre squared** (N/m²). 1 newton per metre squared is also called a **pascal** (Pa).

Sometimes it is easier to measure smaller areas in centimetres squared (cm²). If you measure the area in cm² then the pressure is measured in N/cm².

Reactivate your knowledge answers
1 At right angles/90 degrees to the surface 2 Newtons, N 3 Centimetres squared, cm², metres squared, m²

When you do calculations, it is very important to look at the units of area.

> **B** State three units of pressure.

What produces big and small pressure?

The studs on the bottom of a hockey or football boot have a small area compared with the area of the foot (Figure 3). This produces a bigger pressure. The studs sink into the ground and help the player to move quickly.

The weight of a hockey player is 600 N.

The area of their two feet is 200 cm².

$$\text{pressure} = \frac{\text{force}}{\text{area}}$$
$$= \frac{600\,\text{N}}{200\,\text{cm}^2}$$
$$= 3\,\text{N/cm}^2$$

The total area of the studs is 20 cm².

$$\text{pressure} = \frac{\text{force}}{\text{area}}$$
$$= \frac{600\,\text{N}}{20\,\text{cm}^2}$$
$$= 30\,\text{N/cm}^2$$

Studs on shoes increase the pressure, as do sharp knives and nails.

The tracks on earthmovers, snowshoes (Figure 4), and wide straps on backpacks decrease the pressure. To produce the same pressure on the floor that you exert when you push in a drawing pin, you would need over 5000 people standing on your shoulders.

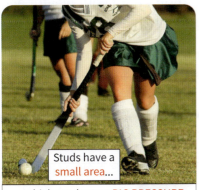

Studs have a small area...

... which produces a BIG PRESSURE, so you sink into the ground.

▲ **Figure 3** The studs increase the grip on the ground.

Snowshoes have a BIG AREA...

...which produces a small pressure so you DON'T sink into the ground.

▲ **Figure 4** Snowshoes decrease the pressure you exert on the ground.

> **C** Explain why wide straps on backpacks decrease the pressure.

Finding the force

Change the subject to work out the correct equation for calculating force.

A force = pressure/area

B force = pressure × area

C force = area/pressure

Summary Questions

1 Copy and complete the following sentences.

Pressure is a measure of how much **force/pressure** there is on a certain **area/volume**. If you exert a **big/small** force on a **big/small** area the pressure will be large. Pressure can be measured in **N/m² / Nm**. (5 marks)

2 A gymnast has a weight of 600 N. The area of each hand is 150 cm². Calculate the pressure on the floor when they are doing a handstand. (3 marks)

3 Atmospheric pressure is 101 kPa, or 101 kN/m². Assume the top of a car has an area of 1.5 m².

a Calculate the force of the atmosphere on the top of a car. (3 marks)

b A giant panda has a weight of 1000 N. Calculate the number of giant pandas that would have to sit on the top of your car to exert the same force as the atmosphere. (1 mark)

c Explain why your car does not collapse under the weight of the atmosphere. (1 mark)

Learning objectives

After this topic, you will be able to:
- describe what is meant by a moment
- calculate the moment of a force and apply the law of moments.

Reactivate your knowledge

1 State the equation for work.
2 State where handles are in relation to hinges: close together/far apart.
3 State the difference between 'balanced' and 'unbalanced' forces.

▲ **Figure 1** Tightrope walking over Niagara Falls.

Key words

pivot, moment, newton metres, law of moments, centre of gravity, centre of mass

A tightrope walker uses a long pole to help them to balance (Figure 1).

What is a moment?

Whenever you open a door, you are using a turning force (Figure 2). A turning force acts a certain distance from a **pivot**. The turning effect of a force is called a **moment**. The moment depends on the force being applied and how far it is from the pivot.

moment (Nm) = force (N) × perpendicular distance from the pivot (m)

You measure force in newtons (N) and distance in metres (m).

You calculate a moment in **newton metres** (Nm).

> **A** Compare calculating work and calculating a moment.

What is the law of moments?

You sit on the left of a see-saw with your friend at the other end. It balances like the apples in Figure 3. The moment of your weight acts anticlockwise. The moment of your friend's weight acts clockwise.

When an object is in equilibrium the sum of the clockwise moments is equal to the sum of the anticlockwise moments. This is the **law of moments**.

▲ **Figure 2** You need to apply a turning force to open a door.

▲ **Figure 3** These apples are in equilibrium.

Reactivate your knowledge answers
1 Work = force × distance in the direction of the force 2 Far apart 3 Balanced = no net force, unbalanced = net force

B Explain why the large apple is closer to the pivot than the small apple when they are in equilibrium.

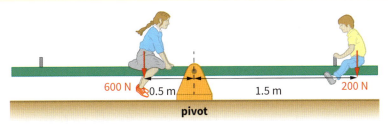

▲ **Figure 4** The see-saw doesn't turn if it is in equilibrium.

You can work out if the see-saw in Figure 4 is going to be balanced by calculating the clockwise and the anticlockwise moments.

$$\text{clockwise moment} = \text{force} \times \text{distance on the right}$$

$$= 200\,\text{N} \times 1.5\,\text{m}$$

$$= 300\,\text{Nm}$$

$$\text{anticlockwise moment} = \text{force} \times \text{distance on the left}$$

$$= 600\,\text{N} \times 0.5\,\text{m}$$

$$= 300\,\text{Nm}$$

The moments are the same. The see-saw balances.

What makes objects unstable?

When you lean back and tip your chair slightly, there is a turning force that brings your chair back (Figure 5A). That turning force is your weight acting about the point where the legs touch the floor. If you lean back far enough you will topple over (Figure 5C).

All the weight of an object seems to act through a point called the **centre of gravity** (or **centre of mass**). If the centre of gravity is above the pivot there is no turning force (Figure 5B). If the centre of gravity is to the left or right of the pivot there will be a turning force.

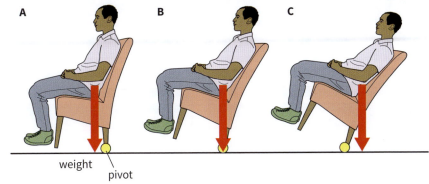

▲ **Figure 5** There is a turning force in **A** and **C**, but not in **B**.

C Explain why it is hard to balance a pencil on its point.

Sitting on a see-saw

A mother and daughter are on a see-saw 4 m long. The mother has a weight of 600 N and the child has a weight of 150 N.

Calculate where the mother must sit to balance the child who is sitting at the other end.

Summary Questions

1 Copy and complete the following sentences.

The _____ effect of a force is called a moment. You can calculate the moment of a force by multiplying the _____ by the _____. If the anticlockwise moments equal the clockwise moments the object will be in _____. This is the _____ of moments. The _____ of an object acts through a point called the centre of _____.
(7 marks)

2 A child applies a force of 5 N to close a door. The handle is 0.75 m from the hinge. Calculate the moment of the force.
(3 marks)

3 Using Figure 4, suggest and explain, using the law of moments, what the girl on the see-saw would need to do to balance the see-saw if:

a the boy moved closer to the pivot (3 marks)

b another boy sat between the first boy and the pivot.
(3 marks)

In this chapter you have learnt how motion graphs tell a story of how the speed of an object changes with time. The speed is the slope (or gradient) of the graph – a steeper slope means the object is moving faster. You have seen how to use distance and time to calculate speed when it is constant, or to use a motion graph to calculate speed.

You have learnt to use the particle model to explain gas pressure in terms of the collisions of particles with the container walls. You have seen that gas pressure increases with increased temperature and decreased volume. You have seen how atmospheric pressure and liquid pressure both increase as you go 'deeper'. You have learnt to calculate the pressure on a solid surface using force and area, and to use their units to figure out the unit of pressure. You learnt how to calculate the moment (or turning effect) of a force around a pivot from force and distance. You have seen how to use those calculations to work out if an object is balanced – if it is then the moments about a pivot are equal.

Metacognition and self-reflection task

Writing questions is a good way to check your understanding. In this chapter there have been lots of calculations; of speed, pressure and moments. Write questions that require the use of each equation. Write model answers, and then write answers with one or two errors. Mix the answers up, and try them out on your friends. Wait until you have almost forgotten, and try them out on yourself.

Journey through P2

Chapter 1	Chapter 2	Chapter 3
Charging up	Food and fuels	Speed
Circuits and current	Energy resources	Motion graphs
Potential difference	Energy adds up	Pressure in gases
Resistance	Energy and temperature	Pressure in liquids
Changing the subject	Energy transfer: particles	Pressure on solids
Series and parallel circuits	Energy transfer: radiation	Turning forces
Magnets and magnetic fields	Energy: forces	
Electromagnets	Energy and power	
Using electromagnets		

YOU ARE HERE

Chapter 3 Summary Questions

1 Choose units of speed from the list below.

m/s   m s h   mph   km/s   km

(3 marks)

2 You can make a hole in a piece of wood if you bang in a nail with a hammer. If you hit the wood with the hammer it does not make a hole. Choose the best explanation for this from the statements below:

A The area of the nail is much smaller so the pressure is smaller.

B The area of the nail is much smaller so the pressure is bigger.

C The area of the hammer is bigger so the pressure is bigger.

(1 mark)

3 Figure 1 shows a graph of a person riding their bike.

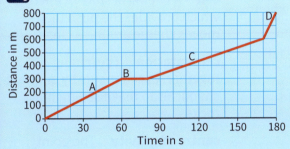

▲ **Figure 1**

a State the letter of the section where the person was:
  i stationary (1 mark)
  ii moving fastest. (1 mark)
b Calculate the speed from 0 to A. (3 marks)
c Describe the cyclist's motion at points B, C, and D. (3 marks)

(8 marks)

4

a State the angle between the direction that liquid pressure acts and the surface. (1 mark)

b Explain in terms of pressure why you have to hold a balloon to keep it under water. (2 marks)

c Suggest and explain what would happen to the force you need to exert on the balloon if it was smaller. (2 marks)

(5 marks)

5

a Calculate the pressure of person with a weight of 700N standing on a foot of area 200 cm². (4 marks)

b Describe and explain what happens to the pressure if they stand on two feet instead of one without doing a calculation. (2 marks)

c Another person exerts a bigger pressure even though their weight is the same. Suggest and explain why. (1 mark)

(7 marks)

6 Look at Figure 2 of an arm holding a phone. The phone has a weight of 1.5 N.

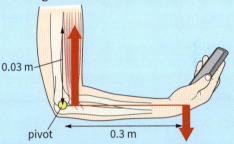

▲ **Figure 2**

a Calculate the moment of the force exerted by the phone. (2 marks)

b Calculate the force that the muscle exerts to keep the phone in equilibrium. (2 marks)

c Explain why the force exerted by the muscle is much greater than the weight of the phone. (2 marks)

(6 marks)

7 You buy a bag of crisps in an airport. After take-off on the plane you take the crisps out of your rucksack.

Explain in detail why the bag has expanded.

(6 marks)

8 A person carries a plank of wood so that it balances on their shoulder (Figure 3).

a Explain why the plank is stable. (2 marks)

b The person moves the plank so there is more plank in front than behind. Suggest and explain in terms of moments how the person can balance the plank. (3 marks)

(5 marks)

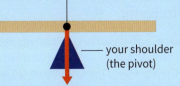

▲ **Figure 3**

Glossary

acceleration   The amount by which speed increases in one second.

acid rain   Rain that has a non-metal dissolved in it.

adaptation   Characteristic that helps an organism to survive in its environment.

adaptation   Special features that allow an organism to be successful.

addiction   A need to keep taking a drug to feel normal.

aerobic respiration   Chemical reaction where glucose reacts with oxygen to release energy, carbon dioxide, and water.

alcoholic   A person who is addicted to alcohol.

algae   Green unicellular or multicellular organisms that perform photosynthesis and live underwater.

ammeter   A device for measuring electric current in a circuit.

amps   Units of measurement of electric current, symbol A.

anaerobic respiration   Chemical reaction that takes place without oxygen. Glucose is converted into lactic acid and energy is released.

anus   Muscular ring through which faeces pass out of the body.

atmosphere   The mixture of gases surrounding the Earth.

atmospheric pressure   Pressure caused by the collisions of air molecules that produce a force on an area.

atom   A neutral particle; everything is made of atoms.

attract   Be pulled together, for example, opposite poles of a magnet attract and positive and negative charges attract.

average speed   The total distance travelled in the total time taken for a complete journey.

balanced diet   Eating food containing the right nutrients in the correct amounts.

battery   Two or more electrical cells joined together.

Benedict's solution   A blue liquid that turns orange-red when heated with a sugar solution.

bile   Substance that breaks fat into small droplets.

bioaccumulation   The build-up of toxic chemicals inside organisms in a food chain.

biodiversity   The variety of organisms living in an area.

biuret solution   A pale blue solution that turns purple when added to protein.

camouflage   A type of disguise, often where the organism blends in with its surroundings.

carbohydrase   Enzyme that breaks down carbohydrates into sugar molecules.

carbohydrate   Nutrient that provides energy.

carbon cycle   The carbon cycle shows stores of carbon, and summarises how carbon and its compounds enter and leave these stores.

carbon fibre   A material made of thin tubes of carbon.

carbon monoxide   A poisonous gas that stops the blood from carrying oxygen.

carbon store   A place where carbon and its compounds may remain for a long time. Carbon stores include the atmosphere, oceans, sedimentary rocks, fossil fuels, the soil, and living organisms.

catalyst   Substance that speeds up a reaction without being used up.

cell   A chemical store of energy, which provides the push that moves charge around a circuit.

cementation   The 'gluing together' of sediments by different chemicals to make sedimentary rocks.

centre of gravity   The point in an object where the force of gravity seems to act.

centre of mass   The point in an object where the mass of an object seems to act.

ceramic   A compound such as a metal silicate or oxide that is hard, strong, and has a high melting point.

chemical property   How a substance behaves in its chemical reactions.

chemical store   Energy stored in food and fuels.

chlorophyll   Green pigment that absorbs light for use in photosynthesis.

chloroplast   The organelle where photosynthesis happens.

chromatogram   An image obtained from chromatography.

chromatography   A technique to separate mixtures of liquids that are soluble in the same solvent.

chromosome   Long strand of DNA, which contains many genes.

circuit symbol   A simple diagram to show different components in circuits.

climate change   A long-term change in weather patterns.

combustion   A burning reaction, in which a substance reacts quickly with oxygen, and gives out light and heats the surroundings.

community   The collection of the different types of organism present in an ecosystem.

compaction   The process of squashing sediments together to make new rocks by the weight of layers above.

competition   This happens when there aren't enough resources available.

composite   A mixture of materials with properties that are a combination of those of the materials in it.

compressed   Squashed into a smaller space.

conduction   A way in which energy is transferred through solids, and to a much lesser extent in liquids and gases.

conductor   A material that conducts charge or energy well, such as a metal or graphite.

consumer   Organisms that eat other organisms as food.

continuous variation   Characteristic that can take any value within a range of values.

convection current   The movement of heated liquids or gasses.

convection   The transfer of energy by the movement of gases or liquids.

core (electromagnets)   A rod of a magnetic material placed inside a coil to make the magnetic field of an electromagnet stronger.

Core (Earth)   The centre of the Earth – made up of the inner and outer core.

crust   The rocky outer layer of the Earth.

current   The flow of electrical charge (electrons) around a complete circuit per second.

decomposers   Organisms that break down dead plant and animal material, returning nutrients to the soil or water.

deficiency   A lack of minerals, that causes poor growth

deforestation   The cutting down or burning of trees in forests.

density   The mass of a material in a certain volume.

deposition   The settling of sediments that have moved away from their original rock.

depressant   A drug that slows down the body's reactions by slowing down the nervous system.

digestion   Process where large molecules are broken down into small molecules.

digestive system   Group of organs that work together to break down food.

discontinuous variation   Characteristic that can only be a certain value.

displace   A more reactive metal displaces – or pushes out – a less reactive metal from its compound.

displacement (reaction)   In a displacement reaction, a more reactive metal displaces – or pushes out – a less reactive metal from its compound.

dissipated   Energy that has become spread out or 'wasted' by heating the environment.

dissolve   The mixing of a substance (the solute) with a liquid (the solvent) to make a solution.

dissolving   A substance (solute) mixing with a liquid (solvent) to make a solution.

distance-time graph   A graph that shows how far an object moves each second.

distillation   A technique that uses evaporation and condensation to obtain a solvent from a solution.

DNA   Chemical that contains all the information needed to make an organism.

drug   Chemical substance that affects the way your body works.

durable   A property of a material meaning that it is difficult to damage.

ecosystem   The name given to the interaction between plants, animals, and their habitat in a particular location.

elastic store   Energy stored when objects change shape

electric charge   A property of a material or particle that can be positive or negative.

electric field   A region where a charged material or particle experiences a force.

electromagnet   A temporary magnet produced using an electric current.

electromagnetic   The electrical and magnetic forces or effects produced by an electric current.

electromagnetic spectrum   The range of all types of electromagnetic radiation.

electron   A negatively charged particle found in atoms. Electrons flow through a wire when a current flows.

endangered   When a population is small and at risk of extinction.

energy resources   Materials or mechanisms for heating or generating electricity.

energy store   Something such as a food or hot object that enables you to account for the energy at the start and end of a transfer.

energy   Associated with changes in temperature or with work.

environment   The conditions found in a habitat.

environmental variation   The variation in characteristics caused by your surroundings and life experiences.

enzyme   Special protein that can break large molecules into small molecules.

equilibrium   Objects are at thermal equilibrium when they are at the same temperature.

erosion   The breaking of a rock into sediments, and their movement away from the original rock.

ethanol   The drug found in alcoholic drinks.

evolution   Development of a species over time

extinct   When no more individuals of a species are left anywhere in the world.

fermentation   Chemical reaction used by microorganisms to convert glucose into ethanol, carbon dioxide, and energy.

fertiliser   Chemical containing minerals, normally applied to soil.

fibre   Provides bulk to food to keep it moving through the digestive system.

filtering   A way of separating pieces of solid that are mixed with a liquid or solution by pouring through filter paper.

filtrate   The liquid or solution that collects in the container after the mixture has passed through the filter paper.

filtration   A way of separating pieces of solid that are mixed with a liquid or solution by pouring through filter paper.

food chain   A diagram that shows the transfer of energy between organisms.

food test   Chemical test to detect the presence of particular nutrients in a food.

food web   A diagram showing a set of linked food chains.

fossil fuel   Coal, oil, and gas made from the remains of trees and sea creatures over millions of years.

fossil   The remains of plants and animals that have turned to stone.

fuels   Substances that can be burnt to release energy.

gas pressure   The force exerted by air particles when they collide with a surface.

gene bank   A store of genetic samples, used for research and to try to prevent extinction.

gene   Section of DNA that contains the information for a characteristic.

global heating   The gradual increase in the Earth's mean air temperature.

global warming   The gradual increase in the Earth's mean air temperature.

gravitational potential store Energy due to the position of an object in a gravitational field.

greenhouse effect   The absorbing of energy by gases in the atmosphere, such as carbon dioxide.

greenhouse gas   A gas that contributes to climate change, such as carbon dioxide.

Group 0   Group 0 is on the right of the Periodic Table. Group 0 elements include helium, neon, argon, and krypton.

Group 1   The elements in the left column of the Periodic Table, including lithium, sodium, and potassium.

Group 7   Group 7 is the second from the right of the Periodic Table. Group 7 elements include fluorine, chlorine, bromine, and iodine.

group   A vertical column of the Periodic Table. The elements in a group have similar properties.

guard cells   Cells that open and close the stomata.

gullet   Tube that food travels down into the stomach.

habitat   The area in which an organism lives.

haemoglobin   The substance in blood that carries oxygen around the body.

halogen   Another name for the Group 7 elements.

hibernation   When animals sleep through winter in order to survive.

Hooke's law   The force to stretch an elastic material is directly proportional to the extension.

igneous   Rock made when liquid rock (magma or lava) cools and freezes.

impure   A substance is impure if it has different substances mixed with it.

incompressible   Cannot be compressed (squashed)

infrared radiation   Radiation given off by the Sun and other objects that brings about energy transfer.

inherited variation   The variation in characteristics inherited from parents.

inner core   The solid iron and nickel at the centre of the Earth.

insecticide   Chemicals used to kill insects.

insoluble   A substance that cannot dissolve in a certain solvent is insoluble in that solvent.

instantaneous speed   The speed at a particular moment.

insulator   A material that does not conduct electricity or transfer energy well.

interdependence   The way in which living organisms depend on each other to survive, grow, and reproduce.

iodine   An orange-brown solution that turns blue-black when added to starch.

joules   The unit of energy, symbol J.

kilojoules   1 kilojoule = 1000 J, symbol kJ.

kilowatt hours   The unit of energy used by electricity companies, symbol kWh.

kilowatts   1 kilowatt = 1000 W, symbol kW.

kinetic store   Energy of moving objects.

large intestine   Organ where water passes back into the body, leaving a solid waste of undigested food called feces.

lava   Liquid rock that is above the Earth's surface.

law of conservation of energy   Energy cannot be created or destroyed, only transferred.

law of moments   An object is in equilibrium if the clockwise moments equal the anticlockwise moments.

lever   A simple machine that multiplies the force.

lightning   A current through the air that produces light and sound.

lipase   Enzyme that breaks down lipids into fatty acids and glycerol.

lipids   Nutrients that provide a store of energy and insulate the body.

liquid pressure   The pressure produced by collisions of particles in a liquid.

magma   Liquid rock that is below the Earth's surface.

magnesium   A mineral needed by plants for making chlorophyll.

magnet   A material with a north and south pole that has its own magnetic field.

magnetic field lines   Imaginary lines that show the direction of the force on magnetic material.

magnetic field   A region where there is a force on a magnet or magnetic material.

magnetic material   A material that is attracted to a magnet, such as iron, steel, nickel, or cobalt.

magnetise   Make into a magnet.

malnourishment   Eating the wrong amount or the wrong types of food.

mantle   The layer of Earth that is below the crust. It is solid but can flow very slowly.

medicinal drug   Drug that has a medical benefit to your health.

metal   Elements on the left of the stepped line of the Periodic Table. Most elements are metals. They are good conductors of energy and electricity.

metalloid   Elements near the stepped line of the Periodic Table are metalloids.

metamorphic   Rock formed by the action of heating and/or pressure on the sedimentary or igneous rock.

metres per second   A unit of speed.

microorganism   A tiny organism that can only be seen with a microscope.

migration   When animals move somewhere warmer or with more food.

mineral   Essential nutrient needed in small amounts to keep you healthy.

mitochondria   Organelles where aerobic respiration happens.

mixture   A mixture is made up of substances that are not chemically joined together.

moment   A measure of the ability of a force to rotate an object about a pivot.

motor   A component or machine that spins when a current flows through it.

natural polymer   Polymers made by plants and animals, including wool, cotton, and rubber.

natural selection   Process by which the organisms with the characteristics that are most suited to the environment survive and reproduce, passing on their genes.

negative   The charge on an electron, or on an object that has had electrons transferred to it.

neutral   Describes an object or particle that has no charge, or in which positive and negative charges cancel out, giving no charge overall.

neutron   A neutral particle found in atoms.

newton metres   The unit of moment.

newtons per metre squared   A unit of pressure.

niche   A particular place or role that an organism has in an ecosystem.

nicotine   An addictive drug that stimulates the nervous system.

nitrates   Minerals containing nitrogen for healthy growth.

noble gases   Another name for the Group 0 elements.

non-metal   Elements on the right of the stepped line of the Periodic Table. They are poor conductors of energy and electricity.

non-renewable   Energy resources that have a limited supply.

north pole   The pole of a magnet that points towards the north.

nuclear power station   A power station that uses uranium as a fuel.

nuclear   Relating to a fuel such as uranium.

nucleus   Organelle that contains genetic material (DNA) and controls the cell's activities.

nutrient   Essential substance that your body needs to survive, provided by food.

obese   Extremely overweight.

ohms   The unit of resistance, symbol Ω.

ore   A rock that you can extract a metal from.

outer core   The liquid iron and nickel between the Earth's mantle and inner core.

oxygen debt   Extra oxygen required after anaerobic respiration to break down lactic acid.

parallel   A circuit in which there are two or more paths or branches for the current.

pascal   A unit of pressure, 1 pascal is equivalent to 1 newton per metre squared.

passive smoking   Breathing in other people's smoke.

period   A horizontal row of the Periodic Table. There are trends in the properties of the elements across a period.

phosphates   Minerals containing phosphorus for healthy roots.

photosynthesis   The process plants use to make their own food, glucose. In photosynthesis, carbon dioxide and water react together to make glucose and oxygen.

photosynthesis   The process plants use to make their own food, glucose. In photosynthesis, carbon dioxide and water react together to make glucose and oxygen.

physical property   A property of a material that you can observe or measure.

pivot The point about which a lever or see-saw balances.

plasma The liquid part of blood, which carries carbon dioxide to the lungs where it is exhaled.

polymer A substance made up of very long molecules.

population The number of plants or animals of the same type that live in the same area.

porous A porous material has small gaps that may contain substances in their liquid or gas states. Water can soak into a porous material.

positive The charge on a proton, or on an object that has had electrons transferred from it.

potassium A mineral needed by plants for healthy leaves and flowers.

potential difference A measure of the push of a cell or battery, or the energy that the cell or battery can supply.

power rating The number in watts or kilowatts that tells you the rate at which an appliance transfers energy.

predator An animal that eats other animals.

pressure A force exerted on a certain area.

prey An animal that is eaten by another animal

producer Organism that makes its own food using photosynthesis.

protease Enzyme that breaks down proteins into amino acids.

protein Nutrient used for growth and repair.

proton A positively charged particle found in atoms.

pure A substance is pure if it has no other substances mixed with it.

radiation The transfer of energy as a wave.

ramp A simple machine that reduces the force needed to lift an object by a certain height.

rating The value of potential difference at which a cell or bulb operates.

reactive A substance is reactive if it reacts vigorously with substances such as dilute acids and water.

reactivity series A list of metals in order of how vigorously they react.

recreational drug Drug that is taken for enjoyment.

rectum Feces are stored here, before being passed out of the body.

recycling Collecting and processing materials that have been used, to make new objects.

relationship How the variables in an equation are related to each other.

relative motion The difference between the speeds of two moving objects, or of a moving and a stationary object.

relay Electrical device that uses current flowing through it in one circuit to switch on and off a current in a second circuit.

renewable Energy resources whose supply will not run out.

repel Be pushed away from each other, for example, like magnetic poles repel or like electrical charges repel.

residue The solid that collects in the filter paper.

resistance How difficult it is for current to flow through a component in a circuit.

respiration The process that transfers energy from plants and animals. In respiration, glucose reacts with oxygen to make carbon dioxide and water.

rock cycle The rock cycle explains how rocks change and are recycled into new rocks over millions of years.

sediment Pieces of rock that have broken away from their original rock.

sedimentary Rock made from sediments.

series A circuit in which components are joined in a single loop.

simple machine Lever or gear that reduces the force required to do something, but increases the distance.

small intestine Organ where small digested molecules are absorbed into the bloodstream.

solubility The solubility of a substance is the mass that dissolves in 100 g of water.

soluble A substance that can dissolve in a certain solvent, often water, is soluble in that solvent.

solute The solid or gas that dissolves in a liquid.

solution A mixture of a liquid with a solid or a gas. All parts of the mixture are the same.

solvent The liquid in which a solid or gas dissolves.

south pole The pole of a magnet that points towards the south.

species   Organisms that have lots of characteristics in common, and can mate to produce fertile offspring.

speed   A measure of how far something travels in a given time.

starch   A type of carbohydrate found in plants, especially grains and potatoes.

starvation   Extreme case of not eating enough food.

stimulant   A drug that speeds up the body's reactions by speeding up the nervous system.

stomach   Organ where food is churned with digestive juices and acids.

stomata   Holes found on the bottom of the leaf that allow gases to diffuse in and out of the leaf.

sugar   A small soluble molecule that your body needs for energy.

switch   A component that controls the current by making or breaking the circuit.

synthetic polymer   A substance made up of very long molecules that does not occur naturally.

tar   A sticky black substance that builds up in the lungs.

temperature   A measure of how hot or cold something is, measured in degrees Celsius.

terminals   The two ends of the battery.

thermal imaging camera   A camera that absorbs infrared and produces a (false-colour) image.

thermal power station   A power station that uses fossil fuels to generate electricity.

thermal store   Energy in objects as a result of the motion of their particles.

thermometer   Instrument used to measure temperature.

tobacco   A substance that contains many toxic chemicals.

transport   Movement of sediments far from their original rock.

troposphere   The part of the atmosphere nearest the Earth.

unit of alcohol   10 ml of pure alcohol.

unreactive   Elements that take part in few chemical reactions are unreactive.

uplift   Uplift happens when huge forces from inside the Earth push rocks upwards.

uranium   A radioactive element that can be used as a fuel in nuclear power stations.

variation   Differences in characteristics within a species.

villi   Tiny projections in the small intestine wall that increase the area of absorption.

vitamin   Essential nutrients needed in small amounts to keep you healthy.

voltage   A measure of the strength of a cell or battery used to send a current around a circuit.

voltmeter   A device for measuring voltage.

volts   Units of measurement of voltage, symbol V.

watt   The unit of power, symbol W.

weathering   Weathering breaks up all types of rock into smaller pieces, called sediments.

withdrawal symptom   Unpleasant symptom a person with a drug addiction suffers from when they stop taking the drug.

work   A way of transferring energy that does not involve heating.

Index

Periodic Table

Group

| 1 | 2 | | | | | | | | | | | 3 | 4 | 5 | 6 | 7 | 0/8 |

Period

Key:
- relative atomic mass
- **chemical symbol**
- name
- atomic (proton) number

1.0
H
hydrogen
1

Alkali metals
Noble gases
Halogens

| 7 **Li** lithium 3 | 9 **Be** beryllium 4 | | | | | | | | | | | 11 **B** boron 5 | 12 **C** carbon 6 | 14 **N** nitrogen 7 | 16 **O** oxygen 8 | 19 **F** fluorine 9 | 4 **He** helium 2 |

Period 2:
| 7 **Li** lithium 3 | 9 **Be** beryllium 4 | | | | | | | | | | | 11 **B** boron 5 | 12 **C** carbon 6 | 14 **N** nitrogen 7 | 16 **O** oxygen 8 | 19 **F** fluorine 9 | 20 **Ne** neon 10 |

Period 3:
| 23 **Na** sodium 11 | 24 **Mg** magnesium 12 | | | | | | | | | | | 27 **Al** aluminium 13 | 28 **Si** silicon 14 | 31 **P** phosphorus 15 | 32 **S** sulfur 16 | 35.5 **Cl** chlorine 17 | 40 **Ar** argon 18 |

Period 4:
| 39 **K** potassium 19 | 40 **Ca** calcium 20 | 45 **Sc** scandium 21 | 48 **Ti** titanium 22 | 51 **V** vanadium 23 | 52 **Cr** chromium 24 | 55 **Mn** manganese 25 | 56 **Fe** iron 26 | 59 **Co** cobalt 27 | 59 **Ni** nickel 28 | 63.5 **Cu** copper 29 | 65 **Zn** zinc 30 | 70 **Ga** gallium 31 | 73 **Ge** germanium 32 | 75 **As** arsenic 33 | 79 **Se** selenium 34 | 80 **Br** bromine 35 | 84 **Kr** krypton 36 |

Period 5:
| 85.5 **Rb** rubidium 37 | 88 **Sr** strontium 38 | 89 **Y** yttrium 39 | 91 **Zr** zirconium 40 | 93 **Nb** niobium 41 | 96 **Mo** molybdenum 42 | (98) **Tc** technetium 43 | 101 **Ru** ruthenium 44 | 103 **Rh** rhodium 45 | 106 **Pd** palladium 46 | 108 **Ag** silver 47 | 112 **Cd** cadmium 48 | 115 **In** indium 49 | 119 **Sn** tin 50 | 122 **Sb** antimony 51 | 128 **Te** tellurium 52 | 127 **I** iodine 53 | 131 **Xe** xenon 54 |

Period 6:
| 133 **Cs** caesium 55 | 137 **Ba** barium 56 | 139 **La** lanthanum 57 * | 178.5 **Hf** hafnium 72 | 181 **Ta** tantalum 73 | 184 **W** tungsten 74 | 186 **Re** rhenium 75 | 190 **Os** osmium 76 | 192 **Ir** iridium 77 | 195 **Pt** platinum 78 | 197 **Au** gold 79 | 201 **Hg** mercury 80 | 204 **Tl** thallium 81 | 207 **Pb** lead 82 | 209 **Bi** bismuth 83 | 210 **Po** polonium 84 | (210) **At** astatine 85 | 222 **Rn** radon 86 |

Period 7:
| (223) **Fr** francium 87 | (226) **Ra** radium 88 | (227) **Ac** actinium 89 # | (261) **Rf** rutherfordium 104 | (262) **Db** dubnium 105 | (266) **Sg** seaborgium 106 | (264) **Bh** bohrium 107 | (277) **Hs** hassium 108 | (268) **Mt** meitnerium 109 | (271) **Ds** darmstadtium 110 | (272) **Rg** roentgenium 111 | (285) **Cn** copernicium 112 | (286) **Nh** nihonium 113 | (289) **Fl** flerovium 114 | (289) **Mc** moscovium 115 | (293) **Lv** livermorium 116 | (294) **Ts** tennessine 117 | (294) **Og** oganesson 118 |

*58–71 Lanthanides

| 140 **Ce** cerium 58 | 141 **Pr** praseodymium 59 | 144 **Nd** neodymium 60 | (145) **Pm** promethium 61 | 150 **Sm** samarium 62 | 152 **Eu** europium 63 | 157 **Gd** gadolinium 64 | 159 **Tb** terbium 65 | 163 **Dy** dysprosium 66 | 165 **Ho** holmium 67 | 167 **Er** erbium 68 | 169 **Tm** thulium 69 | 173 **Yb** ytterbium 70 | 175 **Lu** lutetium 71 |

#90–103 Actinides

| 232 **Th** thorium 90 | 231 **Pa** protactinium 91 | 238 **U** uranium 92 | 237 **Np** neptunium 93 | 239 **Pu** plutonium 94 | 243 **Am** americium 95 | 247 **Cm** curium 96 | 247 **Bk** berkelium 97 | 252 **Cf** californium 98 | 252 **Es** einsteinium 99 | (257) **Fm** fermium 100 | (258) **Md** mendelevium 101 | (259) **No** nobelium 102 | (260) **Lr** lawrencium 103 |

Great Clarendon Street, Oxford, OX2 6DP, United Kingdom

Oxford University Press is a department of the University of Oxford. It furthers the University's objective of excellence in research, scholarship, and education by publishing worldwide. Oxford is a registered trade mark of Oxford University Press in the UK and in certain other countries.

British Library Cataloguing in Publication Data
Data available

978-1-38-202107-4

978-1-38-202095-4 (ebook)

10 9 8 7 6 5 4 3 2 1

Paper used in the production of this book is a natural, recyclable product made from wood grown in sustainable forests.

The manufacturing process conforms to the environmental regulations of the country of origin.

Printed in United Kingdom by Bell & Bain Ltd, Glasgow.

Acknowledgements
The authors would like to thank the following:

Jo Locke

Many thanks to my girls Emily and Hermione for all their support, encouragement, and delicious cakes, and to Dave for providing endless cups of tea and helpful ideas. It has also been an honour to write again with the original Activate team of Philippa Gardom Hulme and Helen Reynolds; I couldn't have done it without you.

Philippa Gardom Hulme

Enormous thanks to Barney, Catherine, and Sarah Gardom for their superb support and sparkling suggestions. Thank you, too, to Helen Reynolds and Jo Locke; I love working with you both. Finally, huge thanks to my parents, Mary and Edward Hulme, for patiently correcting my holiday diaries all those years ago, and getting me into writing in the first place.

Helen Reynolds

I would like to thank Michele, Roh, Lesa, and Bill for their support and innumerable cups of tea and walks. Many thanks also to Oleksiy and all those at the dance studio for their tremendous support and encouragement throughout the writing process. Finally, it has been an absolute pleasure working with Philippa Gardom Hulme and Jo Locke again. Thank you so much for your support, insight, and inspiration.

Thank you to Amanda Clegg and Karen Collins for their expert review of and contribution to the Working Scientifically chapter, and to Lauren Stephenson for the authoring of the Metacognition spreads.

The publisher and authors would like to thank the following for permission to use photographs and other copyright material:

Cover: Michal Bednarski.

Photos: **p6(a)**: Party people studio/Shutterstock; **p6(b)**: EHStockphoto/Shutterstock; **p6(c)**: Alones/Shutterstock; **p6(d)**: ShutterDivision/Shutterstock; **p6(e)**: Pongchart B/Shutterstock; **p6(f)**: Sergio Ponomarev/Shutterstock; **p8**: Vitalii Nesterchuk/Shutterstock; **p10**: FabrikaSimf/Shutterstock; **p12**: Studio Peace/Shutterstock; **p14**: Colin Cuthbert/Science Photo Library; **p15**: Mikkel Juul Jensen/Science Photo Library; **p16(t)**: ART STOCK CREATIVE/Shutterstock; **p16(b)**: Art Directors & TRIP/Alamy Stock Photo; **p20(a)**: hedgehog94/Shutterstock; **p20(b)**: Africa Studio/Shutterstock; **p20(c)**: ALPA PROD/Shutterstock; **p20(d)**: Nicole Helgason/Shutterstock; **p20(e)**: Air Images/Shutterstock; **p20(f)**: Ton Bangkeaw/Shutterstock; **p20(g)**: Matej Kastelic/Shutterstock; **p20(h)**: Ivan Chudakov/Shutterstock; **p22**: SciePro/Shutterstock; **p24**: naito29/Shutterstock; **p25(tr)**: Martyn F. Chillmaid/Science Photo Library; **p25(mr)**: Martyn F. Chillmaid/Science Photo Library; **p25(b)**: Cordelia Molloy/Science Photo Library; **p26**: Andrew Lambert Photography/Science Photo Library; **p27**: Andrew Lambert Photography/Science Photo Library; **p28**: Elena Schweitzer/Shutterstock; **p29**: Biophoto Associates/Science Photo Library; **p31**: Steve Gschmeissner/Science Photo Library; **p32**: Cordelia Molloy/Science Photo Library; **p34**: Gustoimages/Science Photo Library; **p35(t)**: BCFC/Shutterstock; **p35(b)**: Szasz-Fabian Jozsef/Shutterstock; **p37**: Arthur Glauberman/Science Photo Library; **p38**: Mac99/iStock/Getty Images; **p39**: Matt Meadows, Peter Arnold Inc./Science Photo Library; **p42**: Cornel Constantin/Shutterstock; **p44**: NNehring/iStock/Getty Images; **p45(t)**: alanphillips/iStock/Getty Images; **p45(b)**: Science Photo Library; **p46**: vvoe/Shutterstock; **p48(t)**: Nigel Cattlin/Alamy Stock Photo; **p48(m)**: aleori/Shutterstock; **p48(b)**: Nigel Cattlin/Alamy Stock Photo; **p49**: northlightimages/iStock/Getty Images; **p50(t)**: Stephen Mcsweeny/Shutterstock; **p50(b)**: Science Photo Library/Alamy Stock Photo; **p51**: r.classen/Shutterstock; **p52**: Maridav/Shutterstock; **p53(t)**: Power And Syred/Science Photo Library; **p53(m)**: Olaf Speier/Shutterstock; **p56**: Brian Lasenby/Shutterstock; **p60**: Toby Parkes/Shutterstock; **p62**: AMR Image/E+/Getty Images; **p64**: Shutterstock; **p66(t)**: GP232/E+/Getty Images; **p66(b)**: Skyak/E+/Getty Images; **p67(l)**: Studiotouch/Shutterstock; **p67(r)**: photos martYmage/Shutterstock; **p70**: Novi Elysa/Shutterstock; **p72**: Eric Isselee/Shutterstock; **p73**: gehringj/iStock/Getty Images; **p77**: Science History Images/Alamy Stock Photo; **p78**: Steffen Foerster/Shutterstock; **p79(l)**: Michael W. Tweedie/Science Photo Library; **p79(r)**: Michael W. Tweedie/Science Photo Library; **p80(t)**: Grauy/iStock/Getty Images; **p80(b)**: denisk0/iStock/Getty Images; **p81(t)**: Pjmalsbury/E+/Getty Images; **p81(b)**: James King-Holmes/Alamy Stock Photo; **p83**: Tribalium/Shutterstock; **p84(a)**: Davide Zanin Photography/Shutterstock; **p84(b)**: Robert Kneschke/Shutterstock; **p84(c)**: kittirat roekburi/Shutterstock; **p84(d)**: Cryptographer/Shutterstock; **p84(e)**: PR Image Factory/Shutterstock; **p84(f)**: bernatets photo/Shutterstock; **p84(g)**: Gorodenkoff/Shutterstock; **p84(h)**: Starsphinx/Shutterstock; **p86**: Peter Hermes Furian/Shutterstock; **p88(tl)**: Soonthorn Wongsaita/Shutterstock; **p88(m)**: Piotr Krajewski; **p88(bl)**: Love Silhouette/Shutterstock; **p89(tr)**: Hulton Archive/Getty Images; **p89(ml)**: cigdem/Shutterstock; **p89(mr)**: Bjoern Wylezich/Shutterstock; **p90(t)**: JK Brown, Graze, 2015, Stainless and mild steel; **p90(b)**: Bjoern Wylezich/Shutterstock; **p91**: Sebastian Janicki/Shutterstock; **p92(t)**: Piu_Piu/Shutterstock; **p92(b)**: Axel Jung/Shutterstock; **p93**: helfei/Shutterstock; **p94**: dien/Shutterstock; **p96**: Mike Flippo/Shutterstock; **p97(l)**: Turtle Rock Scientific/Science Photo Library; **p97(r)**: Martyn F. Chillmaid/Science Photo Library; **p98**: Andrew Lambert Photography/Science Photo Library; **p99**: Andrew Lambert Photography/Science Photo Library; **p100(l)**: Djburrill/Dreamstime; **p100(m)**: Anatoly Vartanov/Shutterstock; **p100(r)**: Slobo Mitic/iStock; **p101(l)**: stocksolutions/123rf; **p101(m)**: Valerie Loiseleux/iStock; **p101(r)**: Baranozdemir/iStock; **p104**: Science Photo Library; **p106(b)**: Mind Pixell/Shutterstock; **p106(t)**: Mongkolchon Akesin/Shutterstock; **p108(bl)**: Martyn F. Chillmaid/Science Photo Library; **p108(br)**: Martyn F. Chillmaid/Science Photo Library; **p108(t)**: WRLVON/Shutterstock; **p109(b)**: Chamille White/Shutterstock; **p109(t)**: Leonid Altman/Shutterstock; **p110**: Martyn F. Chillmaid/Science Photo Library; **p111(b)**: Carbonell/Shutterstock; **p111(t)**: Martyn F. Chillmaid/Science Photo Library; **p114(l)**: Andrew Lambert Photography/Science Photo Library; **p114(m)**: Darren Baker/Shutterstock; **p114(r)**: Cookie Studio/